ELEMENTS

OF

TACTICKS.

ELEMENTS
OF
TACTICKS,
AND INTRODUCTION TO
MILITARY EVOLUTIONS
FOR THE
INFANTRY:

BY

A celebrated PRUSSIAN GENERAL,

WITH PLATES.

Translated from the ORIGINAL in GERMAN,

By I. LANDMANN,

PROFESSOR OF FORTIFICATION AND ARTILLERY TO
THE ROYAL MILITARY ACADEMY AT WOOLWICH.

The Naval & Military Press Ltd

Published by

The Naval & Military Press Ltd
Unit 5 Riverside, Brambleside
Bellbrook Industrial Estate
Uckfield, East Sussex
TN22 1QQ England

Tel: +44 (0)1825 749494

www.naval-military-press.com
www.nmarchive.com

In reprinting in facsimile from the original, any imperfections are inevitably reproduced and the quality may fall short of modern type and cartographic standards.

TO

General Eliott

THIS WORK

IS MOST RESPECTFULLY DEDICATED,

BY

HIS VERY OBLIGED

AND MOST OBEDIENT

HUMBLE SERVANT,

I. LANDMANN.

PREFACE

BY THE

TRANSLATOR.

THE study of tactics, as well as all other sciences, should begin from the most simple principles; these should be fully known, and already learned, before the higher parts are meddled with. The following work contains the first elements of this science, which are so directly laid down, that I do not know of any book now extant that treats the subject in a more elementary, or proceeds with so compleat and connected a gradation; the application and reference that may be continually made from any one part of the work, to some former rule or principle, makes it, if one may say so, the Euclid of the tacticians.

The author leaves off at his entrance into the manœuvres of large corps; and the little he has said on this subject so well illustrates the utility of his principles, that it is much to be regretted he had not pursued the subject further; had he done so, we might then have hoped to have had a system of tactics compleat in all its parts. An attentive reader will however observe from what has been by this great master wrote on the subject, with what celerity, compactness and precision the great and essential movements of an army, in all the various operations of war, will be performed, when the officer and soldier have been gradually trained up, and brought forward by such principles as are laid down in the following treatise.

The rules and principles here laid down do not essentially differ from the regulations lately published by royal authority, to establish uniformity amongst the troops of the

British.

British army; where they may be found so to do, the regulations will of course be kept to, and this the author observes with regard to the regulations established in his own country: a country, the discipline of whose armies as formed by the late king of Prussia, has been the admiration, and thought worthy of the imitation of most of the military powers of Europe; it will however not be unacceptable, or unuseful to military readers to see these same subjects more fully extended, and very methodically treated. It will rather serve to enable them to follow those regulations with more accuracy, facility and precision.

I shall now say something respecting the following translation. Where passages were doubtful or obscure, I have endeavoured to explain freely what I conceived to be the author's meaning, and have sometimes used notes for such purpose; but on the contrary, where the sense might have been injured by a too free translation, I have used his own words in as literal a sense as possible, in preference to a close attention to either language or stile. I have likewise
endea-

endeavoured to give a set of plates with some improvements upon the original ones; and I have also given for a better elucidation of the manœuvres, some additional ones.

The encouragement I have met with in the prosecution of this work from the generals Eliott and Fawcett, particularly the former, is too flattering for me to let it pass unnoticed, and shall ever be gratefully remembered.

I have used my utmost endeavours to make my author understood in the language I now present him to my reader, which language as I do not profess myself a thorough master of, I hope the candid reader will excuse all defects of grammar and stile. I profess no more than to communicate to the public, the sense of a very useful military author; and if I have succeeded in this, my end is answered.

CONTENTS.

CONTENTS.

PART I.

	Page
How, and in what Manner a Recruit ought to be exercised	1
Of the Deploy, or Lock-step	16
Of the Firings	
With Platoons standing	18
To the Right about, and to fire by Platoons	20
In advancing by Platoons	21
By Platoons retreating	23
By Platoons in advancing, to fire to the Rear	26
By Platoons retreating, to fire to the Front	27
Of the Parapet, or Street Fire	28
Of the Parapet, or Street Fire in retreating	ib.
Of the Parapet, or Street Fire, in Flank	29
When charging by Battalions	30

[xii]

PART II.

Page

Essay upon the Evolutions.
What is necessary to the Soldier, for the Execution of the Evolutions — — — 33
Of marching in General — — — ib.
Of marching to the Right by Files — — 39
Of marching to the Left by Files — — 43
Of Inclining — — — — — ib.
Of Inclining to the Right and Left by Files 48
Of the Deploy March — — — 49
Of Closing — — — — — 50
Of Wheeling — — — — — 52
Of the Evolutions themselves, and what an Officer should observe here — — — 58
Of the Marching off — — — — ib.
Of breaking off in Divisions — — — 64
Of Marching up — — — — 68
Of the Alignment — — — — 73
Of marching a Battalion into the Alignment 81
Of the Point D'Appui — — — 88
Of Wheeling to form the Line, when extended along the Alignment — — — 91
Of the Countermarch — — — 98
Of taking Distances backwards — — 101
Of Deploying — — — — — 105
To deploy to the Right, when marched off from the Right — — — — — 110
When marched off from the Left, and deployed to the Left — — — — 112

When

	Page
When marched off from the Right, and deployed to the Left	113
When marched off from the Left, and deployed to the Right	114
Of advancing with a Battalion	118
Of Retreating	132
Of breaking off in Advancing	137
Of breaking off in Retreating	142
Of dressing a Battalion when it Halts, after Advancing	143
Of the first Line passing through the second	147
Of the March of the Flanks, before a retreating Battalion	154
Of Wheeling with a Battalion	156
Of the Square	159
Of bringing a Wing forward, or Advancing it	164

PART III.

Of Evolutions with a whole Corps	169
Of the March in Column	188
Of Marching into the Alignment	192
Of Marching up to form the Line	198
Of Dressing a Line	202
Of Advancing	219
Of the Dressing the Wings in a Line	239
When a Line halts, after advancing	244
Of Retreating	246
When a Line in retreating, fronts again	253
Of Inclining with a Line	256

	Page
Of the Attack, *en Echellon* — — —	259
Of what is called throwing oneself upon the Enemy's Flank — — — —	268
When a Corps, which is not yet formed, is to march into the Flank of the Enemy —	273
Of Paffing Through — — — —	277
Of dreffing a Line from the Center, after having Paffed Through — — — —	281
Of refufing a Wing of a Line that has Paffed Through — — — — —	287
Of the Retreat, *en Echiquier* — — —	292
Of the fame Retreat, when a Wing is to be refufed — — — — —	297
Of the Retreat, *en Echiquier*, in Two Lines	299
Of the Square and Oblong — — —	304
Of the March of a Square or Oblong, and how the Movements which may be made with it are to be executed with Order — —	309
Of wheeling with a Square or Oblong —	314
Of the breaking off a Square and forming an Oblong — — — — —	315
Of forming again a broken-off Square —	319
Of marching into the Alignment, in Order to deploy with clofe Battalions — —	323

N. B. The Arrows marked in the Plates fhew the Direction of the March.

INTRODUCTION.

INTRODUCTION.

ALL such sciences as are treated of upon established principles, are doubtless those whose execution is attended with the best success.

This is too evident a truth to need any demonstration; why then should we not endeavour to reduce to the principles of science, the exercise of the soldier; and at the same time, give rules for all ranks of officers? such an undertaking would put an end to that variety, which is found to prevail more or less in all the regiments of the army; and would further produce this great advantage, that both foldiers and officers in corps, however difperfed, might pafs from one regiment to another, without being obliged to learn anew, by what principles the recruit was drilled in that particular corps he comes into, how the platoons were managed at exercife, and in what manner the evolutions are performed: convinced as I am of the truth of this, I propofe for fuch purpofe the following rules.

PART I.

PART I.

How, and in what manner a Recruit ought to be exercised.

THE most essential thing in the instruction of a soldier, is the march; he must be perfectly exercised in this, as well in small as in large bodies, so that he may act of himself when he comes to exercise in corps. He must know the different cadences and length of paces, so that he may not lose the step except on very uneven and rough ground, or through want of strength.

ſtrength. In marching, he will learn how to keep himſelf dreſſed in line without being told; and it is known by frequent exerciſe a large body moves with as much facility and order as a ſmall one, which conſtitutes the baſis of this ſcience.

Neatneſs in the clothing, and a body upright and well formed, ſets off every man, and particularly the ſoldier, who being under arms, muſt keep himſelf upright without ſtiffneſs. A forced poſition becomes painful and fatiguing, but a natural one is eaſy to every body. The officer who has the charge of exerciſing a recruit, muſt examine well what he is capable of, ſo that he may give leſs time to one, who is eaſy of comprehenſion, and more to one who is not ſo quick; for this reaſon it is better that each captain and officer ſhould exerciſe ſuch recruits as are deſigned for his company, and not as it uſually happens, that one perſon only exerciſes them for the battalion; becauſe it would be impoſſible for one perſon to diſtinguiſh the capacities of ſo many men; if he treats them all alike, he never will qualify one who wants capacity. To uſe recruits with ſeverity,

rity, is improper and inhuman; patience is neceſſary where there is no wilful obſtinacy; their confidence is gained by this means, and they learn with more facility, than when they are obliged to take their arms with fear; ſeverity muſt only take place with thoſe who are lazy and inattentive; circumſpection is neceſſary when you want to obtain any end; there is not much occaſion for ſeverity, when men are kept in awe of it. A ſoldier ſhould be always conſidered as a man; the greater part of them may be brought to any thing by good treatment, and the ſoldier will do more for an officer who uſes him well, and in whom he has confidence, than for one who inſpires him with fear. Thoſe who mean to effect all by rigour, are commonly ignorant of the means by which they could aſſiſt the ſoldier, and for want of knowing thoſe means, they fall into an exceſs of ſeverity. It would be needleſs here to ſhew the methods how a recruit ſhould be inſtructed; becauſe they are already known, and with a trifling difference uniformly practiſed through the whole army. The firſt thing a recruit is to learn, is a good poſition; that is to ſay, to keep his body very upright, his head inclined to the right, his eyes turned a very little towards the flank man; by this means his shoulders will be so placed, that one will not be more to the front than the other, which is the main point, and cannot be too carefully observed. He must bring his breast forward, and keep his shoulders and arms back; his arms must hang close to his side without stiffness, so that his elbows may come back, and that the seam of his sleeves may be seen, that is to say, to keep his arms so as to touch his thigh with the flat of his hand. His toes must be turned outwards, but not too much*. In this position you begin to shew him the facings, and instil well into his mind, not to move his left heel, but only to turn himself upon it, by lifting up his toe; this is to be continued till he knows the position well, and performs the facings properly; after this he is to march; because it is natural that he should learn first how to stand, before he is

---

* The angle A B C (Pl. II. fig. 1) formed by the two feet, is about 60 degrees, consequently the cord A C from one point of the foot to the other, will be nearly equal to the length of the foot A B or B C; because A C B is an equilateral triangle.

taught

taught to march; and he muſt then directly be uſed to the cadenced ſtep, of which 75 are to be taken in the ſpace of a minute, and he muſt be likewiſe taught to keep an equal length of pace; ſo that he may gain in the ſame minute 175 feet; by this he learns at the ſame time the meaſure of his pace, and you will not be obliged, when he has firſt been taught to march ſlow, to break him of a thing that has been ſhewn him with ſo much trouble.

To march well, it is further neceſſary that the ſoldier ſhould move with a ſtiff knee, and carry his body rather forward; the firſt is obtained, by accuſtoming him to bring his toe to the ground before his heel, ſo that when he brings down his foot, he touches the ground more with the toe than with the heel; by this means the knee will keep ſtiff. The ſecond is obtained, by making him underſtand, that the body always reſts upon the leg on which he ſtands, and not upon that which he intends to lift up. This is another reaſon, which will oblige him to keep his knee ſtiff. Therefore, an officer who teaches recruits or a body of men to march, muſt keep himſelf at a certain diſtance from them, and not to ſuppoſe that his men march well, until he can no longer ſee the ſoles of their feet; it is only then that they march well. When ſeveral recruits are collected together, ſo that they may march in a rank, you muſt make them march with intervals of about the length of a ſpan between their files, until they are able to carry themſelves properly, otherwiſe they will be apt to fall upon one another, or ſupport one another; to croud, to remove their arms from their ſides, to feel their neighbour, and to contract many other habits, which it will be difficult to break them of.

In this manner make him march, for two, or three days; after this you may make him take his pouch, that he may be uſed to it; then he is to be taught the facings: he muſt know all this perfectly, before you make him exerciſe with the firelock. When he is arrived ſo far you muſt not hurry on too much, that is, begin too many things at the ſame time, nor proceed further, until he is well acquainted, with what has been already ſhewn him. The officer ſhould regulate

gulate himself according to the easy or slow conception of his recruit. You must not directly require of him, that he should perform the motions with quickness, because this will come of itself, when he has learned to perform them well; the officer begins then, to teach him first how to carry his firelock, his arms and elbows being kept in the position that has been shewn above; the back of the left hand must be turned outward, so that he can embrace the butt end of his firelock; the left elbow must be a little bent, without being too far removed from the body, only so much, that the hand may be placed behind the hilt of the sword, the breech pin must be so placed, that when you front the soldier, you see it full, and not sideways; the barrel must lie in such a manner upon the shoulder, that it may neither fall from it, nor come too near the head. In this position the recruit is to be exercised again in marching, and at the same time care must be taken, that he does not move his elbows from his side; because this is of great consequence when he is to advance or retreat; for if he does so, one of his neighbours

bours muſt naturally give way; and if he comes too cloſe again, there is an unneceſſary interval between him and his comrade, who is obliged to cloſe; this occaſions what is commonly called a *waving*, when advancing or retreating; and which is too dangerous, not to make uſe of every poſſible means to prevent. It is true, that in the beginning the recruits will be ſomewhat fatigued; and they generally try to eaſe themſelves, by bending the elbow on which the firelock reſts; but when this is prevented they at laſt are uſed to it, and it then becomes natural to them. When the recruit marches with his firelock, and the time is ſhewed him, the officer places himſelf on the left of his men, ſo that they may not ſee him; but have only their eyes fixed upon the flankman, (flügelman), for, if he ſtands near to or before the center of his men, their attention is taken off, particularly of recruits. At every ſtep, in the beginning, you muſt go up to them and ſet right their firelocks, fingers and elbows, which is already well enough known; in this reſpect nothing ſhould be neglected; and you muſt go on by the regulations, be-

cauſe

cause it contributes much to preserve uniformity; but when they become more instructed, you must neither move nor touch them, the officer only calls to them, by this means they learn to correct themselves and become more attentive; the motions which are difficult must be repeated more frequently than those which are easy, which will perfect them in both at the same time. The recruits must first learn to carry their arms, to ground them, and at the same time to present their arms, and shoulder: this is the beginning, and before they are perfectly well acquainted with this, you must proceed no further. Then, when the exercise of the firelock is over, they are again to march without it, in order that they may be still more perfect, and learn to carry themselves: afterwards they will learn to present arms, to ground their firelocks, to take them up, to advance them, to secure them under the left arm, to club and shoulder; after they have been taught how to fix and unfix the bayonet, then they are to march in close files, arm to arm, to wheel often, observing what has been mentioned against pushing

and

and crouding their neighbours; at the same time they are taught the facings with the firelock, that they may by this means learn to hold it steady; this is what at first they are to learn respecting the manual exercise; for, that part that relates to the firings must be added to it; because it belongs only to the firings. Now you proceed with the recruit to the next part; but he must previously take off the cover of the pan, and have some wooden cartridges in his pouch, after which you must observe as follows.

1. When the word is given: *cock your firelock!* he must, as is usual, at the first motion, place his thumb upon the cock, and at the second motion he cocks; for, why should not the recruit directly learn this part of his exercise, so as to acquire a habit of performing it *?

2. *Present!* the right foot must be brought back as far as possible, the left arm stretched, the breast forward and the belly drawn back; the butt end must press hard

---

* This is the nearest phrase I can imagine to convey the sense of the original, which literally is to do it with the eyes shut *(blind arbeiten)*.

against

against the right shoulder, and the cheek must lie firm upon the butt end. The soldier must be taught to take his direction along the line of the barrel to the point of sight, so that he may properly learn to aim, because an undirected shot, is as good as lost.

3. Upon the word: *fire!* he fires at the same instant with the flankman, and the firelock is then brought down to the position, where it must lie, when he is to half cock. Here is a threefold distinction to be observed; the first rank lays the firelock against the buckle of the sword belt, the second against the navel, and the third on the pit of the stomach; in consequence of this the recruits are taught to bring the firelock down to the right side, according to the rank he stands in, at the same time the right foot is placed before the left, and not behind as above; so that the heel may lie close to the under strap of the gueters; the reason why will be explained afterwards; the left heel must remain immoveable.

4. Upon the word: *half cock your firelock!* the cock which lay upon the pan, is drawn back.

5. The

5. The cartridge is seized as quick as possible, not with two but with one motion, and in taking it out of the pouch, is brought directly to the mouth; this teaches the recruits in future to exercise briskly with bran, or powder cartridges.

6. The pan being shut, the word is given: *cast about to charge!* the soldier standing faced to the right, brings the butt end of his firelock down; but instead of throwing it to the left, and lifting up the right foot, he only turns gently to the left, so as to face the enemy on whom he has fired, both his heels remain as they were, and the soldier by this means will stand with his heels close, as it should be.

This is the reason, why the right heel is placed before the left under-strap of the gueter, because by this means, the soldiers are prevented when they shoulder from being obliged to bring the right foot back to its place; by which means this advantage will be gained, that they will stand steady, and not lose the time when loading.

7. The cartridge is put into the barrel, not in two, but at one motion; the strong

motion

motion on the rammer is omitted, which is only made when the cartridge falls into the muzzle.

8. When the word is given: *draw your rammers!* this is done in two motions, and at the same time you count 1, 2; at 1, the rammer is drawn by the thumb, and the two fore fingers, and you directly flip your hand down, without turning it, so as to seize it by the middle; at 2, you intirely draw it, and put it into the barrel about an inch, the left hand at the same time keeps the firelock close to the thigh, and as steady as possible.

9. When the word is given: *ram down your charge!* this is likewise done in two motions, and you also count 1, 2; at 1, the rammer is pushed down with force upon the cartridge, and again directly drawn out, and as before, is seized by the middle close to the barrel, without turning the hand; at 2, it is quite drawn out, and placed in the first loop.

10. Upon the word: *return your rammer!* you again count 1, 2. At 1, you push down the rammer which is in the loop, with as quick a motion as possible; at 2, you give

a stroke

a stroke to the rammer and bayonet with your hand, to make it steady; as the weight of the ramrod may have loosened it, and at the same time the right hand must come briskly down to the right thigh.

11. When the word is given: *shoulder!* the recruit throws up the firelock with his left hand, and catches it by the but, without the least assistance from the right hand; this is called loading by the numbers, or the words, one, two; and the recruit will again be in the position in which he was, before he loaded. After he has gone through this three or four days, bran cartridges are given to him, and he is taught how to bite them off well and quickly; he is no longer to load by numbers, but by the word of command, that he may particularly attend to the words: *ram down your charge!* and to make of two times only one; which he will easily learn, having been previously shewn it in detail. In the same manner, when the word is given: *rammer, shoulder!* having now the ramrod in the loops, he strikes it with the flat of his hand, at the same time raising it high with the left hand; all this will teach him

[15]

him to load quick; and care muſt be taken, to inſtil well into the recruit, how he is to make uſe of the cartridge and ramrod, that he uſes the laſt in the manner ſhewn him in the tellings, without this all the trouble taken will be uſeleſs, and he will never learn well. You will do well alſo to teach thoſe of the front and rear rank, in what manner, in coming down, they may make ready with the left hand, or without making uſe of the right hand till the word of command is given, *cock!* by this means they learn to come down ſtrait, and to reſt well upon the ground; becauſe they cannot reſt upon the but, nor hang forward. Marching muſt not be omitted; but always conclude the exerciſe. Now you come to loading; and you teach the recruits the manner of bringing down the firelock, obſerving, that he keeps the firelock in the manner as has been ſaid § 3, according as he ſtands in one of the three ranks; as likewiſe that he ſlips the right heel, at the ſame time that he brings down his firelock, to the under ſtrap of the gueter of the left foot. From this time the recruit has conſtantly bran cartridges, until he is perfectly inſtructed; for,

by

by this means he learns to excercife brifkly with powder cartridges. The recruits are then daily brought more forward, and all the parts of loading are fhewn them; however they muft be well grounded in one part and perform it well, before you proceed to another. Here it is to be remembered that in retreating, and advancing, they muft load backwards, and in parapet firing, the firelock is caft about to load according to the ancient cuftom, but the pofition of the feet remain, as has been prefcribed in bringing down the firelock, fo that there muft not be two different rules given to the foldier to do the fame thing, becaufe he is likewife obliged to advance the foot when he cafts about to load.

The recruits are taught to march to the right and left, by the deploy ftep*, which they

---

* This Deploy ftep which General Eliott calls *Lock-ftep*, is according to the defcription of the author performed in the following manner. Suppofe (Pl. 2. fig. Y. Z.) A B to be the firft rank, or the head file, when inclining to the right or left by files, C D the 2d, and E F the 3d rank or file, the word, *March!* being given, they all ftep on at the fame time, and fuppofe here that they begin with the left foot, the man in D who fucceeds his

leader

they muſt know, when they fire by platoons or battalions; this will enable them to keep the cadence as well as the ſtep in advancing; but it is as much ſhortened as that the heel of one foot only comes to the joint of the great toe of the other foot; he is then taught to incline to the right and to the left, and when they know the whole, they are not to be put on duty, until they have been previouſly exerciſed amongſt a body of men, who are well diſciplined; by this means they become bold and ſteady.

Theſe are the rules, which I have thought neceſſary to eſtabliſh for uniformity, that all

---

leader B, is to place his left foot G in H in ſuch a manner as that the heel H does exactly come oppoſite the joint of the great toe I of the leading man's foot B; the ſame is to be performed with the right foot. Now if the diſtance D B of the ranks is 20 inches, the length of the pace K L, or G H will be 28 inches, or 2 feet 4 inches, which is the length of paces fixed upon in this work.

The above deſcribed ſtep has always been allowed to be of the greateſt conſequence; but ſuppoſed impoſſible for troops to accompliſh: the contrary however is clear, as the Pruſſians do it, and General Eliott has introduced it into his garriſon at Gibraltar, and very properly calls it the *Lock-ſtep*, which he has brought to ſuch perfection, that when a Corps of 1500 men march off the parade by files, the rear of the line gains ground at the ſame inſtant of time as the front.

the recruits may be drilled according to one principle, and confequently that the reft of the exercife may be alfo performed with the fame uniformity. It appears fuperfluous, to give more rules, fince there are already fo many upon the fame fubject. Neverthelefs there is found here and there fome deviations, which partly through forgetfulnefs, and partly alfo from other unknown caufes, prevent a perfect equality, the moft of them arife from the officers themfelves, and from the difference with which the words of command are given for loading. I fhall endeavour to remedy this likewife, by eftablifhing in the fecond fection the following rules.

A

With PLATOONS ftanding.

1. The officers give the word: *toon, ready!* and not, as it fometimes happens, one to fay, *ready!* another, *platoon, ready!* The word *toon* muft be pronounced fo fhort, as to be juft fufficient to awake the attention of the foldier.

2. Be-

2. Between the interval of the fire of the firſt platoon, and the preſent of the following, muſt ſcarcely be counted one, becauſe a greater delay would ſlacken the fire of the battalion; in general the words of command muſt be taken as ſoon as the preceding one has finiſhed his.

3. They leave to the preceding platoon, whom they follow, no more than one word of command; becauſe the officer of the third platoon commands: *toon ready!* when the firſt preſents; and after his fire, this other one preſents; and ſo on, the 5th with the 3d, and the 7th with the 5th.

4. The chief attention reſts between the firſt and ſecond officer; it is almoſt impoſſible for the others to fail, and it is conſequently uſeleſs, for them to look at the preceding platoon, which would make one believe that they were not ſure of what they were about.

5. The officer of the ſecond platoon is to make ready when the ſeventh preſents; but as it might be too far for him, to ſee it, he gives the word at the fire of the fifth, then he will fall in with the preſent of the ſeventh,

at whose fire, which he can hear, he commands present.

6. The first is to make ready the second time, when the eighth presents; but as he is too far off to see him, he commands upon the firing of the sixth, by which he will fall in with the present of the eighth, at whose fire he presents; if he should still be too far from him, he may at the firing of the fourth platoon, count 1, 2, 3, 4, 5, and instead of 6, give the word, *ready!* by which means he will equally obtain the time; but it is better if it can be done, to give the word at the firing of the sixth.

7. All the officers are exactly to present at 4, and instead of 5, to give the word: *fire!*

B

To the right about, and to fire by PLATOONS.

The same as when standing; it must only be well instilled into the mind, that now the eighth platoon becomes the first, and the seventh the second.

C

In advancing by PLATOONS.

1. All the above rules remain, except that the officer inftead of, *toon ready!* commands: *toon, march, ready!* There fhould be left no more time between thefe words of command, than is neceffary for the foldiers to perform the following without hurry.

2. The officer of the following platoon gives the word: *toon, march!* when his leader makes the third ftep, which he can meafure, even if he does not fee him (being obliged to look at the colours), by counting upon the word of his leader *march*, 1, 2, and inftead of 3, gives the word: *toon, march!*

3. The officer of the fecond, fhould upon the third ftep of the feventh, give the word: *toon, march!* but it would be perhaps requiring too much, if this fhould be fcrupuloufly performed; it is enough if he moves at the making ready of the feventh, which

muſt be done, when the fifth preſents, or, which is the ſame, when the third has fired. Conſequently he will not be out, when he gives the word, whether it be at the firing of the third, or the preſenting of the fifth.

4. The officer of the firſt platoon, muſt begin to give the word, the ſecond time, when the officer of the fourth has fired; ſo that he meets with the *preſent* of the ſixth, and with the *make ready* of the eighth. But both muſt obſerve, before they preſent, the ſecond platoon to wait for the fire of the ſeventh, and the firſt, for that of the eighth.

5. The (feldwebels) flag ſerjeants are to remain during the firings, as well as every ſoldier, both in advancing and retreating, at the cadenced ſtep, of which 75 are made in a minute, and to take care that the heel does not come either more before or behind, than the joint of the great toe.

6. The platoons muſt advance three common ſteps, without over ſtepping them, becauſe otherwiſe they never would advance in a ſtraight line, neither muſt they make them too ſhort, becauſe they would then fire from behind the colours.

7. For

7. For the falling in again, four or six men muſt not be waited for; becauſe they are by this means accuſtomed to move quicker; the left file leaders of the four platoons, muſt be told, that they muſt come in by the left of the colours; this muſt be underſtood of the four laſt; which the officers muſt do without being told of it.

D

By Platoons retreating.

1. The following of the platoons is the ſame as when ſtanding and advancing; and here likewiſe there muſt be only one word of command left, that is, the officer of the third platoon gives the word: *toon, about!* in as ſhort a manner, as he did before in advancing; when the firſt is making ready, the fifth gives the word upon the *make ready* of the third; the reſt is the ſame as when ſtanding.

2. The officer of the ſecond platoon, who gives the word: *toon, about!* when the ſeventh makes ready, may guide himſelf,

when he begins to give the word, by the prefenting of the fifth, or directly after the fire of the third.

3. The officer of the firft, who muft give the word: *toon, about!* when the eighth makes ready, will likewife guide himfelf, when he cannot well fee, by the prefenting of the fixth, or begin to give the word directly after the fire of the fourth.

4. As neceffary as it is to keep the ranks in a line advancing, ftill more attention muft be paid in retreating, becaufe the foldiers are then left to themfelves, and the officer is not able to direct them; for this reafon, as the noncommiffioned officers who have divifions, are fuppofed to have more judgement than the reft, it will be better to leave the care of falling in, rather to them, than to the others, to which in the exercife by divifions they muft be drilled. But it is required that the noncommiffioned officers of the four laft platoons, bring back their divifions into the line again, becaufe the foldiers fee them; wherefore, their platoons having fired, they raife their right arm and make a fignal, when the platoons are 4 or 5 deep;

deep; at that sign they directly march, and look to the left to the colours, and thus they lead their platoons close to the platoons on the left hand division; the soldiers must be practised in this, that they may follow them; because they are no longer to look back. The four first platoons have the noncommissioned officers of their divisions, when they fall into the line, on their left hand, and as they look to the right, they cannot see them; therefore some other method must be found, to obtain this end; which is this; when the officer of the first division gives the word: *toon, about!* the noncommissioned officer of the flank of the second division stops, keeps his right arm high up, when the first has fired, and makes a signal as the preceding one; when the platoon has shouldered, as far as four or five men; he then turns his eyes to the right, pays no further attention to the platoon falling into the line, which is to mind him, and it advances with a common step without running towards the right flank of the second platoon; thus, the noncommissioned officer of the third proceeds with the second, and the

the fourth with the third; and the noncommiffioned officer who breaks the files of the colours, with the fourth platoon. By this method, the battalion is always kept in clofe order, without lofing their intervals.

E

By Platoons in advancing, to fire to the rear.

Upon the word: *by platoons in advancing, fire to the rear!* the officers of the platoons, as is well known, ftep into the third rank, and the officers and noncommiffioned officers who are behind them, clofe the firft; the following of the platoons is, as when ftanding, when they go to the right about; that is to fay, the eighth will become the firft; and the firft the eighth; the words of command follow each other as when retreating; in falling into the line again, the noncommiffioned officers, who lead the divifions, are to obferve the fame as in retreating, that is to fay, thofe who are actually of the 5th, 6th,

6th, 7th, and 8th platoon, lead their own divisions; and those of the 4th, 3d, 2d, and 1st, by the noncommissioned officers who are to their right; thus he of the second, leads the first; the third, the second; the fourth, the third; and he who breaks the division of the colours, the fourth.

F

By PLATOONS retreating, to fire to the front.

The officers and noncommissioned officers who close, step at the word of command behind the first rank; and the noncommissioned officers who lead the divisions step into the third rank; the firing is, as when standing to the right about; that is to say, the eighth which must be looked upon as the first, begins first; as to the rest, the word is the same as in advancing.

G

Of the Parapet, or Street Fire.

Any observations upon the parapet or street fire is unnecessary, as it is a thing well known. I believe that the paces made by the divisions in advancing should not be too long, because it produces a bad effect, as the men appear to hurry out instead of marching; besides which they would gain by this, more ground than is necessary for them to come into the line again, which would still produce a worse effect; the object of being more advanced is but trifling, as to its contributing to a greater range of the shot; the falling in again of the files is made, as much as possible, towards the immoveable flank.

H

Of the Parapet, or Street Fire, in retreating.

Here the officer commands: *two divisions about, ready!* and so on; the divisions do not

not come in till the officer gives the word: *march!* this word of command seems to me to be very useless; for, why is it not done when standing, where the soldier is placed the same as here, and casts about his firelock the same, and when he casts about, falls in of himself; by this will be gained, when it is omitted, that the soldier will always fall equally into the line.

I.

Of the Parapet or Street Fire, in Flank.

When a battalion marches, and makes flanks with the first and eighth divisions which march with them; it is then natural to begin to charge, there, where the flank joins the battalion; as the enemy will naturally come rather this way, than from any other side: The officers command thus, e. g. he of the first division his two last files, and when broke, it is to be understood of itself that he begins likewise in the center:

ter: *two files, front, march!* whereby these files take their three steps towards the right, to which the flank marches; because before they have fired and primed, the flank will certainly have gained ground enough, for the soldiers who come out, to fall in again, without hindering the others in their advancing; the men of this flank make ready to charge, as in retreating; and load when marching, by which they keep farther to the right, in order to regain the places they occupied before. The left flank does quite the contrary, beginning the word of command by the two first files, and makes them march forward to the left, to gain likewise as much ground as possible: the soldiers here cast their firelocks to the left, to load according to the old method; they load during the march, and move to the left, so as to gain their places again.

K

When charging by BATTALIONS.

The captain upon the word: *battalion!* must advance some paces, because then the whole battalion cast their eyes upon him.

Upon

Upon the word: *march!* he advances three paces, or more, according to his orders; and after he has done this, he gives a signal with his spontoon, to affift the battalion in cafe any of the foldiers fhould have been inattentive. As neceffary as it is, in order to advance in a right line, that the paces be not taken too long, fo is it, as effential to a battalion whofe number is greater. The motion from the captain in fhouldering, is the fignal for the whole battalion, to look again to the colours, and to fall directly in again, with the *charging ftep*; (chargir fchritt); he muft not ftop here for the fake of 12, or 15 men. When in retreating, the retreat is beat, the battalions refume again an eafy ftep, that is they march with a flower cadence than ufual, keeping however the fame proportion of fteps; this, in my opinion, is likewife a fault, which ought to be remedied; becaufe the foldier would in this cafe be obliged to learn a new cadenced ftep; otherwife the battalions, making unequal fteps, would lofe their line. Therefore I believe, that it would be better, to fix upon a ftep, and keep

keep it always, which should be that which is made when charging, that is, an established cadence; but however in such manner, that the heel of the one foot, shall never be further than the joint of the great toe of the other.

PART

PART II.

Essay upon the Evolutions.

SECTION FIRST.

What is necessary to the Soldier, for the Execution of the Evolutions.

§ 1.

Of Marching in general.

MILITARY motions, to be good, require the most exact uniformity in their execution. Nothing is more essential than certain established rules, according to which, the troops are to be practised and so exercised as to execute them with the greatest quickness, but without being hurried. To obtain this end, the soldier must be first accustomed to a bold, free, and easy march; for which purpose it is necessary,

1. That each soldier should be in an upright position; his body must not incline either to the right or the left, so as to incommode his neighbour, nor must it lean too much forward; no idea is so wrong, as that he should think he stands upright, when he throws his body back; for in that position he never can step out properly; because being overpowered by the weight of his body, he will be obliged to draw back the foot he has lifted up, in order to preserve his balance; whence it happens, that one single soldier dressed in this manner, will put into disorder, not only a whole division, but sometimes the whole wing of a battalion; because not only he himself, but likewise all those near him, will not be able to dress in a line; he will always remain behind those who march strait, and who keep their breast rather forwards than backwards; consequently those who are on the right or left of him, when they dress by him, are obliged to do the same; from whence arise openings in the wings, a very dangerous waving *(schwanken)*,

ken), the stopping and pressing of a division; and every officer must know, the great influence this has upon a battalion, and much more upon a whole line.

2. The soldier must never be permitted to advance or throw back either of his shoulders. It commonly happens that he will bring his left shoulder more forward than the right, because perhaps by a false judgment, he imagines that he then caries his firelock better; suppose it to be so, though it is far from being proved, yet I think, it would be better rather to overlook this fault, than through this apparent advantage, to fall into a greater error; which as well as in the first case, would produce the waving and other inconveniences; a soldier dressed in such a mistaken manner, occasions a fault which is directly seen; because, if for example, he brings his left shoulder forward, let it be ever so little, he naturally obliges his neighbour to step out, in order to see the wing or center by which he is obliged to dress; the second man will advance somewhat more; the third, still more; and the rest in proportion; which will naturally make the whole front unequal;

unequal; on the contrary, the same thing will happen, when the soldier draws back his left shoulder more than the right; because in that case the wing will also fall off. These faults, little as they appear, must by all means be avoided; having upon the whole too great an influence. But as of two evils, the least should be chosen, it will be better to accustom the soldier to turn the shoulder to where he looks, and rather bring it back than forward; as the falling off will by this means be better avoided, and you can much easier keep a soldier back, than bring him forward; but the best, I say, is the upright position.

3. You must never permit the soldier to turn his head too much to the side to which he is to dress; though it should be in some manner allowed; but however as little as possible; because from this it will infallibly happen, that the shoulder will be brought out; he must be rather accustomed to look across his neighbour's face in order to perceive the flankman (*Flügelman*).

4. It would be of great importance if it could be done, to bring the soldier to take

equal

equal paces; by this means, not only too fcrupulous a dreffing would be prevented, but likewife the waving of the line would be avoided; in this we cannot come to an entire perfection; but we muft endeavour to approach as near as we can to it; a little confideration will make us conceive the great advantage that will arife from it, as alfo what will be obtained, when,

5. We endeavour to accuftom all the foldiers to march with equal celerity. On all occafions the march fhould be kept equal, as well in advancing as in retreating, either when they march by divifions or by files; you fhould inftil well into them the cadence, by which they are to regulate their march; but as it is eftablifhed, that in advancing 75 fteps fhould be made in one minute, and only 70 in retreating; the prefcribed orders muft in this cafe neceffarily be obferved; however as the march by divifions is nearly the fame in advancing, we may combine the two together, in order to imprint in the foldiers memory thefe two cadences, which they will naturally remember with more facility than three or more. Two exceptions

only take place, where the cadence once adopted cannot be kept; the one is in the wheelings, and the other in the deploy; in both these cases, the quickness of the steps must be doubled. If it be objected that this cannot always be executed, particularly in advancing or retreating, where sometimes it is ordered, step out *(vom leibe zu treten)*, I say that he who believes, that upon the word step out; they march by a faster time, is mistaken. It is no such thing; the same quickness of the step is kept, but only the length of paces is somewhat increased; and on the contrary when ordered to march slow, the paces are to be a little shortened.

But it will be difficult to teach a soldier to march well, if you do not pay attention to make him march with a stiff knee, and to slip his foot along with the toe pointed towards the ground, in such a manner, that when you stand before him, the sole of his foot cannot be seen, either in lifting it up or putting it down.

§ 2.

§ 2.

Of Marching to the right, by Files.

Suppose a division or a battalion is to march to the right by files, the soldiers, must previously observe all that has already been mentioned, § 1. of marching in general. But besides this, on the word: *march!* all must begin to move, and at the same time; not as it commonly happens for one to begin to step after the other; the false notion they have of treading upon the feet of each other, is the reason, why they begin with an unequal step, and some of them with a waving motion. But when it is clearly explained to them, that this first unequal step, occasions their being a hindrance to each other, and they are made to understand, that when they lift up their feet altogether, and put them down at the same time, and step out with an equal length and quickness of pace; it will then be impossible for them to obstruct one another; because it will certainly happen, that the rear man's foot will be placed where the leading man had his; I believe that they might by this means be brought out of their error. The first rank of a division, marching to the right muſt remain ſtraight upon the line, on which the wing marches; for which purpoſe each ſoldier muſt be accuſtomed to have his eyes conſtantly fixed upon the nape of the neck of his leading men, and never to look either to the right, or to the left; becauſe otherwiſe the march will be ſerpentine; this is alſo as great a fault as that of waving is in a right line. This we may be eaſily perſuaded of, by obſerving that a diviſion marching thus in a ſerpentine form, muſt naturally take up a greater ſpace, than the one which marches in a right line; becauſe between two given points, the right line is the ſhorteſt; thus it is natural, that the diviſion A, and that of B (Pl. 1, fig. 1) ſhould take up a greater ſpace, than that of C, which marches in a right line.

Therefore, this principle being adopted as demonſtrated, it follows,

1. That,

1. That, if the soldiers keep an equality in the quickness and length of paces, the distance in the divisions A and B between the files, must, when the word: *halt!* is given, be more open, than in that of C; because the line described by these divisions, taken in the whole, is longer; but as useless spaces cannot be admitted, this division and all the following ones, must close more. Now when the word: *front!* is given, and the divisions A and B, are to be dressed in a right line, they will not have ground enough; if on the contrary they keep,

2. Their distances, it will be then impossible to preserve an equal march; the men will be obliged to lengthen their steps; because those in their rear, in order not to lose their distance, are obliged to run, from whence arises a pressing up. When they are to front and to dress again, the staff officer, or general, will have an infinite trouble to give to the prest out divisions, or files, their proper distance. Before they can bring them to front, it will undoubtedly happen, that as soon as the word: *halt!* is given, the soldier will fall back of himself;

self; because he observes, that his distance, when he comes to front, will be too close; from whence it will naturally happen, that the men will tread upon each others feet, and fall into the greatest confusion; those of the second and third rank must look to the left at their leading man, and constantly follow that file; for otherwise, when the front is made, they will not only have lost their leading man, but even if the first rank should have marched well, they will fall into the same fault, as the first did; as mentioned in the above second remark. A soldier must in general be used to the keeping of his file; and he will be brought to this, when he has been made to understand, that they are only placed in files, to support their leading man, and the three men must look upon themselves, as one body only, which by this position is made capable of more resistance; but this can never be effected unless they properly attend to it.

§ 3.

§ 3.

Of Marching to the left by Files.

In this march besides the above rules, nothing farther is to be observed, than that the second and third rank, must look by the right to their file leaders.

§ 4.

Of Inclining.

This motion is without dispute, one of the most essential; being on almost all occasions necessarily made use of. It is therefore very necessary to attend with the greatest care, to exercise the soldier well in it. To effect this, you must, for example, (Pl. 1, fig. 2) when a division is to incline to the right, accustom the soldiers to lift their right feet strongly from the side, placing them however as much as possible forwards; with the left one also forwards, but along and beyond the right foot.

foot*. This motion will naturally induce the soldier, if he follows the natural position of

---

* As the above inclining, is performed by the oblique step, which can only be made of a certain length, and in a direction forming an angle of a certain number of degrees, it will be proper to explain to what degree of obliquity this step may be made, so as not to occasion any confusion in the march.

Suppose (Pl. 2, fig. 27) each man to occupy a square of 20 inches, his feet to be placed so as to form an angle A B C of 60 degrees, when he is facing perpendicularly to the line B D.

The men to perform the oblique step, may go in the direction of the diagonal E L, or in the direction E F, forming an angle F E D equal to 49°: If this line was less oblique, suppose it to be in the direction E G, the left foot E H of each man would knock against the right foot I K of his leading man, or else the pace would be extremely short.

If the step is made in the direction of the diagonal E L, or nearly so in the direction E F, the length of the pace can be of no more than about 26 inches: because the side of the square E I, or I L, being 20 inches, the diagonal E L will be about $28\frac{28}{100}$ inches, consequently the heel of the left foot E H cannot be brought farther than 26 inches from E to F, without knocking against the right foot L M of the preceding man, who is in this same oblique direction.

Thus the distance of the ranks being 20 inches (fig. 28) and the men facing perpendicularly to the front, cannot in this direction by each oblique pace gain more ground straight forward, than about $18\frac{1}{2}$ inches: because the
square

of his body, to bring his right shoulder back and the left forward. A fault which must

square of the diagonal N P, is equal to the sum of the two squares of N S, S P, and the length of the oblique pace being the diagonal N P, the ground gained forward will be the side N S of the rectangular triangle N S P; but this side N S will be the square root of half the square of N P; therefore this diagonal being 26 inches, the square of 26 is equal to 676, its half is 338, and its square root is $18\frac{38}{100}$ inches for the side N S.

When the direction is taken a little more obliquely than the diagonal as N Q, the ground gained forward N T will be about 17 inches; and if less oblique as N O, the ground gained forward N R will be about $19\frac{1}{2}$ inches.

If the distance A B (fig. 29) of the ranks was 22 inches, the oblique step would be no longer; because the diagonal A C being that of a parallelogram, in which the side A B is equal to 22 inches, and the side B C equal to 20 inches, the diagonal A C, or the hypothenuse of the rectangular triangle A B C will be equal to nearly $29\frac{66}{100}$ inches; therefore the oblique pace would then be $27\frac{1}{2}$ inches, so as not to knock against the right foot of the preceding men who march in the same direction. This oblique step which goes in the direction of the diagonal A C, forms an angle C A D equal to 48 degrees. Now as the distance A B of the ranks is here 22 inches, the oblique step may be performed with more facility, than in the preceding distance of 20 inches; and if this direction is less oblique as A F forming with A D an angle F A D equal to 52 degrees, there will also be gained more ground by it.

The above may serve as a general rule to calculate the length of the oblique step, according to the distance of the muſt be abſolutely avoided; we muſt not think we remedy this, when we make the ſoldier bring his right ſhoulder forward when he inclines to the right, and his left ſhoulder when he inclines to the left. But what will happen from the frequent calling to them to do this? a ſecond fault, which if not worſe, is however analagous to the firſt; for when the ſoldier brings his right ſhoulder too forward, he will alſo be as ill dreſt in the line, as when he keeps it backward. With one ſingle diviſion indeed,

the ranks E I, and the ſide E D the ſpace given to each man.

But if according to the opinion of General Eliott, the poſition of the feet is brought to an angle of 90 degrees inſtead of 60 as before mentioned, the men will have more facility in performing the oblique ſtep; becauſe ſuppoſe (fig. 27) the inclining to be performed to the right, and the two feet E H, E N forming an angle of 90 degrees, the right foot E N will then naturally keep the direction of the diagonal E L, and the left E H, will be brought with more facility along the right one, when paſſing it to form the pace which is to be deſcribed by this foot: this angle of 90 degrees will eaſily be preſerved, by the feet of the men, particularly when they keep their ſhoulders *ſquare to the front*. Now if the diſtance E I, or the opening of the ranks is taken a little more than 22 inches, ſuppoſe it 24 inches, the men will then be able to perform longer paces, and conſequently gain more ground forward.

ſuch

such a fault is not so striking; but with one or more battalions, that march *in front*, and which at the same time are to incline, the confusion must be unavoidable, when a division brings the right shoulder too forward; because all the divisions and battalions who are on the right, are then obliged to run, in order to keep the line; and on the contrary, those who are on the left are obliged to stop; and when the second motion is added to this, namely, to incline to the right, you may easily conceive what confusion will then happen.

An officer should then take the utmost care, to avoid both these faults, which he will obtain; when it is well explained to the soldiers, that the word: *the right shoulder forward!* will only mean, do not let your right shoulder fall back; but remain on your feet with the rest of your body in the same position as you did before you begun to incline. The officer must endeavour to understand this distinctly himself; and he must not imagine that his division marches well, until he be very sure, that at each step, made by it, it comes in a line C D parallel to that A B from whence

whence it set out. When a division is to incline to the left, the above rules are also to be observed; but are to be taken in an opposite sense: however it must be noticed, that in inclining to the left, the soldier must still keep his eyes to the right; an officer also who is to command a division to the right of the colours, as for example, the fourth, third, second, and first, will do well, to march them often to the right, with their eyes turned to the left. He will reap great advantage from this, when he is to perform that motion with his division in a battalion, where the soldiers are obliged to keep their eyes to the left.

§ 5.

Of INCLINING to the right, and left, by FILES.

When a division marches to the right or left by files; it should be accustomed to incline as when marching to the front; that is; each man must as well as in front carry his right shoulder inclining to the right, and his

left

left shoulder when he inclines to the left, in the same position, as he had it when he marched straight out; each file must according to fig. 3. be supposed to represent one rank which is to march inclining to the front; and when they all comprehend this, and likewise observe, what has been said § 2 and 4; such a division will move as well and as easily, as a division which marches inclining to the front. An officer cannot too often repeat this manœuvre with his division, in order that they may be well practised in it. What follows will shew the great advantage the above will be of, particularly when marching in flanks.

§ 6.

Of the DEPLOY MARCH.

When a division is to be practised in this march, the officer is to give the word: *deploy, to the right or left : by files!* the division then without stopping or marking any time, is to incline to the right or to the left by files. Upon the word: *march!* all step together at the same time, besides which every thing must be observed, that has been said § 5 of inclining to the right, and left, by files; the quickness of the step in this march must be doubled, so that in the space of time that two common steps are made, four, of these deploy steps are taken. It will however naturally happen, that the quick steps will be made shorter, than the common ones; but it would be also well, when the soldiers are exercised, that they should keep a limited length in the deploy step, as well as in the common ; at least I think that by this means the irregularity, and unnecessary time which is taken up to bring the men into their proper distance again, will be somewhat spared.

§ 7.

Of Closing.

Closing is marching with a division, or with one or more battalions to the right or to the left, and keeping the front. Thus when a division, for example, is to close to the right, and the officer has given the word:

to the right clofe! then all the foldiers upon the word: *march!* bring their right feet according to the given line towards the right, and bring their left to it; this they continue to do until they come to the given fpot. Here it is to be obferved;

1. That the noncommiffioned officers of the right flank, or the flank man of the left flank, muft not take very long paces, but fhort ones, and in proportion quicker.

2. That the foldiers keep the line the fame as when inclining, that is, that they do not bring either of their fhoulders forward, or backward.

3. That they conftantly keep their proper diftances.

4. That it be not allowed them to bend their knees in this movement: and,

5. That they do not overrun the given line, as fometimes happens.

To avoid this it will be neceffary, that, when an officer exercifes his divifion in this movement, he fhould keep himfelf at a certain diftance either to the right, or to the left, and in the fame line with his divifion, by which means he will very eafily obferve, if his divifion keeps the alignment properly,

[52]

and what man has prevented it. If he does not make use of this means, but goes on with his division, he never will be certain whether he himself has not lost the given line, nor know who has occasioned the running forward, or the remaining behind. (Pl. 1. fig. 4).

But when a division is to close to the left, besides the above rules it is to be observed; that the men upon the word: *left close!* must cast their eyes to the left, and keep them to the left, until they are dressed in line again.

This essential rule is also to be observed, that no man is to halt, when he has lost his distance, until he has regained it, even though his officer should have already given the word: *halt!* yet they must not be alto push or croud each other.

§ 8

Of WHEELING.

Wheeling is nothing else, than to give to a division just the same position as is given to a single man, when commanded to the
right

right or left about face; from hence comes the movement, *to the right or left about, wheel!* in the same manner as the different positions can be given to a single man; so the positions of a whole division may be obtained. As for instance, if a division is to wheel to the right, the word is given (supposing the ranks to be in close order) *by divisions, to the right, wheel!* upon the last word of command, *wheel!* the whole division must cast their eyes to the left; so that the men may dress themselves by the left flank and keep an equal step with it, and neither push forward, or remain behind; the men must at the same time remain in close order to the right, that is they must feel their right hand neighbour, without crouding him; they must also not be allowed to hide their heads; but the greatest attention must be paid that they are also upright, and keep their knees as stiff as when marching forward; otherwise the wheeling will never be well performed. But the principal rule which should here be observed, is, that a division which wheels, must make their steps twice as quick, as when they march straight for-

forward; becaufe if this is omitted by a divifion, it never will keep its diftance; and I believe when carefully examined, it will be found, that the repeated running and ftopping in a column, is chiefly owing to the unequal wheeling of the divifion: the following example will make this clear; I fuppofe that two divifions of 24 files each, march with the moft exact diftance between them, as E B (Pl. 1. fig. 5.) of 18 paces, the fecond divifion muft then be juft at the fame diftance of 18 paces from the firft, when it begins to wheel; but the quarter of the circle b d, which muft be performed by the left flankman b, will come when calculated to fomething more than 28 paces; if the firft divifion in wheeling keeps alfo the foregoing equal march; the fecond divifion will arrive at the wheeling point b, 10 paces before the firft is marched up; if to this is added the fpace of time in which are given the words: *halt, wheel! halt, drefs, march!* and when marching into the line, the word: *eyes to the left!* and at the fame time, that with the quicknefs of the ftep, they are not to ftep out too far; it will then eafily be feen, that
this

this delay takes up so much time, that nearly 8 paces more may be taken; these 8 paces being added to the above 10 will make 18 paces, by which the second division would arrive too soon at b; and as this one must not be hindered as to the equality of its march, because it would occasion a stop in the whole column; it follows, that the first division must regain their 18 lost paces, so that the second division may just begin to wheel, when the first marches up from the point of wheeling. This cannot be otherwise obtained, than by marching twice as quick. If (fig. 6) on the contrary in the second case, the second division was to order its march so, as not to wheel sooner, than till its foregoing division begins to step forward (which however would always be a fault) it would both when marching with the common pace and wheeling, have made 28 paces, before the left flankman A at the second would have described the quarter of the circle; and consequently by the delay of the 8 paces which have been lost by the words of command, they would have further lost the distance of 10 paces, which afterwards must be regained by a quicker pace;

pace; faults which muſt be abſolutely avoided, and which proves, how neceſſary it is to practiſe a diviſion very well in the wheelings. There is nothing more to be obſerved in wheeling to the left, than what has been ſaid in the above rules; except, that the men then keep their eyes to the right.

To the right and to the left about, means nothing more, than that a diviſion inſtead of a quarter circle is to deſcribe by wheeling the ſemicircle. It commonly happens, that the men of a diviſion and particularly the flankmen, ſtop, before the officer gives the word: *halt!* or that they overſtep one or more paces, before the officer has given the word; this happens, becauſe a ſoldier is more accuſtomed to what he is often doing, than to what ſeldom occurs to him; and as wheeling is commonly done by a quarter of a circle, he will be ſo mechanically uſed to this motion, that it will be difficult to him to ſtop ſooner or later, when once he has adopted a point to come to, whether he has reached the point or not. It will then be difficult to an officer, to give to his diviſion the proper line when

wheeling

wheeling is required either below or above a quarter of a circle; from whence it follows, that a division should never be practised in the same wheelings; but you should make it wheel sometimes more, and sometimes less; nor must the soldier be permitted to stop in the division, until the word: *halt!* is given; nor to step further out, when it is already given; but the whole division must in wheeling, always remain at the once established march, till the word of command is given.

The division must be like a machine, which by the word: *march!* is put into motion, and which upon the word: *halt!* stops at once its course.

These few rules above, are those evolutions according to which the soldiers must be drilled; and it would be more hurtful than useful, if more was shewn to them, which would be of no other use than to confuse the mind. They will be sufficiently instructed by these few rules, to perform all the possible evolutions, which may be commanded by their officers.

SECTION SECOND.

Of the Evolutions themselves, and what an Officer should observe here.

I suppose a battalion formed into eight divisions, and in close order to charge, with the evolutions which have been hitherto used; and I suppose, that the men who compose them are drilled according to the above rules, and so qualified, that the officer need only pay attention to himself, and the manœuvres which are to be made; otherwise that officer, (and experience teaches us this), will fall into unavoidable faults, who, during the manœuvres, should give too much time to the men; and he will do well, to remit the care of them to the officers and noncommissioned officers who close the files.

§ 9.

Of the Marching off.

A battalion marches off either to the right or to the left by files, and then there is
nothing

nothing further to be obferved, than what has already been faid § 2 and 3; only that all officers, who have divifions, are to ftep out three paces before them, keep the ftep with the flank captain, that their divifions may drefs themfelves by them, and that the officers may be able to take proper care of them. Or the battalion marches off by divifions, which is the common method. Should it march off by divifions from the right, or left, and the word given by the commandant of the battalion: *by divifions, to the right, or left, wheel!* then all the eight divifions wheel about together, and obferve, what has already been faid of wheeling with a fingle divifion. As foon as the firft divifion is come to the ground, the word of command is given by the right flank captain, when marched off from the right, and by the left flank captain, when marched off from the left, and as foon as the eighth divifion is about: *halt, drefs!* the other feven divifions, give the word of command at the fame time, with him; and they naturally muft agree, when it is fuppofed that all the divifions wheel with the

fame

same quickness and length of paces. The eighth division must also endeavour to give the word: *march!* at the same time, so that all the eight divisions may at once begin to step with the same foot, and may fall into the same step as is given by the first division, and which step they are absolutely to keep. If it is not done so, it will follow, that the officer who stops, must lose the space of the two paces. For example: if the second division is too slow, and does not give the word of command at the same time with the captain, it cannot then step out, until the first division lift up for the second time the left foot; because it must march off with the same foot, as the preceding division, consequently it has lost two paces; now if all the divisions do the same, there will be lost in the battalion the distance of 14 paces. Therefore it will be proper that the commandant of the battalion should give the word: *march!* But as this is not customary, it should be endeavoured to fix for the captain, and all the other divisions, a certain point of time according to which they are to give the word.

It might, for example, as at the prefent of the platoon firing, be eftablifhed, that after their divifions have wheeled, and the word is given: *halt, drefs!* they fhould let pafs juft as much time, as to enable them to count as at the prefent, 1, 2, and inftead of 3, to give the word: *march!* If this is not brought to an entire perfection, it will come however pretty near to it, and though it be ever fo little there will be ftill enough gained. The officers as long as they not to march in the *line*, march in the front and center of their divifions, at the diftance at moft of 4 to 5 paces from them; they are to look often at their divifions, to make them keep the fame ftep, and likewife to preferve them in good order.

There are alfo other methods of marching off, which indeed are not practifed, but are however of great utility, particularly during a campaign; and it will not be amifs, to give now and then to the officers an idea of this; thefe are to march off from the flank with four or fix files. Nothing further is here to be obferved, except that the officer divides his divifions into as many
fections

sections of four or six files, as he is strong in the number of his men; if then each section is considered as a division, the noncommissioned officers, or flank men being accustomed to keep the distance, it will be seen that no further remark is necessary.

The marching off with six files, is however, to be preferred to that with four; because a division of 24 files, is then only divided into four sections, which as to the keeping the distance may be left to the care of the closing officers and noncommissioned officers, besides which such a regulated march, gives to the soldiers much ease, as they are not in close files; but may march at double distance, without altering by that, the distance of one section from another. Because in the distance of six files, there must be just room enough for six men. But there are only three men to march in this distance, consequently each may take double his distance. Besides this by such an order of march, the frequent falling off in the divisions will be prevented, which fatigues very much in a march; you will also seldom meet with a defile, where six fix files cannot pafs; but fuppofe there was one, where only three would pafs, this would ftill make but little hindrance; becaufe, as the files march with a double diftance, they may be broke off in the following method.

For example; if marched off from the right, and to be broke off from the right; the three men of the firft rank of the left flank of the fection, incline behind the 1ft, 2d and 3d men of the 3d rank of the right flank.

And on the contrary, when marched off from the left, then the ranks march in clofe order, as muft be done in the breaking off of ranks, till they have paffed through the defile, and it is obvious that this will make no alteration in the diftance of the fections. But this is only a propofition, which I give to accuftom officers, who have not yet made a campaign, to marches in the field, and to make them fearch for every means that may be proper to leffen the fatigue of the foldier.

§ 10.

§ 10.

Of breaking off in Divisions.

A division breaks off into 3, 6, 4, or 2 sections; and this is commonly done from the center. In the first case, the officer divides his division into three equal parts (Pl. 1. fig. 7), the center section continues marching; when he gives the word: *break off!* (this is to be understood when they march with close ranks, otherwise the ranks must first be closed), the two other sections remain halting. As soon as the third rank of the center section has passed the first of the two others, the section of the right flank marches, and inclines to the left behind the 2d. And as soon as the 3d rank of the 1st section, has passed the 1st of the 3d, they incline to the right behind the 1st. If on the contrary, it is marched off from the left, as (fig. 8) the 3d is first to take place behind the 2d, and then the 1st behind the 3d.

Should

Should it happen, that in a division, the sections have not an equal number of files; it must then be observed, that the center section is to be always the strongest; and the last that breaks off, to be always the weakest.

For example; in a division of 23 files, when it is to march off from the right, the 3d section is to have only seven files; if on the contrary, it is marched off from the left, the 1st section is then only to have seven files. If this division, on the contrary, had only 22 files, then the strength of the 1st and 3d sections, would only be seven files.

Should a division (fig. 9) with six sections, or which is the same with four files, break off from the center; the officer must then, when marched off from the right, divide his division into four, and four files; beginning from the right flank, and when marched off from the left, to begin from the left flank. If it should happen that all his sections have not four files, the last one which is to break off, must be the weakest, if not less than three files. In case a section should have only two files, then the

officer

officer muſt rather make one ſection leſs, and add one file to the two firſt advancing, ſo that the two firſt ſections may be of five files. But if there is only one file remaining, it muſt be added to the firſt advancing ſection. Then he gives the word: *break off!* upon this word of command, all the ſections are to proceed, as has been ſaid before, when this is performed with three ſections. In marching off from the right, the 3d marches firſt, then follows the 4th, then the 2d, the 5th, the 1ſt, and laſtly the 6th.

If marched off from the left, as in (fig. 10) the 4th begins to move, followed by the 3d; then the 5th, the 2d, the 6th, and the 1ſt moves laſt.

The officer is to proceed in the ſame manner of dividing, when the diviſion breaks off with ſix files, or into four ſections (fig. 11); that is, inſtead of four he divides them into ſix, and then marches; and when breaking off, by marching off from the right, the 2d ſection advances, is followed by the 3d, the 1ſt, and then the 4th.

In marching off from the left (fig. 12) the 3d advances, the 2d follows, and then the 4th, and laftly the 1ft.

But when a divifion is to break off into two fections only, as in (fig. 13); the officer is then to take off the fourth part of his divifion from each flank, and make them break off behind the center of it; and thefe fections are then to join behind the center of the advanced ones.

It may alfo happen, that the divifions are obliged to break off, from the right or left flank; here nothing further is to be obferved, than that the fections muft naturally follow inclining, either behind the right, or left flank fection (fig. 14 and 15).

In all breakings off, the following general rules are to be obferved.

1. A divifion muft not break off, before it is at the place where the firft broke off, that is clofe to the defile.

2. The arms to be carried very fharp.

3. The ranks, as well as the fections, muft remain in clofe order; the men muft particularly keep an exact ftep.

4. A broken-off divifion, muft never wheel, but incline about. There is one fingle cafe only that can take place, where a divifion is not to keep the ftep; that is, when paffing over light bridges, and particularly when marching over bridges made with boats, where the keeping of the ftep would produce fuch a motion, as might be hurtful to the bridges.

§ 11.

Of Marching up.

When a divifion has broke off from the center, and is to march up again (fig. 16); then all the fections belonging to the right flank, upon the word given: *march up!* incline out to the right, they endeavour with a quick ftep, but however, without running, to drefs again in the line, with the center fection. Here the men caft their eyes to the left, until they are dreffed in the line with the center fection, and have the ftep; then they caft their eyes again to the right. The fections of the left flank
incline

incline in the same manner, as those of the right, did, outwards to the left.

If on the contrary, a division is broke off from the right or left flank, then all the broken-off sections incline out, either to the right or to the left. It would be useless, to give more rules upon this; because the preceding marching section, may only be considered, as one broke off from the center; and the same may be imagined with regard to the others, which are standing above or below it.

You may proceed in the same manner, when a division marches to the right, or to the left by files. Because a single man, or file, may then be considered only as a section, and made to march off, according to the above rules (fig. 17 and 18).

The following general rules are here necessary to be observed.

1. The front marching section of all the divisions, however broken off, must, in marching up, go straight forward after each other. The first section must take particular care, not to deviate either to the right, or to the left. The above first rule proves,

that it was not unneceffary to eftablifh certain fundamental principles, according to which the fections are to break off; becaufe if the officers of the divifions were fo undetermined, that one divifion fhould make the 3d fection advance, the other the 4th; it would undoubtedly happen in marching up, where the advanced fection muft move ftraight on, that one divifion would overflank the other by a whole fection.

2. All the divifions marching with the fame ftep, and in clofe order, when marched up, will have their proper diftance. But as there may be fome obftacles in the defile, which will prevent the officer from attending to his men properly, this muft not be ftrictly required. Wherefore the firft divifion in marching up, is to continue in its proper march; but not to let their men ftep out fo wide, as is cuftomary, in order that the other divifions may recover their diftances without running.

3. When the divifions of a battalion do not march up in the fame time, but divifion by divifion; none of the divifions, as when breaking off, is to march up before it is
come

come to the place where the first began to march.

§ 12.

An officer of the least experience, will easily see how necessary it is, that the divisions should with the utmost care, keep their exact distances; that is, the interval of one division from the other, must be such, as that when wheeling in, the space be just filled up by the files of which the division consists; so that the men may not stand either too far, or too close, from each other. If this is not observed, the battalion must then either open, or close, when wheeled in.

These movements are not only unnecessary, but may likewise be of dangerous consequence in action; because if the men are too close, it will naturally happen that some files will be pushed out, whose fire will be lost. If on the contrary, they are too open, the resistance would be diminished, which they otherwise would oppose to the enemy;

enemy; and particularly against cavalry; besides that dangerous waving, which would undoubtedly happen in the advancing of the battalions.

Let a line be supposed to consist of 20 battalions, in which each battalion, would have lost only eight paces distance, which is one in each division; this would in the whole line make 160 paces, which a commanding general would be obliged first to order to close or to open, so as not to fall into the above mentioned ill consequence. It is inconceivable what time will be lost by this, which certainly on a day of battle might be more usefully employed. It may be taken for granted, that by this movement, the dressing in line will undoubtedly be lost; and consequently you will be obliged to dress it again.

This shews how necessary it is, for every officer, to perfect himself in the exact keeping of distances, and to give him the means to obtain it, by an easy method; my advice would be this, suppose a certain distance (which may be done in walking) to consist

of

of a certain number of paces; then pace it, and this will shew what is deficient in the exact number. This being often done, the practice of it will enable you to judge with accuracy, and make you more ready, not only to make use of it with your platoon, but it will likewise enable you to judge on other occasions, how many battalions are wanted to occupy such or such a spot of ground. As a second rule, you must never accustom yourself to take the distance from the 3d, but from the 1st rank of the preceding division; because the ranks are often not close enough, and have not in themselves, the exact distance.

§ 13.

Of the ALIGNMENT.

The *alignment* (fig. 19 .and 20) is an imaginary right line given between two points A and B (fig. 19), and which are called *points des vuës*. To march in the alignment is nothing else, but to make the troops march in that right line. But you are not to imagine, that this right line, which is the only one that can be drawn between the two given points, can be so easily found by one single man, and still less by an officer, who is to direct his division to it; particularly, when the *points des vuës* are far distant, which is then quite impossible. But if on the other hand, the points are so given, that by one of them, you may wheel in; as for example, by A (fig. 19); then indeed, the beginning of the line which is to serve to direct the alignment, will be obtained. But it is difficult to keep it, when there cannot be found more objects, which come in the same right line with the other point, and which consequently must lie in the same direction. Because, an officer being either in C, D, or E, will always believe he is in the alignment; having from all these points, the same *points des vuës* in sight, as if he was in F; in which three several points C, D and E however, he will make an angle, which he does not perceive. Whence it follows, that if there are not two objects before him, by which he can direct himself, it is im-

possible

possible he can come in a right line with them; but if he has them, nothing is easier; for, then the officer is only to march, so as to have always the furthest object covered by the nearest, or which is the same thing, to have both in the same line. For example, the officer at A (fig. 20) will not deviate from the line B C, when he marches, so as to keep C covered by the point D.

It is however possible, to obtain this line by another method: when there are two officers that understand it. But, as it is necessary here, that he should often look back, it will then happen, that he will partly change his position, but mostly his step; this will occasion a stop in the whole column, which must be avoided as much as possible.

The officers who are marching in the center, will by this means lose their distance, which is likewise a fault; therefore it will be better, to forsake this method entirely.

I come then back to the first, to shew, how to make intermediate points, when the nature of the ground does not of itself give any. If there were any, it would then

then indeed be needlefs to look for them; but as this very feldom happens, and as an officer may eafily lofe them when going through a valley that lies between; it will then be better, in order not to multiply the rules, to keep to one fixed method, which fhall be given here.

The fureft points which can be had, are the adjutants, who are exercifed to this, and who are to practife themfelves in it, in the following manner.

The points A and B (fig. 21) are the two *points des vuës*, by one of which, namely A, you may wheel into the line. As foon as thefe points are given, the firft adjutant, either of the general of the brigade, or of the leading battalion, is to ride on from A, towards B, from 150 to 200 paces, but not farther; becaufe this would retard the march; here his commandant, or any other perfon, who remains at the point A, is to drefs him upon the point B; he is then to make a mark on the ground where he ftands, and then rein back his horfe, until the horfe's head correfponds with the point marked on the ground.

N. B.

N. B. The adjutants muſt always face the men, when they are wheeled into the line. By this means there will be found an intermediate point, that is, the head of the horſe, which the diviſions march cloſe by, and which muſt be kept in a right line with the point B. But this is not ſufficient, for when the officer of the firſt diviſion has paſſed this adjutant, he will be in the ſame caſe as when at the point A; conſequently another intermediate point muſt be got, before he marches on, which point will now be eaſily found. The adjutant (fig. 22) of the ſecond battalion of the line, or ſome other adjutant of the general rides on, as ſoon, or even before the head of the ſecond battalion comes up to the firſt in C, and relieves him, placing himſelf ſo, as that the head of his horſe, may be juſt where the firſt one ſtood.

The firſt adjutant is again to ride 200 paces further on, from C to D, directs himſelf by the adjutant C, and the point A; and as before, reins his horſe back, ſo that the head of it is placed the ſame; and by this means he procures another intermediate point.

point. If the line is to be continued, a third adjutant must relieve the second in C, that one again the first in D, and that one to place himself again at 200 paces further in E, in the direction of the horses heads of those in C and D, and proceed as before.

Three adjutants will in this manner be sufficient to give the direction to a whole line, and to keep them in it, when they alternately relieve one another, as has been said above, and the third is necessary; because the first adjutant cannot always see the point, which must be marked by him. However when the line is long, it will then be necessary, to have one or two adjutants more, to relieve the others, that the center and rear may not lose the line.

But when in the second case, the *points des vuës*, are far distant, and so placed, as not to admit the wheeling into the line by one of them; as for example, A and B (fig. 23), there will then be no other means, than that the alignment should be first taken by two adjutants, one of whom will be as in the first case at A (fig. 22) at the wheeling in point; then there is nothing else to

be

be done, than to prolong the line by the adjutants; to find out then this alignment in a ſhort time, ſo that the column may not be ſtopped, the following rules muſt be made uſe of, and by practice they will be enabled to perform it with great readineſs.

Let then A and B (fig. 23) be the given *points des vuës*; L the column which is to wheel in; d and e the two adjutants, who are to take the alignment. As ſoon as the *points des vuës* are given, the adjutant e rides about 50 paces to the right, or to the left, and a little ſide ways, according as the column is to wheel in. The adjutant in d, endeavours to place himſelf as quick as poſſible in the direction of that in e, and the point B; however, ſo as to remain always before the head of the column; after he has thus placed himſelf in the direction with e, he has nothing elſe to do, than to look conſtantly towards the right at the one in e, that he may always keep with him in the direction of the point B, however he moves; on the contrary, the adjutant in e, is to look conſtantly to the left at the

one

one in d; and as this one sees, that the point A is yet before him, then the one in e has nothing else to do than to ride on forwards, until he in D comes to be in a line with A, who constantly has directed himself by e and B; it will then naturally follow, that he will come in the direction of A; as soon as he sees this, he stops, and both D and E will then certainly be in the alignment A D E B.

If two adjutants exercise themselves in this, they will find that but a little practice is wanted, to come into the alignment on the gallop, whence there will be no fear of any stop in the column.

Should it happen, that the alignment was already passed in F, it will directly appear to the one at C; because he will see the point A out of the direction C F; wherefore he will then be obliged to come back, and to proceed as before.

But it is not enough, that the staff officers, and those who are on horseback, should take on themselves this trouble, and know, how to take the alignment; every officer should know this equally well; because

cause besides that, he may occasionally be employed as an adjutant; he will likewise learn by these few rules, how to lead his division more perfectly. Should his preceding division deviate from the alignment, he will, if he knows the rules according to which the adjutants keep it, correct this fault, before it shall have an influence upon the whole line; and how easy is it for officers walking two and two, to practise themselves in this rule, by taking points of sight; between which they may direct themselves?

§ 14.

Of Marching a Battalion into the Alignment.

When a battalion marches off from the right, it may wheel in, into the alignment, either to the right or to the left. In both cases the principal rule to be observed, is, that the left flank must be placed upon the line of alignment; by observing what we shall now say of the equal march, keeping distances, and marching into the alignment, nothing will be easier; yet nothing will be more difficult, if one or more of the following rules are omitted. Suppose, then (fig. 24) the given *points des vuës*, to be C and D, E the wheeling-in point, and F the adjutant, who directed himself by it. The battalion then is marched off from the right, and is to wheel in to the left. In both cases, the principal rule is, that not only the noncommissioned officers of the right flank of the first, but also all the noncommissioned officers of the other divisions, are to march straight on towards the wheeling-in point.

When the officer is come as near to the point E (fig. 24), as the distance wanted for his division; he gives the word: *halt, wheel!* he will then if he has kept the distance well, just come in with his left flank-man upon the wheeling-in point E; after having without delay, given the word: *halt, dress!* he steps to the left flank, and gives the word: *eyes left!* and *march!* he is not to make any stop in these words of command, but only to let just as much time pass,

pass, as will enable his men to perform them; because he would otherwise keep back his rear man. Then he marches, (without looking back, or minding any thing else) with the established cadence of step towards the second *point de vuë*, in such a manner, that his body passes close to the horse's head of the adjutant, whom he has besides the point D, constantly in a right line, and which he must never deviate from. This is a rule which must be observed by the officers that follow; and should any division happen to deviate from it, the one that follows must not fall into the same error; but regulate his march again by the adjutant.

The principal attention of the first officer, must be never to change his step with regard to its length, and cadence; because otherwise, either a running or a stop would undoubtedly happen in a battalion, and still more so in a large column. He must further endeavour to march, so as to keep his division, as much as possible, in such a direction, that his first rank may make a perpendicular with the line, upon which he marches;

marches; but his mind being sufficiently employed, and not being able to attend to his men, they muſt be ſo exerciſed, as to dreſs themſelves. The ſame is to be underſtood with reſpect to all the other officers, who lead the other diviſions; beſides which the officers muſt yet further obſerve what follows, and they cannot pay too much attention to it.

Theſe rules are,

1. That the rear diviſions, upon the word: *march!* of their front diviſions, give the word: *halt, wheel!* and there will be a perfect agreement, when the officers keep exact diſtances, and make their diviſions wheel with a double ſtep, as has been before ſaid.

2. At the point, where the front or firſt diviſion wheels, all the other diviſions muſt wheel, whatever number there may be; (this muſt be done when not wheeling-in to the alignment). Therefore, all the diviſions march ſtraight forward towards the firſt rank of the preceding diviſion, which already has wheeled. But it commonly happens, that the diviſions of a battalion

in

in wheeling to the right, diverge to the left of the wheeling-in point. A fault, which when not quickly repaired, will have a great influence in causing a bad marching up in line. To make this clear; suppose (fig. 25) that the first division of the battalion had already wheeled-in, into the alignment A B; now instead of the second division, marching upon the first rank of the first division; it generally happens, that the flank of the third rank of the second division, and so on, will always deviate more and more from the wheeling-in point. There are only two causes that can occasion such a fault: either the officers before the wheeling-in, have taken too short a distance, endeavouring by this to gain some steps; or the division does not wheel with the required quickness, and, apprehensive of losing their distance when wheeled in, they make use of this resource, to wheel in so much the sooner. But consider what will be the consequence of this: now, taking the depth of a division, that is, two steps from the first to the third rank; then each division which marches upon the rank of the preceding divifion, deviates two fteps from the wheeling-in point, it confequently lofes two fteps; this amounts to 14 fteps for the whole battalion, the fecond and all the other battalions will lofe 16 fteps. Now the queftion is, how to regain the lofs of thefe fteps? by running; fuppofing the line of eight battalions, the laft divifion of the 8th battalion, muft then regain 126 fteps, which have been loft. How neceffary is it then, that the flanks of all the divifions, whether they have marched off from the right or the left, fhould march in a ftraight line upon the firft rank, or upon the wheeling point, where the firft divifion begun.

If a battalion is marched off from the right, and is to wheel-in to the left, into the alignment; the firft divifion begins to wheel upon the line of alignment itfelf, inftead of remaining as before at the diftance of a divifion from it; and whan has been faid above, concerning the flank-noncommiffioned officers, with regard to their marching ftraight forward to the wheeling point, and on the firft rank of the preceding divifion,

fion, is now left to the care of the flank-man, who confequently muft be an intelligent man. All that has been faid of the wheeling-in of a battalion, when marched off from the right; muft likewife be obferved when marched off from the left; to which then there is nothing more to be added.

The only difference confifts in this, that you act juft the contrary with the wings; and you do the fame with the left of the divifions, as was done with the right; and with the right, the fame that was done with the left.

For example; when you are to wheel into the alignment to the left, the left flank-men are to march towards the wheeling-in point, and upon the firft rank of their preceding divifion, and with the right they come out of the alignment. If on the contrary, they wheel in to the right, the noncommiffioned officers of the right flank, march upon the alignment, where the wheeling-in point is.

§ 15.

Of the POINT d'APPUI.

The *point d'appui*, is that point, to which the wing of a battalion or corps of an army is fixed. From which fixed wing, as soon as the line has wheeled in, it is then to begin to make the alignment with the opposite *point de vuë*; and one single cafe only can alter this principle. The reason why in marching off from the right, it is to be dressed by the right wing; and when marching off from the left, by the left wing; is, because it is supposed that it is marching towards the *point d'appui*, to fix there; excepting when you take distance to the rear, of which more will be said hereafter.

§ 16.

The main point in evolutions, and particularly in advancing and retreating, if you will

will have them well executed; confists in the dreffing of the battalions. The beft practifed foldiers will advance ill, without any fault on their fide, if they ftand ill dreffed in the battalion.

Two examples will make this clearer: fuppofe that the battalions A and B, confift of men perfectly well exercifed, but ill dreffed in the battalion; thofe in A, when they advance perpendicularly to their line as required, will by degrees concenter more and more, as they advance; confequently they will crowd, and in the end confufion will evidently happen (fig. 26). And thofe in B on the contrary, will fall into the oppofite fault, becaufe they muft naturally open by degrees, as they advance.

If it be however objected, that the faults arifing from a defective dreffing, may be corrected while advancing. I agree, that it might be done with one battalion; but it will be difficult, if not impoffible, to effect it with a whole line, confifting of a number of battalions. Therefore it is always better, to drefs well at firft; and each officer fhould endeavour to attend carefully to this in ad-
van-

vancing, as it is one of the moft effential parts.

For this purpofe it is neceffary,

1. That the officer fhould drefs in line, by the faces of the men of his platoon; and not as is often done by their breafts, and oftner by their feet; becaufe the man who has a large and prominent breaft, will naturally be behind him who has a fmaller one; confequently he cannot look acrofs the face of his neighbour to fee the flank-man, whom it is neceffary he fhould fee. From whence it follows, that, as the foldier does not fee with his breaft, but with his eyes; it is preferable for him to drefs himfelf in the line by his eyes.

2. He muft never drefs in the line, without having firft fixed upon a line, or at leaft imagined one, on which the platoon or battalion is to be drawn up.

3. He muft conftantly remain upon the point that has been chofen for the *point d'appui*, and on which the wing is to fix, fo as to drefs by it, until the whole platoon, or at leaft a part of it has been dreffed in the line, by the adopted *points des vuës*. If it is to

go further on, the laft man of the part which is dreffed, is then to be confidered as the *point d'appui*. But he muft never go along the divifion during the time of dreffing, as by that means, the line which has been propofed will feldom be kept; from whence an ill dreffing in the line will happen.

In the fame manner, a battalion may be eafily dreffed in line, by fuppofing the platoons to be fingle men; and by not riding away from the wing, until the fecond battalion, or at leaft a wing of it, is come into the given alignment. In the fame manner, the wheeling-in wing of the fecond platoon, is alfo not to be left, until that of the third is dreffed in line, &c.

§ 17.

Of Wheeling to form the Line, when extended along the Alignment.

When one or more battalions are, according to the method above prefcribed,

to

to march into the alignment; it will then be very eafy to march up well, either by a given fignal, or by the word of command only. But I fhall fuppofe it to be done by a fignal: as foon as it is heard, the commandants of the battalions without exception, and abfolutely muft give the word: *halt!* whether the diftance in their battalions has been loft or not, (this is to be underftood when exercifing, or on a day of action). The officer, upon the word: *halt!* being given by the commandant, muft not advance half a ftep further, but muft only place forwards the lifted up foot, and bring the other to it. If it is not done fo, and one officer ftops, while another goes on one or more fteps, all the reft who follow him, muft ftep on again and advance; which will not only caufe a confufion, but will likewife raife in the mind of a fpectator, who underftands the fervice, the idea, that the officers of that battalion or line, are not acquainted with the firft principles of their duty, namely, that of keeping the diftance. Now as foon as the word: *halt!* is given, the officer directly looks to his

files;

files; if those of the wing are well dressed in the line, he then places himself, when marched off from the right, and closed to charge, at the right flank of his division. Then if it is further commanded: *by divisions*, (to the right, or to the left) *wheel!* (according as they were marched off), upon the word: *march!* all the divisions are to wheel about at the same time.

Here it is to be observed,

1. That all the flank men, who stand in the alignment, must stand steady, and not turn about; it would be still better that they should directly front, as soon as the word: *march!* is given; if this is not done, all the pains that have been taken to be well placed upon the alignment is lost.

2. The opposite wing wheels to the flankman of the preceding divisions, who are in the alignment; then the word of command is given again: *halt, dress!* upon which all the officers step quickly out, and dress their divisions in the line. Here I refer to what has been said before about dressing; and it will be very easy, to dress well a division,

division, or a whole battalion, as eight flank-men are so many fixed points in a battalion, upon which the whole line may be dressed. The officer of the third division for example, has only to consider the left flank-man of the second division, as the *point d' appui*, and his own flank-man, as the *point of alignment*. It will then be perfectly easy for him to dress his platoon well in the line, without moving from the spot; particularly if he observes, that he is to step beyond the flank-man of his preceding division, and to begin then to dress in the line. This will convince him that his own right flank stands well dressed in the line, for otherwise, all dressing in the line would be needless. If all the officers do the same, a battalion, if the men are only a little accustomed to dress by themselves in the line, will be put with the greatest celerity in order, and the major or commandant, will then find very little to do. If it is objected, that the battalion would be ill dressed, when the flank-men do not stand exactly in the alignment; I shall give for answer, that no wheeling up must take place, until this is done, and as

there

there remains not much time to dress in the line, after signals are given; care must be taken not to fall into such faults.

3. The commandant, or major must dress according to the same principles, that is, by the left flank-men; the alignment however will be always about one step before him; but it cannot be otherwise; because the alignment was taken before by the officer in marching; the left flank-man will consequently be out of the alignment, the distance of the whole breadth of the officer; if he should then dress very exactly upon the *points de vuë*, all the flank-men would by this means be put out of order, and stand rather in a curve line than in a straight one.

4. A commandant must as seldom as possible dress the line from the center. Unless he has first directed himself in the alignment, which he ought to do, if he would assist his divisions while still marching in the alignment, and he must also not ride between two divisions, as is commonly done: because then he himself is not in the direction, besides which the whole body of his horse, being before the officers, obliges them to
march

march about him, and confequently they muft lofe the alignment.

But if he would fee, if his divifions march well; I fay again, that he muft firft drefs himfelf in the line by the adjutant who ftands behind him, and give his horfe fuch a pofition, that the divifions march along his flank. But when a battalion is marched off from the left; it cannot proceed otherwife than to wheel in to the right. All what has been faid § 9 of wheeling up to the left, likewife takes place here, and muft be done in the fame manner; the only difference is this,

1. That the right flank-man performs what the left one did; namely, to front as foon as the battalion begins to wheel in. However, it might be objected, that the officer being in the true alignment, it would be better, he did it himfelf, becaufe it would then exactly ftand in the line. But by this, the officers would be obliged to ftand ftill, in order to drefs by them as has been done before upon the left flank-man; but they themfelves are to drefs, confequently they cannot ftop; for this reafon it muft be done

by

by their right flank-man. Besides which you gain this, that two different things are done by one principle.

2. As the *point d'appui* is at the left flank, the dressing in the line is to be done from thence; consequently, the men must keep their eyes to the left; and as the officer, in order to dress his whole division, must run from the right to the left flank, by which a stop must naturally happen; it will be better, that the officers should dress those platoons which are on their right hand. As for instance; the captain of the left flank, dresses his own division, steps on this side the flank-man of the 8th division, and dresses the 7th platoon upon the flank-man of the 7th division; the one of the 7th division, steps on this side of the right flank-man of his own division, and dresses the 6th by the right flank-man of it; the one of the 6th, dresses the 5th; the 5th, the 4th; the 4th, the 3d; the 3d, the 2d; and the one of the 2d, the 1st division. By this mode, a battalion will be sooner dressed in the line, than by any other, where the officers dress their own divisions.

§ 18.

§ 18.

Of the Countermarch.

This evolution is, without doubt, one of the moſt important; it being abſolutely neceſſary for many other movements.

I ſhall ſuppoſe one caſe. For inſtance; a battalion is marched off from the right, by diviſions, into the alignment A B (Pl. 3. fig. 30). Its *point d'appui* would therefore be B; but circumſtance requires, that it ſhould be changed, and taken in A, without changing the alignment. But as it will then naturally happen, that the ſame way muſt be taken back again, to ſave ſo many movements of to the right about face, and to front again; the ſhorteſt way will be to make uſe of the countermarch, which is practiſed in the following manner. As ſoon as the commandant has given the word: *battalion, halt! countermarch*; all the officers immediately command: *to the right by files, march!* the right flank file is then to turn to the right about, and march

march close behind their third rank, with the lock-step, (which, as has been said above, is to be twice as fast, as a common one, only a little shorter; one may suppose it to be only half that length) till they come to the flank, where their left flank file stood; in like manner, the other files of the division are to do the same. When the whole division is thus come about, the officers, without waiting for one another, give the word: *halt, front!* and so on for the rest; then the battalion will stand marched off from the left, and be able to march on, wherever they are ordered to go.

This, hitherto, has been the method commonly used, and is the same which must be observed, when a battalion is not yet marched into the alignment; but if it is so already, it will be better then, that the officers should remain standing on the line of alignment A B, and only give the word of command to their divisions; but leave the rest, that is the leading of the right flank file, to their noncommissioned officers; who, as well as the whole division, must know what should be observed.

The reasons, why this will be better, are,

1. The officer, who is only to turn to the right about, does not lose the alignment; and consequently, is not obliged to look for it again.

2. As a division is two paces deep, the officer may advance only four paces (two for the depth of the division marching off to the right, and two for the same depth by marching off to the left, after having gone to the right about) and wait there for their flank, to give the word: *halt, front!* by this means you will lose no distance; and when particularly required, no time will be lost in wheeling-in.

With regard to the two above advantages, it certainly would be better, when a battalion is marched off from the left, that it should likewise perform the countermarch to the left (Pl. 3. fig. 31); but as this is not adopted, the usual method must be followed, which is to perform the countermarch always to the right; however it would not be amiss, if the soldiers now and then, were to countermarch to the left, in order that they may not fall into confusion, when this is occasionally required.

§ 19.

Of taking Distances backwards.

It would be superfluous, to endeavour to shew all the advantages that may arise from such or such evolutions, these are subjects which belong to the science of tacticks; it is enough to shew, how, and not why, such or such evolutions are performed; and one example is sufficient to point out the utility of it, and why it is necessary to take distances backwards.

Thus suppose the case, that the column A (Pl. 3. fig. 32), was closed to deploy, so as to deploy to the right, upon the rising ground before them, in order to be in a parallel line with the enemy, who is supposed marched up in a line in B. But if the report was found to be partly false, and that the enemy had changed his position, and now stood in C; then it would be a great fault, if the above proposed disposition was taken; becaufe, by the pofition D F, the left wing would be given to the enemy.

Now to prevent this, and at the fame time, not to lofe the advantage of the rifing ground, which the left wing of the corps is to occupy; the means of taking diftance backwards, is made ufe of, fo that by keeping the height E, the ground E G or E H, may be gained. If the diftance was taken forward, as is cuftomary; then either the rifing ground, or the interval between the battalions, would be loft;—If any one officer had loft the diftance, or the commanding officer had perhaps given the word: *halt!* too late.

When then it is ordered, to take the diftance backwards; the whole column marches on with a lock-ftep; after having, as before, taken the precaution of dividing the alignment, by the adjutants, to give the proper diftance to the firft officer; who, as well as all the reft, muft be at the left flank, as foon as the laft divifion of the column, is come to the point E, which has been chofen for the *point d'appui*, he

gives

gives the word: *halt!* The officer of the 7th division, who precedes him, looks then behind him, and takes for his rear man, such a distance, as to be able to wheel in. The 6th is to proceed in the same manner; likewise the fifth; and lastly the officer of the first division. But as the officers, cannot come exactly into the direction of the alignment, which partly arises from the quickness of the march, and partly also by their looking behind them, so as to take the distance; the following rules are to be observed, which will easily correct any faults that have been committed. The officer of the eighth division, who is upon the *point d'appui*, directs the man who stands before him, in the point of alignment, which he can do with a little attention, if he makes use of the rules mentioned about the dressing in a line; namely, that he constantly calls to his front man to go to the right or left, till he has him in a direction with the point of alignment; or which is the same thing, till it is covered by him.

As soon as he is in the direction, which will be known, when the officer of the 8th division gives the word: *halt!* then the officer of the 7th division, directs the 6th in the same manner. He then looks upon himself, as being the *point d'appui*, as the one of the 8th did; and proceeds according to the same rules. In like manner, the 6th proceeds with the 5th; the 5th with the 4th; and so on to the first of the column. It appears here, as if it was needless to have the alignment marked by adjutants; but this is absolutely necessary; because in a long line, a number of obstacles might intervene, which would hinder the officers from seeing the alignment. Though for single battalions, this would indeed be unnecessary. When every thing is fixed, then the wheeling-in to the left is performed; the men keep their eyes to the left; and this then is the case, where the line is dressed by the left wing, although it was wheeled in to the left. If on the contrary, the column is marched off from the left, all the above rules are to be observed, but taken in an opposite sense. The right wing does what the left did before; and you proceed with the left, as you did above

with

with the right. The men keep their eyes to the right, and dreſs in the line by the right wing. In general, an officer will not be at a loſs how to dreſs in the line, if he pays a proper attention to his *point d'appui*, and ſolely directs himſelf by it to the point of alignment.

§ 20.

Of Deploying.

There are four different methods of deploying.

1. Marched off from the right, and deployed to the right.

2. Marched off from the right, and deployed to the left.

3. Marched off from the left, and deployed to the left.

4. Marched off from the left, and deployed to the right.

There might be added a fifth, which is to deploy from the center; but as this is only compoſed of the above four methods, it will be needleſs to deſcribe it: Becauſe, when

when a battalion deploys from the center, the grand divisions compoſing it, muſt deploy according to ſome one of the four above mentioned methods. There are ſome movements belonging to the deployings, which muſt precede, before the evolution can be performed. For example;

1. To march at half diſtances.

This is done, as ſoon as it is intended to deploy; and it is to be remarked here, that the firſt diviſion keeps a ſhort ſtep, until thoſe behind have got their half diſtance; then the common ſtep is taken again.

2. To march into the alignment.

As ſoon as the order is given, to march into the alignment; which commonly is done at the diſtance from 100 to 200 paces behind it; the battalion marches on with a double ſtep, in order to reach it as quick as poſſible; and however neceſſary it is, to be well in the alignment, when marching up by diviſions; it is yet indiſpenſably more ſo, that the head of the deployed battalion ſhould be directed with the utmoſt accuracy. The method of marking it firſt by the adjutants, is ſtill more neceſſary here.

3. To

3. To march up by grand divisions.

There are two different methods of marching up the grand divisions: The first (Pl. 3. fig. 33) and most common is, when all the second sub-divisions of a grand division, or, which is the same thing, all the even sub-divisions, as the 2d, 4th, 6th and 8th, incline out to the left, and fall in towards the 1st sub-division of the grand division to which they belong, so as to be in a right line with them.

The second method, and which, in my opinion, is better than the first, for the deploy is, that the sub-divisions, whether they be the first or second sub-divisions of the grand division, incline out; and all that deploy to the right, incline their 1st divisions to the right; and all that deploy to the left, incline their second divisions, towards those that remain on the line, however the march may be performed. The following principles will prove, that the preference is to be given to this last method.

I suppose the case to be, that the battalion A (fig. 34) is marched off from the right, and is to deploy to the right, in the alignment B C, where the *point d'appui* is underſtood to be at the left wing.

The *point d'appui*, muſt be taken as quick as poſſible, ſo as to be able to dreſs at once in the line, by the given point of alignment; and this will be obtained much quicker by the laſt method, than by the firſt: becauſe by this laſt, I ſhould be firſt obliged to go to ſuch a diſtance from the *point d'appui*, as to give the ſecond ſub-diviſion of the grand diviſion, the required ſpace to go back again, from whence they came; this is a loſs of time, which ſhould be avoided: ſhould a ſecond fault be added to this, which may eaſily happen, namely, that a battalion ſhould deviate too far, ſo as that the 2d ſub-diviſion cannot fill up the diſtance between the 1ſt and the *point d'appui*; I ſhall by this occaſion, that not only all my 1ſt ſub-diviſions, but likewiſe all the next battalions, when deploying with a column, compoſed of ſeveral battalions, will be obliged to cloſe again to the left. All which movements, hinder a quick dreſſing in the line. If marched off from the left, and deployed to the right (fig. 35), the
advan-

advantage will be more confiderable; becaufe the 8th divifion may be already dreffed in the line, before the 7th arrives; which laft may then be dreffed fo much the eafier. The fame is to be obferved in an oppofite fenfe, when deploying to the left.

4. To clofe in order to deploy.

As foon as the grand divifions are marched up, they clofe in order to deploy; that is, all the grand divifions clofe fo to one another, that the clofing officers and noncommiffioned officers, may juft ftand between them. While this is doing, the grand divifion, which is ftanding in the alignment, muft be very accurately dreffed in it. All the drummers march behind the battalion, becaufe they would otherwife be only a hindrance. The officers who have platoons, ftep into the fub-divifions. When thefe movements, which muft always precede, are performed; the word: *deploy!* is given; and, as we fuppofe it here.

A

To Deploy to the Right, when Marched off from the Right.

As soon as this is commanded, the commandant without delay, gives the word to his battalion: *to the right by files!* (Pl. 3. fig. 36). The whole battalion is to perform this movement, without marking any time, and without stopping, till they come to the 4th grand division, which keeps the front, and which is then called the *head: march!* the 1st, 2d and 3d grand division, step directly on with a lock step; the captain of the 1st marches straight to the alignment, and the adjutant who marked it: (I believe it is unnecessary to repeat here, that in this march, every thing must be observed that has been said § 2, 3 and 6); as soon as the three first grand divisions, have with their last files, passed before the right wing of the 4th; the captain of the 4th gives the word: *forward, march!* and

he

he steps upon the place where the first one stood; that is, with his left wing to the *point d'appui* C; and from thence directs his division to the alignment A B. The commandant of the battalion further commands, when he sees that the 3d grand division, comes with its left wing to the right of the 4th: *third division, halt!* upon this the wing of the grand division must directly stop; and the files, should they have lost their distance (which however ought not to happen), must advance: *front!* upon this the commandant runs to his left wing, gives the word: *eyes to the left!* and orders his men to close. When the grand division has deviated too much, and the second has passed him, he goes to the 4th and dresses by it to the alignment; all the other grand divisions, are to do the same. When all are thus drawn up, the commandant dresses his battalions from the left wing, if any corrections are wanted.

B

When MARCHED off from the Left, and DEPLOYED to the Left.

In the same manner, as the left wing of the 1st sub-division was led to the *point d'appui*; the same is now done when marched off from the left, with the right wing of the 8th division (fig. 37); because the *point d'appui* C, is then at the right wing; and if, what has been said above of deploying to the right, is now considered in an opposite sense, there remains almost nothing to say: because when the word is given: *to the left by files, march!* the 4th, 3d and 2d grand divisions, are to proceed to the left by files, in the same manner, as has been performed above, with the 1st, 2d and 3d, with to the right by files. The 1st, which is then the head, marches into the alignment A B, as the 4th did; the 2d performs the same movement, as the 3d did before; and in the same manner, as the

dressing-dreffing in the line was done by the left wing, fo it is now on the contrary done by the right one.

C

When Marched off from the Right, and Deployed to the Left.

As the deploying is to be to the left (fig. 38) it muft be underftood, that the *point d'appui* C, is again to be at the right wing; confequently, the right wing of the 1ft divifion, muft be led to it; from whence the dreffing into the alignment A B is made. When the word is given: *deploy! battalion, to the left*; the firft grand divifion which is the head, keeps the front; and all the others turn to the left, and march ftraight on in the direction, which the 1ft grand divifion ftands in, and not obliquely, as it commonly happens; until the commandant gives the word: *fecond divifion, halt, front!* As foon as it has fronted, the commandant of the divifion, dreffes it in the direction which is parallel to the alignment A B; but without any delay, orders it to clofe to the right. If his divifion has marched too far, he gives the word: *forward, march!* and fteps towards the 1ft grand divifion, by which he directs his own divifion into the alignment. All the other grand divifions muft proceed in the fame manner.

D

When Marched off from the Left, and Deployed to the Right.

When this deploying is taken in an oppofite fenfe to the former, there is nothing further to be added; but it is only to be obferved, that the *point d'appui* C (fig. 39) is now at the left wing; and confequently, the left wing of the 8th divifion muft be led to it. The 4th grand divifion will be the head, and keep the front. The 3d does what the 2d did before, and fo on. The commandant muft only take care, that as his *point d'appui* C, is at the left wing,

to

to order his division before it falls in, to cast their eyes to the left, and to close.

The major or adjutant of the battalion, must always ride near the deploying wing, that he may in time stop the grand division, in case the commandant should give the word too late, or the division should not hear him; or should also the files, during the deploying, not keep close to each other; and when in coming to the front, they are again to close—Faults which may be avoided, by stopping in time the succeeding divisions. A fault which often happens in deploying, is, that the deploying left wing, almost always passes over the alignment; this however more frequently happens, when marched off from the right, and deployed to the left; or when marched off from the left, and deployed to the right. This fault arises from this, that when the word of command is given: *to the right, and march!* the wing (fig. 40) of the 3d division, that of the 2d, or that of the 1st, march obliquely to the *point de vuë* A, so as to gain ground, and by this means diminish the space for falling in. But it happens, that

by this, the 3d divifion when the word is given: *halt, front!* will certainly be in the pofition C; becaufe the left wing of the divifion, not having been able to follow the right in an exact direction, being hindered by the 4th, which ftands before it; the 2d and 1ft, will in like manner, come in the pofition D and E. Now I fuppofe then, that the 3d divifion is falling in, it cannot fall in otherwife but obliquely: becaufe it will not do to drefs it firft, and give it a pofition parallel to the alignment, as it is preft upon by the whole depth of the 2d column which is behind it, on account of the direction it takes. He is greatly miftaken, who believes that it may be dreft as foon as it is fallen-in; becaufe, not only the wing of the falling-in divifion; but likewife thofe that ftill deploy, have certainly fo over paft, that the captain who leads it, will fcarcely be able to fee the *point de vuë* A; and fuppofe it could be done, ftill all thefe movements are needlefs, by which more time is loft, than could have been gained by obtaining the ground quicker. Formerly, when they deployed with deep
columns,

columns, this method could be in some sort excusable. But now it must be entirely rejected; because, the depth of the column, when they deploy, consisting only of four grand divisions, that is, 12 men deep; the 1st sub-division consequently, when straight in the direction with the head, including the space for the closing officers and noncommissioned officers, requires at most only ten paces to fall in. It would be very easy, to determine the number of paces wanted for a division to fall in, if there was no fear of occasioning by it some errors. Because if for example, nine paces are fixed for the 1st division to fall in; now if the 2d and 3d rank do not remain in close order, it will be impossible for this division to reach the alignment with their nine paces. But the officer who has taken his nine paces, will believe he is in it, at least he will excuse himself, by having followed the given order; and then I should be glad to know, who could discover the origin of this fault? Besides this, the officers would be inattentive to the dressing in the line, and would think they had done all,

all, when they had taken the determined number of paces.

Therefore in my opinion, it is better to attend merely to the dressing, and to refer the commandants of the divisions, to what has been said § 16. of dressing; namely, that they should consider the wing of the standing division, as their *point d'appui*, and step beyond the 1st or 2d file from the flank, and from thence dress the division by the opposite *point de vuë*. If the officer, only steps out two paces to come to that point, he will prevent the running out of his division; because looking constantly at the *point de vuë*, he will see in an instant, when his division steps into the alignment.

§ 21.

Of Advancing with a Battalion.

I suppose, all the soldiers that compose a battalion, exercised in the manner mentioned § 1 and 4: because the advancing well of the battalion, depends upon those principles; and it is no longer necessary to
attend

attend particularly to single men; they ought to know, what dressing is; they must not croud, still less must they open; the cadenced step must have become natural to them; and they must neither take longer or shorter paces, unless ordered so to do; till then they must keep the prescribed pace; they must not bring either of their shoulders too forward or backward, that they may not by this be obliged to turn their heads. The colours which march in the rank, must constantly be their direction to dress by, therefore they must never lose sight of them. The flag sergeants *(feldwebels)* who march in front, are of no other use to the men, than to enable them to recover the step again, in case any one should have lost it; and as this will seldom happen to well exercised soldiers, they are then only to look at them when particularly necessary. This being supposed, every one will easily comprehend, that it depends only upon the preceding marching colours, and flag sergeants, to keep the battalion when advancing, in a good line, and which by this means will be obtained. But before I proceed

ceed further in fixing rules, according to which I believe a battalion would advance well, I shall first shew, how the colours have been exercised, and what errors result from it.

1. The flag sergeants, and particularly the one of the right wing, must march perpendicularly to the line, where his battalion stands; this appears evident and absolutely necessary; for no battalion will march well, if this is not done. But it is more certain, that it will be impossible for a flag sergeant to find this perpendicular, or, if by some method it has been given him, to remain upon it.

It is obvious, that an officer who is to march into the alignment, will not be able to keep in a straight line without assistance. But you require this of a flag sergeant, who is however supposed to have less knowledge than an officer.

I shall now show how erroneous the method, which has hitherto been made use of, is, and how little may be depended upon it. Upon the word: *colours advance!* the flag sergeants advance six paces; and

atten-

attention is seldom paid, whether they advance straight on, and step out at the same time, notwithstanding, the calling to them to take a perpendicular position; and when much is done, the commandant places himself before the three flag sergeants, who form the right flank file of the 5th division, and afterwards makes them advance towards him. This would in some sort be the best method, to obtain the perpendicular nearly; but however, notwithstanding all the pains that have been taken, it is still very erroneous: because (Pl. 3. fig. 41) if the flag sergeant, standing in E, deviates only two degrees from the perpendicular, which is trifling, when taken without an instrument; and where even the most practised engineer, would perhaps commit a fault of five degrees or more; this, at the distance of 2000 paces, which are commonly taken in advancing, would make a great difference: By this, instead of coming in A, he would at last find himself in B *; and by this means,

* At the distance of 2000 paces, the direction E B, forming an angle of two degrees with the perpendicular; the

means, he would have thrown the whole line to the left, when several battalions advance together at the same time.

2. It is further told to the flag sergeants, to take a *point de vuë*, without considering whether there is any, which chance has placed in the direction of the perpendicular: supposing it to have been found exactly; this is not enough, there must be also found one point more, which must likewise fall within the direction of the perpendicular; because otherwise the flag sergeant would not be able to keep it, as has already been proved § 13.

It is further then not considered, that even when standing upon the perpendicular, the least turning of the eyes, will fix upon another object, which is without this line, by which the preceding fault will be also committed; or if the sight of the flag sergeant is not good enough, as that, at a distance of 2000 paces, he could distinguish a small object, though the want of a larger

---

the point B, will have deviated from A, 70 paces; and if it forms an angle of three degrees, the deviation from the perpendicular will be 105 paces.

one.

one. I suppose however all this to be possible.

The flag sergeant E (fig. 42) standing perpendicularly to A B, and C, D being the two objects, which are found in the perpendicular; it will then indeed be easy for the flag sergeant E, to keep the line E C, as long as he does not meet with a valley, which prevents him from seeing the two objects D, C. But should this happen, as undoubtedly it will at such a distance as 2000 paces, what will then become of the perpendicular, and all the trouble that has been taken? If it is said, that at coming out of the valley, they must endeavour to regain the objects; give me leave to ask: how often during that time, the battalion, and if there are more, which are to direct themselves by it, will have inclined to the right, or to the left, have changed their position, and by this means been put into confusion?

3. The end for which the flag sergeants, are taught to step out straight on, or perpendicularly, is, that by this method, a line, consisting of several battalions, may be

be kept ſtraight; that is, by giving them at each ſtep, ſuch a poſition, as will be parallel to the line they have left, and not inclining one way or another.

Now I will ſuppoſe again (fig. 43), that the flag ſergeant E of the right wing, upon whom commonly the whole attention is fixed, is exactly in a line perpendicular to A B; but the others, who are in an oblique poſition E D, are conſequently not parallel to A B; if then the battalion is to dreſs according to this line E D, will it advance well? it certainly will not.

It is then clear that to advance well, depends not ſolely upon the flag ſergeant, who marches perpendicularly to the line A B; but this is rather to be endeavoured at, by keeping on in a parallel line. The ſequel will ſhew, that the principles which I ſhall lay down here, if obſerved, will facilitate the advancing in a good line, as well as the above troubleſome method of ſeeking the perpendicular. But when a line is to advance well, the battalions of which it is compoſed, ſhould be already of themſelves expert in advancing properly.

For

For this, it is neceſſary to give to theſe battalions, certain directions, according to which they are to regulate their march and poſition. Theſe are the flag ſergeants and colours; one part of which is to keep the men in a proper cadence, and the other to keep them in a proper line.

From hence it follows, that all poſſible attention ſhould be paid to the giving them all imaginable aſſiſtance, ſo that they may firſt underſtand how to keep a good line, and what is meant by advancing well.

1. The flag ſergeants and lance corporals *(gefreyten-corporals)* ſhould not only know perfectly the cadence of the march, and the length of paces; but ſhould conſtantly keep the cadence during the march, even though the pace ſhould be made longer, or ſhorter; which however is difficult to perform, unleſs they employ their mind about ſomething relative to it. For example; they may count at each pace, 1, 2, 3, and ſo on, ſhould it be even to 10 only, and then they may begin again. This employs their mind about ſomething, and will prevent their fixing their attention to the battalion,

talion, in cafe it has fallen out of the ſtep; and by this means they are not put into confuſion.

The majors and adjutants, will perfect them in the cadence, if, when exerciſing the noncommiſſioned officers, they place them in one or two ranks; make the flag ſergeants ſtep out, and make them advance, and ſtep with the ranks; ſometimes in quick, and ſometimes in ſlow time.

2. As ſoon as they advance, they muſt place themſelves parallel to the battalion, in caſe it is to march in the ſame poſition it ſtands in; as they cannot do this of themſelves, it is the buſineſs of the commandant, who is to dreſs them.

Now to obtain this, upon the word: *colours, ſtep out!* the four flag ſergeants and colours of the firſt rank, who as well as the whole battalion, ſhould be dreſſed in a ſtraight line, muſt ſtep out together ſix paces, that is 14 feet with a common ſtep. By this means four points are obtained, which notwithſtanding they are out of the baſe line, are of equal diſtances from

it,

it, and may be confidered as a line drawn and paffing through thefe four points.

3. Their fhoulders muft be exactly dreffed in the direction of this imaginary line; that is, muft be parallel to the battalion: for it will be of little ufe that the feet ftand parallel with the battalion, unlefs the reft of their body, and particularly their fhoulders, have an uniform pofition; becaufe, the line is to be directed by their fhoulders, and not by their feet.

4. As long as it is not otherwife ordered, they muft keep their body and fhoulders in the fame pofition which has been given them, whether they incline or not. If they do not obferve this, not only their own battalion, but likewife all the reft who are to drefs after them, will fall into confufion. Therefore, it cannot be too much inftilled into their mind, that all poffible attention fhould be paid to the not turning their fhoulders. They muft therefore keep their heads ftraight forward, and neither look to the right, or to the left, becaufe they will otherwife undoubtedly turn their fhoulders. The falfe idea they have, that

this

this affifts the battalion, when, in marching, it lofes the cadence, inclines them often to this motion; but when this is abfolutely not allowed and attended to, when exercifing them in grand divifions or companies; you make them comprehend, that this wrong idea of affiftance, will rather occafion a greater confufion, than keep it in order.

5. They muft not fuffer themfelves to be led into an error, by any perfon whatfoever of the battalion, otherwife they will not be certain of what they are about. It very often happens, that the flag fergeants of the center, or even the officers, call to them, to go to the right or left, to gain ground more or lefs; they tell them that they fall off too much, and fuch like words. If they follow thefe directions, one may be fure there will be a waving in the battalion. To avoid then the committing fuch faults, no one in the battalion fhould fpeak to them, and they on the contrary, muft give their attention to no body elfe but their commandant; or, if he is otherwife engaged, to the clofing major or adjutant, whofe
bufinefs

bufinefs it is to keep the colours in a line. They alfo muft be bold enough, to tell their commandant, who marches four paces before them, whenever he obftructs them; he is to pay attention to what they fay, as he cannot look behind him; otherwife, a flag fergeant would not take fuch liberty.

6. The flag fergeants and lance corporals, of the fecond and third rank, who replace thofe who ftep out of the firft rank, muft endeavour to take the fame pofition, which the commandant has given to the latter.

It is by them that the colour files drefs, and by them again the whole battalion muft drefs, as they drefs according to the 1ft. If they fee that the advanced colours take another direction, they muft endeavour to drefs accordingly. If the advanced colours incline, they muft incline alfo with them; and in cafe they do wrong, they muft do the fame. It is fufficient that they conftantly remain behind them. They are always to be fix paces behind thofe that march in front, that is, the flag fergeant D (fig. 44), muft conftantly keep his fix paces from the one in A; and the one in C,

C, his six paces from the one in B; they must neither of them, him in D as well as him in C, come nearer, nor remain farther off; by this means the parallel will be kept, or those who march in front are not then to dress by the battalion. It is often therefore very unjust to find fault with the flag sergeants in front, it being rather very often the fault of those who march in the ranks.

It may happen, that the flag sergeants advance very well, and still the battalion ill; this rests entirely, either on the men being badly drest in the line, from a neglect of what has been said § 1; or, because all the companies or grand divisions, have not been drilled according to the same cadence.

This happens, because no commandant of a company will regulate his march, according to his flag sergeant; if the company takes a different step from that of the flag sergeant, you may be sure it never will be imputed to the company, but always to the flag sergeant; from hence will arrive five different cadences. Now let all

these

thefe men, who are drilled according to different cadences come together; and let the beft flag fergeants march in front; I am fure, that fuch a battalion, will never march otherwife than with a waving. It will then follow, that all the companies, with regard to cadence and length of paces, muft ftrictly follow their flag fergeants, to have the fame; and as well as all the other noncommiffioned officers, to march well, is under the care of the adjutant, or in his ftead of the ftaff officers; thefe muft endeavour to perfect them in this, and they will certainly obtain it, if they obferve the rules which have been given, and the non-commiffioned officers make ufe of what has been faid, with regard to the men. The nearer to the colours thefe faults are committed, the more dangerous they are; therefore, for the colour files, and thofe who are next to them, the beft men muft be chofen; and not, as is often done, the worft; becaufe, next to the colours, they are thofe, who muft give the line to the whole battalion.

§ 22.

Of Retreating.

It would be needless to say any thing about this, as retreating, is nothing else than advancing with the third rank; it must only be observed, that the closing noncommissioned officers, are to dress themselves; because, otherwise, they would obstruct the rank which is marching behind them; the third rank must not march in as close order as the 1st, because the men of the first rank are taller, and have commonly larger shoulders; therefore, there must be something allowed for this difference, otherwise, the first rank would be obliged to march too close, or would not be able to follow their file leaders.

But when a battalion bends, or falls off; it is common to call to no other grand division, than to the 1st and 4th; notwithstanding, it is seldom their fault, and is only owing to the center platoons, and arises from one single man; if an endeavour

is

is made to find him out, the rest of the wing will right itself. If this is not done, the frequent calling to them, will bring the wing either out, or keep it back; and in 10 or 20 paces, it will undoubtedly fall again into the same fault, having not previously corrected the original one. It is further imagined, 'that a wing remains behind, when it cannot be seen; but this may be owing to some of the center platoons. For example; to the 3d or 6th, which steping too far out, prevents the seeing the 1st division, without any fault of that grand division. But the question is; can a fault in the platoon where it happens, or at least in the next to it, be stopt, before it is communicated to the wing? I believe not always; but yet, it may in many cases. For example; I suppose the flank of the 4th sub-division, remains in the line (Pl. 3. fig. 45), and the left one of the 5th presses out; this will occasion a waving, which will not cease, till it has gone through the wings of the battalion. But if the officer of the 4th division, or if it comes further on, the one of the 3d or 6th, do not mind it; but remaining in an equal march, obferve the proper cadence and length of paces, and endeavour to direct himfelf more by the center colours, than by the rank, in cafe they can perceive them, the waving will ceafe; becaufe they will affift the platoons, who are to their right and left in dreffing by them. The major and adjutant can remedy this fooner: becaufe, being on horfeback, they are better able to fee which platoon remains dreffed with the colours. They then tell thofe platoons as foon as poffible, to remain on their march, and not mind thofe that run out or fall back, which will then be eafier brought into order again.

In retreating, this is ftill eafier, becaufe the clofing officers, together with the majors and adjutants, can affift them; for, the one who clofes the 3d, keeps, for example, his divifion in line, when the 4th preffes out; and keeps on as before, in a regular march when it falls off. But this officer, is only to affift the divifion he clofes. He muft likewife, without running to and fro (and here it is neceffary

he

he should know the men) keep the division constantly closed, as well in advancing as in retreating; must call to them, and take notice of those men who are not attentive; which he is afterwards to report to the officer, who commands the platoon, or grand division; and who then is not to spare them, otherwise, he will discourage the officer from taking any further care of the men. It must not be imagined, that the frequent calling and roughness, used to a battalion, will bring it into order again; the more quietly the men of a platoon are called to, the sooner what you want is done.

Those cries: *will you hear*, *keep back*, or *step out*, are of no use; because, as all the men in the battalion, think themselves called upon by, *you*, they either pay no attention, or they act all together; and by this means fall into an opposite fault: This fault, must consequently be thus corrected, so that the 2d platoon, may not hear that the 3d has committed any fault, otherwise, the fear they have of being ill dressed, will make them waver; and the uncertainty to which they are brought by this, not knowing if they are right or wrong, is, in my opinion, also a fault. The hallowing and calling out loud to a battalion, serves no other purpose, than to make the spectator who hears it, believe, that the battalion is fallen into some fault, which by his eyes he would not have perceived.

When a battalion is to incline, and to step with longer or shorter paces; the command is to be given loud, so as it may be heard by the whole battalion; because, in the first case, one of the wings will crowd, and an opening will happen in the other; and in the second case, will arise a stopping or pressing out.

Further, there must be no sign made; because then the men would be used rather to look at the commandant, than at the center colours. If a commandant intends to give another direction to his battalion; for example, if the battalion A B (fig. 46), is to take the position C D; then the flag sergeants who precede, are not to turn about at once, but must perform it by degrees; so that the left wing may describe the arc B D with a shorter pace: for all

vehe-

vehement and hasty movements, are of no use to infantry. I believe it might in this case be permitted to the commandant, to give notice to the right wing to advance, by a signal from his spontoon, and by a signal with his hand to the left wing, to keep back.

§ 23.

Of breaking off in ADVANCING.

This method of breaking off, is quite different from that, which has been observed in the divisions: for, it consists in nothing else, than that the breaking-off divisions, should fall behind the flank of the next advancing division, with to the right or left by files. For example; a grand division, as here the 2d, is obliged to break off before the pond (fig. 47); then the commandant gives the word: *halt! to the right and left by files!* thus he joins the 2d division to the right by files; and the officer of the 4th joins the left, at the right flank of the 5th division; both remain thus joined,

joined, until one of them has gained room enough to form-up again. If it happens, that one single divifion is to do this, as for example the 6th, then the officer of that divifion, gives the word: *halt! to the right and left by files!* and they join their next divifions, in like manner, as when a grand divifion break off; therefore, each officer divides his divifion into two equal parts, and muft inftil well into the minds of the men, how they are to break off. To which purpofe, the following rules muft neceffarily be followed.

1. Without the greateft neceffity, there muft be no breaking off, not even for a fingle file.

2. No file muft remain ufeleffly broken off; but an officer, muft manage his ground as much as poffible, and as foon as he gets room, muft make them form-up file by file.

3. All fingle divifions break off, half to the right, and half to the left, behind their next divifions.

4. The wing platoons break off, one half behind their own, and the other half behind their next platoons.

5. Whole grand divisions break off, with one sub-division to the right, and with the other to the left, behind their next divisions.

6. Two different divisions, which together do not make up a grand division, consider themselves however as a grand division.

7. When a division is to break off, behind which, a part of the other is already broken off; it must not then break off, half to the right and half to the left; but must break off entirely, either to the right or left by files.

8. When the line, or the battalion halts; all those who broke off are to front, and place themselves close to the impediment, before which they broke off; so that nothing can pass between them; wherefore, in this case, you are not obliged to adhere to the dressing. But, when a battalion goes to the right about, and is to retreat, nothing is then more inconvenient than broken-off divisions, which you will then have at once before you, and which, respecting their position, are not able to keep so regular a distance, as not to be either too far off from the battalion, or to stop it.

In

In this cafe, you muft endeavour to bring as faft as poffible, fuch divifions behind again, which is performed in the following manner (fig. 48).

Suppofe the 1ft grand divifion, 1, 2, of the battalion A, which on account of the marfh B, at its right wing, was obliged to break off; the flank of the 2d grand divifion, 3, 4, will confequently join clofe to it, and will alfo hinder the 1ft, to pafs through between it and the marfh to join again.

Now to procure room for this, the officer of the 3d divifion, as foon as the battalion goes to the right about, gives the word to his three firft files, who remain fronting: *to the left!* and as foon as the battalion begins to march, the 3d file wheels to the left, behind the 4th, 5th and 6th; confequently, the 3d rank of thefe three files, will be placed upon the 4th; the 2d upon the 5th; and the 1ft rank upon the 6th of the 1ft rank of this divifion.

The 3d file is followed by the 2d; this one by the 1ft; and thus the whole grand divifion, which, as foon as the battalion halts,

halts, wheels to the right about by files, and joins behind the battalion. This movement muſt be performed with great quickneſs, in order, that the grand or ſub-diviſion, may come behind the battalion, as faſt as poſſible, ſo as not to impede it when retreating. The grand diviſion, marching through the opening made by the 3d diviſion, muſt keep cloſe to the marſh; ſo that, not only the 3d diviſion may bring up its three broken-off files, but that likewiſe, the 2d diviſion may march up as many files, as the ground will permit. Here it is to be obſerved, that it is the 3d rank that begins to march up.

The ſecond method: which, in my opinion, is better than the firſt, to put a broken-off diviſion behind the battalion (fig. 49). All that is broken off, ſtands faſt and keeps front; for example, here the 4th and 5th diviſion; becauſe then preſenting to the right and to the left, they may ſtill annoy the enemy, which cannot be done in the firſt caſe. The movements of the three firſt files of the 3d diviſion, when the battalion has gone to the right about,

remains

remains as in the firſt caſe. But the broken-off platoons, perform by files either to the right or left, and not at once with the whole diviſion, either to the right or left; and wheel likewiſe by files upon the ſpot, either to the right or left about, and join behind the battalion.

§ 24.

Of breaking off in RETREATING.

When in retreating, a breaking off is to be made, it is performed in the ſame manner, as when advancing; and the officer, gives the word: *to the right and left by files!* it being adopted, that the movement firſt commanded, is that which is given to the right wing. When marched up again in retreating, the 3d rank is then to be conſidered as the firſt; and they march up with it.

§ 25.

Of Dressing a Battalion when it halts, after Advancing.

When the word is given: *battalion, halt!* the flag sergeants and lance corporals, who march in front, step back again into their respective ranks, and dress themselves as true as possible, in the position that is given them; they must further keep here, as well as in advancing, their halberds and colours firm and upright, and not let them hang over; because, otherwise the dressing in line cannot be performed. Upon the word: *dress!* the captain of the right wing, looks for his colours, and dresses himself by them. This indeed is rather difficult, when standing in the rank, where the men prevent him from directly seeing them. Therefore in this, much practice is required; if they cannot be seen before the rank, it is a sign that the wing has stept out too far, one must consequently, endeavour to find them, either between the 2d

and

and 1st, or between the 2d and 3d rank. But, if it should be impossible for the captain to find them, which might happen, when obstructed by standing on a lower ground; in this case, the major or adjutant, who is on horseback, and consequently can see better, must assist him; he is the first who should be dressed, otherwise, the dressing of the battalion, will never be obtained: For in this case, the captain must consider himself, as the *point d'appui*, and the colours, as four points of alignment, which are standing one behind the other. Now if the captain does not stand in the prolonged line of these four points, it will be impossible for him to form any other line, than a curve one. I suppose now, that the captain, stands exactly in the direction of the colours; he then tells his division to dress by him. The flank-man places himself close to him, and he without moving from his place, dresses his division by the colours, as he did by the *point de vuë*, § 16. The officer of the 2d division waits until the first is dressed; he then steps to the 3d file, on the left flank

flank of the first division, and dresses his division as the first did, by the colours, without moving from his place. The same is performed by the officer of the 3d and 4th division. The officer of the 5th division begins to dress directly; and as soon as his colours are fixed, he steps beyond them, and considers himself as the *point d'appui*, on which he is to fix his division; and he dresses it, either by the colours of his battalion; or, when there is besides these another one, he then may consider it as the point of alignment; especially if there is none in the prolonged line formed by the four colours.

When the 5th division is dressed in a line, the officer of the 6th division, steps beyond the three files of the left flank-man of the 5th, and proceeds in the same manner as the second did; the officer of the 7th, proceeds as the one of the 3d; and the 8th, as the one of the 4th.

It would appear, that this method of dressing was very slow; but make the trial; and let the officers as they are posted, dress directly by the colours, (which must

L always

always be done), without waiting for one another. The battalion will be certainly then in a curve line, and will ſtand as in (fig. 50). Every one now thinks he is in the right; and why? becauſe he dreſſed by the colours, without conſidering that his own perſon did not ſtand upon the line A B, which however, is the only one upon which the battalion can ſtand, when required to be dreſſed in a right line. Now the conteſt, who is right or wrong, ends always in this, that the commandant is obliged to dreſs a-new; by which, certainly more time is loſt, than when the officers wait for one another; for then he will dreſs with exactneſs, having a fixed point upon which he can ſet his flank; and when for example (fig. 50), the one of the 3d, ſteps beyond the three files of the left flank of the 2d, he muſt be very much deceived by his eyes, if he does not ſee the ill dreſſing of his diviſion.

However, it muſt not be imagined, that either oneſelf or the platoon is well dreſt, when this direction is obſerved by one of the colours only or halberds in C: No! one

one may be (fig. 51) at A, or at B, and conftantly believe one is in the line, becaufe one colour is feen. But this is erroneous; for the lines A C and B C being produced, will come to F and G, inftead of being in another point, in the line of alignment D E, which is the true line of direction.

From hence it follows, that to get into the true alignment, you muft be fo placed, as to be in the fame direction with the four colours; that is, the firft muft cover all the laft, or the three firft muft be covered by the laft. This is the reafon, why the flag fergeants and lance corporals, are to keep their colours and halberds fteady and upright.

§ 26.

Of the firft Line paffing through the Second.

The method commonly ufed (fig. 52), and which has been adopted, to pafs through the fecond line, is as follows; it either paffes through in advancing or retreating.

In the firſt caſe, the ſecond line advances, to occupy that poſt which the firſt leaves. As ſoon as it is come near at hand, the commandant of the battalion, gives the word: *paſs through!* and all the officers afterwards, give the word: *to the right!* and each wheels with his right flank file to the right about, which is to be followed by the whole diviſion, marches with a lock-ſtep, ſtraight to the 2d line, and paſſes through it; therefore, the officers of the 2d line muſt break off four files, upon which the diviſions come, but as ſoon as they are paſſed through, the broken-off files are to march up again.

Now to form again the 1ſt line, as quick as poſſible; nothing is better, than that the commandant of the battalion ſhould fix to all the officers, a certain number of paces which they are to make, as ſoon as they begin to paſs through the 2d line with their 1ſt files; when they have performed them, they halt, order the diviſion to cloſe and front. They then ſtep to the left flank, take their proper diſtance, and dreſs by their leading men; wherefore, the three firſt

first divisions, must be directly placed by the major.

If it is objected, that in dressing by the leading men, it would be unnecessary to fix upon any number of paces; it must be considered, that this number of paces is taken, only to perform, as nearly as possible, the dressing, and to prevent the divisions from stepping out too far; because, you must then bring them back again, with a great deal of trouble, in order to prevent the rest from falling into the same fault. Another rule is also to be observed: which is, that the strongest division, as for example, the colour division, must, according to their degree of strength, take some paces more, and the grenadier divisions, as smaller in number, some paces less than the common divisions. When all are posted, they wheel up to the left; and the greater part of the battalion, if not the whole, will be then dressed.

In the second case (fig. 53), the 2d line, on the contrary, remains at its post; the 1st retires as far, as to about three paces from the 2d; then the commandant, like-wise, wife, gives the word: *pafs through!* each officer gives the word to his divifion: *to the left!* he wheels again with his right flank file to the right, and both lines proceed as has been faid above, with the determined number of paces.

But there may be cafes, where a line or battalion, is obliged to pafs through, in fuch a manner, that when through, it ftands marched off from the left. Then the officers command to their divifions in the 1ft cafe: *to the left!* the officers brifkly ftep to the left flank of their divifions, and wheel to the left with their left flank files; inftead of to the right as above.

The reft is performed as above; it is only to be remarked, that the diftance is then to be taken from the left flank, as is ufually done, when marching off to the right and left.

But if neceffity requires another pofition to be taken with the battalion, which paffes through, or that you fhould crown a rifing ground which is behind it; it will eafily be feen, that it is then impoffible to determine upon a number of paces, according to

which

which the battalion is to form again; thus in the firſt caſe (fig. 54), the commandant, muſt, with his two firſt diviſions, take directly the poſition which has been preſcribed to him, and give orders to all the other officers, to dreſs by theſe diviſions. As ſoon as this is done, he muſt wheel in, without loſs of time; becauſe, when ſeveral battalions paſs through the line, this will facilitate the dreſſing. It is therefore proper, that the battalions ſhould be practiſed to this beforehand; and at the ſame time, it will accuſtom the officers, to obtain the line of direction with more expedition.

In the ſecond caſe, it is a fault, if the officer ſhould dreſs upon his preceding diviſion. He muſt obſerve nothing elſe here but the diſtance, and direct himſelf by the riſing ground which is to be crowned; that is, he muſt (fig. 55) halt with his left or right flank, according as he is marched off, juſt at that part of the riſing ground, where he can ſee its entire ſlope. It ſometimes happens, that in paſſing through, diſtances muſt be taken backwards, becauſe one wing is to be fixed, and the other refuſed; this however, must be avoided as much as possible, and it can be done, by passing through in another manner. For example (fig. 55); if I had passed through, in retreating to the left by files, then I should have marched off from the right; but if I am obliged to fix the left flank on the rising ground, then I should be obliged to take the distance backwards, where the movement of the passing through, and the refusing of the wing added to it, is liable to many difficulties. But I obtain this end, so much the quicker and easier, when in retreating, I pass through with to the right by files, and march to the *point d'appui*; by this means, the officer will, with more facility, keep both the distance and dressing.

It should be in general adopted as an absolute principle, that of two movements which converge to the same end, the most simple one, or that which is liable to the least difficulties, should be always chosen. But when it is absolutely ordered to pass through, in such a manner, and not otherwise; and if in this case, I am obliged to take the distance backwards, it will then
be

be obtained, when what has been said § 19. is observed. There is still another method of passing through, which is called the *passing through forward*. This method is made use of when coming before a wood, which is too thick to go through in front in good order, and this is performed in the following manner: as soon as the battalion A B (Pl. 4. fig. 56) has reached the wood, the commandant gives the word (when very close to it, and not before): *pass through forwards!* then all the officers immediately command: *to the right! wheel!* with their right flank files to the left, which are followed by the rest, and march with the longest paces that the thickness of the wood will permit; as soon as the officer has reached the other side of the wood, he directly gives the word to his division: *march up!* without waiting for the rest, so that he stands with his back close to the wood; and then he waits for the other divisions, and for the order to march, in order to dress again with the battalion.

§ 27.

§ 27.

Of the MARCH of the FLANKS, before a RETREATING BATTALION, (Pl. 4. fig. 57).

Nothing is more difficult to an officer, then to lead a divifion, which is to march *en flanc* * before a battalion retreating: becaufe, his march muft be fo regulated, as not to be either too far off, or come too near to it, fo as to obftruct it in its march. He muft keep a direction perpendicular to the battalion, and not an oblique one; nor incline either to the right or left.

To obtain this end,

1. The noncommiffioned officer of the right flank of the 1ft divifion, and the one of the left flank of the 8th, muft ftep on in a ftraight line without looking about

* Divifions marching *en flanc*, are thofe which are broken off, as A and B, from the wings of the battalion, and march in clofe order perpendicularly to the front C D.

them;

them; and pay attention to their officers only, who are to direct them; and who for this reason, are obliged to march on that side of their divisions, where they join the battalion.

2. The division must keep a very exact pace, and remain constantly in close order, without losing the position which has been given it.

3. He must, according to what has been said § 5. know how to incline to the right and left, without deviating from his position.

4. When the officer orders longer or shorter paces, the whole division, must take that pace at the same time. A division practised in this manner, will be managed with more facility than any other one; and an officer will have nothing else to do, than to pay attention to give that direction to his division, which he shall think proper with respect to the battalion. To give rules upon this, would be very difficult, if not impossible; because, the movements of a battalion, have too great a variety to fix a particular rule for each. An officer must know, that when he stands with his divi-

sion *en flanc*, that this is done with the intention, to cover the wing of the battalion, or which is the same thing, its flank, according to which he is to direct his movements. When the battalion steps out quick, he must do the same, that he may not stop it; and when marching slow, he must take the same pace, so as not to deviate from it. When the 2d and 7th division fires, he is to halt and front, to assist it in case of necessity; and as soon as they recover, he must again face to the right, or left, and directly step on, that the division who fired, may have room to fall in again.

§ 28.

Of Wheeling with a Battalion.

When, for example, a battalion **A C** (Pl. 4. fig. 58), is to wheel to the right, the word is given: *battalion! to the right wheel!* upon this word of command, all the officers who have divisions, step before the 3d file of their right wing. The captain of the right wing, is the only one who

who commands to his divifion: *eyes! to the left!* all the other divifions are to keep them to the right; upon the word: *march!* the 1ft divifion wheels as ufual, according as the commandant thinks proper: and the captain, dreffes his divifion without ftopping, at the given direction A B. If on the contrary, the 2d divifion fhould wheel in the fame manner, it would come behind the 1ft, which however it fhould be at the fide of; confequently, it may be eafily feen, that he muft firft ftep forward with his divifion; and fecondly, that he is to wheel, at the fame time that he fteps out, fo as to come in the direction with the 1ft. To obtain this, he muft wheel with both wings; however with this difference, that his right wing, muft not wheel fo quick as the left one; therefore, his right wing muft take fhorter paces, and by bringing out the left fhoulder, give the dreffing to the left wing; fo that the whole divifion, before it comes to the alignment, may come fquare in. It will be eafier, if the officer of the 2d divifion, imagines himfelf to be ftill at the fide of the 1ft, notwithftanding, he is broken

off

off from it; and describes, that quarter of a circle with his right flank, which he would have described, if he had remained joining to the left flank of the 1st division. The bringing out of the left shoulder more, will procure him the facility of giving sooner the position which the 1st already has to his division; it must only be observed, that in this case, as well as in wheeling to the left, that the shoulders are not turned at once and in a hurry; because, a needless inclining would happen, and in the end, confusion. The 3d, and all the other divisions, are to observe the same, which will be easier to them, because the further off they are, the more time they have to direct their platoons. The same rules are to be observed, when a battalion is to wheel to the left, with this difference only, that the 8th division keep their eyes to the right, and all the others to the left. The officers, step before the 3d file of the left flank. According as a division falls in, the officer is to dress by the 16th and 17th §, so that the one who follows him, finds a fixed

point

point d'appui, by which he may dress his division.

There are some cases, where the 3d rank must wheel, and others, where it is to march up, and front. But it would be useless to give rules for this; and an officer of any tolerable degree of knowledge, will easily conceive, that none are wanted, if he only considers, that the 3d rank in such cases is made the 1st.

§ 29.

Of the SQUARE.

The forming of a square with a battalion, which will be treated of here, may be performed in different methods. I shall here mention three only. The first and shortest is (fig. 59), for the 4th and 5th divisions of the battalion, to keep the front, but only to close, in order to fill up the openings made by the colours, on entering into the square; the other divisions face to the right about, and wheel as has been said above with the 3d rank; the three of the right wing

wing to the right; and the three of the left wing to the left. As soon as each division has wheeled in, it is to front, and to dress perpendicularly to the flank of the standing grand division; that is, the 1st rank of these divisions, must come behind the 3d rank of the flank file. The 1st and 8th division wheel again, when they are come in a right line with the 2d and 7th, the 1st to the right, and the last to the left, and close the square forming the 4th flank. It seldom happens, that these two divisions, or when the square is greater, that the battalion, which is to form the tail, can cover properly that part of the square; because, either the distance from the 2d to the 3d flank, is too great for them to be able to fill up; or it is too small, so that they cannot come into it, and consequently, both sides will shoot out; but from whence arises this fault? It is, because the two side flanks A E, B F, are not dressed perpendicularly to the head A B, but stand one way or the other obliquely. To remedy this, I propose the following expedient, which, if not entirely, will however,

ever, in some measure contribute to lessen the trouble which has hitherto been taken. Being placed in A and in B (fig. 59), as before the two flank files of the head of the 1st ranks, you make them take exactly the direction of their file leaders; this file will serve to dress by, which may be considered as the beginning of a line; upon the prolongation of which A C, B D, the side flanks A E, B F, must be directed, which will then certainly be a truer perpendicular to the head, than the method hitherto made use of.

A second method of forming the square (fig. 60), is, for the 4th and 5th divisions to remain standing; the three divisions of the right wing, wheel to the left by divisions; the three of the left wing to the right: then the 1st faces to the left, and the last to the right; and being in flank, they dress in line by the head, whose wing they look upon as their point of alignment; then they wheel in, and dress as in the first case. The 1st and 8th divisions march together to the right and left by files, and form the tail, where the 3d rank will face outwards. But, if it is required to form the square, in such manner (fig. 61), as that the 1st rank of the tail is to be outwards, then the three first divisions must wheel to the right, and the three last to the left; the first are then to face to the right, and the last to the left, and thus march into the flank. But the 3d and 6th divisions must then march with the 3d rank, close behind the 3d rank of the head; so that after having fronted, they may stand back to back. The 2d and 7th divisions take their distance backwards; and when wheeled in, dress as in the two above cases. The 1st and 8th divisions march together, with to the right and left by files, and form the tail, where the 1st rank will then face outwards.

There is very little to be said about the defence of such a square; because it must be always bad. The only thing to be observed, is, that both divisions of each flank, must well defend each other: That is, when the 5th fires, the 4th makes ready; and when the 5th recovers, the 4th presents; and so *vice versa*.

When

When such a square is to march, a non-commissioned officer as flag sergeant, must step out six paces from between the 4th and 5th division; then the 4th division looks to the left, and the 5th to the right; and these divisions march as when advancing, but not with too large paces. The tail is to do the same with the noncommissioned officer, who steps out into the square, from between the 1st and 8th division, and both are then to march, as when advancing or retreating. The noncommissioned officer, who marches thus, must march in a direct line with the head. The side flanks must take care, first to march well to the right, or left by files; and secondly, to keep the line so, that the head and tail are not broke by a wrong dressing; this is to be taken care of by the major or adjutant.

The particulars about breaking off, and marching up of a square, shall be mentioned *, when we treat of a square composed by several battalions.

* See § 54. of the square and oblong.

§ 30.

§ 30.

Of bringing a Wing forward, or Advancing it.

This is a movement, which is made use of to change the front of a battalion, or a line; for example (fig. 62), the battalion A C, is marched off from the right by divisions, whose front, after having wheeled in, will be towards B B; but circumstances require, that it should be towards D D. To obtain this, the left wing must advance, so that the battalion may stand as marched off from the left, and be able to wheel in again to the right, so as to front D D.

There are several methods to perform this manœuvre. But I shall suppose only three of them, as being the most practised, and preferred to those, where the divisions are to open, and let the advancing ones march through; because then, one part of the battalion is separated, and the other closed in; and both are useless. There is only one case where this method may be made use of,

and

and which hereafter will be introduced as the 4th method.

When the left wing of a battalion is to advance, and that there may be still more ground gained in advancing; the commandant of the battalion gives the word: *halt! left wing, advance!* the officer of the 8th division, gives the word: *to the right!* and marches with a lock-step, so far, as that the left flank of his division, may march close by the right of the others. Then he commands: *halt! front!* and marches with the lock-step, to the right flank of the preceding division; as soon as the 8th division comes to the 7th, the officer of that division, gives the word: *to the right!* and as soon as he can pass behind the 3d rank of the 8th, he then likewise marches with a lock-step behind it, and proceeds as the 8th did. All the divisions are to perform the same, as far as the 1st, and when this last is fallen in, the whole battalion then takes again the usual pace.

The second method is this (fig. 63); the battalion is first to march at half or quarter distance, and at the same time, all the divisions are to go to the right by files, and proceed with the rest as before; but here, the officer of the 7th division, as soon as he has fronted, is to take his distance, before he begins to step off.

The third method is, when the front is to be changed upon the same ground, so that the right wing is to be where the left stood; and *vice versa*.

In this case (fig. 64), the 8th division is to perform the same movement as before; the seven others go to the right, and march as the 8th did, with a lock-step, to the place where they came from; as soon as the 7th has reached the place where the 8th stood, the officer gives to his division the word: *to the left!* passes behind, fronts, and follows the 8th; the other divisions perform the same, and then the 1st division, after having fronted, will stand where the 8th stood.

The fourth method of advancing the wing (fig. 65), is only to be practised, when no enemy is to be expected. For example; when on the parade marched off from the right, and a wheeling to the right, was

was to be performed, then all the seven first divisions, *halt*. Upon the word: *to the right and left, open!* the right hand platoon of each division, inclines to the right; and the left one, to the left; so that a division may march in front, through the opening. The 8th division does not open, but marches through the others with a lock-step; the 7th closes with its right and left, as soon as the 3d rank of the 8th has passed the 1st rank of the 7th, and follows the 8th. The same is performed by all the rest, till the whole battalion is marched off from the left, then they take the common pace again.

When a battalion is marched off from the left (fig. 66), and intends to perform this movement, it is to proceed in a contrary sense, but in the same method, just as if it had been marched off from the right. But it is to be observed as a principal rule, that the divisions which advance, are always drawn out from the side, to which you are to front, or, to where the enemy stands; because, at his approach, I am directly able to oppose him with these diviſions; and the others, may paſs behind the line which is formed. But if a battalion is already formed in the line, and is to change its front; the eaſieſt method will be, to perform it with the four firſt diviſions to the right, 'and to wheel to the right about by files on the ſpot, and thus to march off behind the 3d rank of the battalion. The left wing performs to the left, and wheels likewiſe to the right about by files, and marches in this manner, before the 1ſt rank of the battalion, until each of theſe two wings, have reached their preceding oppoſite wings. The colours will then be the center or pivot, about which the battalion revolves.

PART III.

Of EVOLUTIONS with a whole CORPS.

IT has been shewn in the first part of this work, what a soldier should know in order to exercise well with the firelock; and, how an officer is to proceed when commanding.

The second part shews, how the soldier, and the officer, must be practised to the evolutions with a single battalion. And this third part, will serve to establish rules, according to which, a whole line or corps may be manœuvred upon the same principles, and kept in order.

But,

But, as the rules which will be given here, are a sequel of the two firſt parts; one may therefore, I think, be eaſily convinced, that this end will never be obtained, if theſe rules are not followed with the utmoſt rigour and accuracy; and, if the battalions, of which the corps is compoſed, have not been exerciſed accordingly.

It muſt alſo be adopted as an unalterable, and a fully demonſtrated principle, that the advancing and manœuvring with a line, will never be well performed, if the battalions are not ſo perfectly well exerciſed, as that you may not be obliged at the manœuvres, to enter into ſome detail with them. If any battalion is not ſo well exerciſed as another, it will have nearly the ſame effect, as an ill exerciſed ſoldier in a platoon. As unable as the one will be to act with the platoon, ſo it will be with a battalion in a line; the commandant of it, will himſelf fall into unavoidable errors, when he is obliged to pay more attention to the correcting his battalion, than to what he is to perform with it. He is then in the ſame caſe, as an officer, who

who bufies himself with single men in his platoon, at the time, when he should exercife in the battalion. If then, the commandant falls into errors, by too frequent corrections, it will naturally follow, that no commandant, fhould, during the manœuvres, pay attention to fingle platoons; but, fhould leave that care to the major, adjutants, and thofe officers who lead them; and thefe alfo, are to leave the care of their private men, to the clofing officers and non-commiffioned officers.

A general, who leads a brigade, is in the fame cafe, during all the time of the manœuvres, as a commandant of a battalion would be, who fhould bufy himfelf with the interior arrangement of it; for, during the time that he is rectifying the confufion in one battalion, the others perhaps of his brigade, upon which he is then not able to fix his attention, will fall into faults, which perhaps he will not correct fo eafily and fo quickly, as to prevent its having an influence upon the whole line.

But before I proceed further, and come to the manœuvres themfelves; I fhall further

ther mention here, some duties which particularly respect the commandants of regiments and battalions.

The remarks of a commandant himself, have given occasion for this, whose knowledge in the art of war, is so well known, that we should endeavour to put them into practice.

I shall therefore make use here of his own words. He considers a commandant as the instructor of his officers, and says:
" I think one should endeavour to make
" all the officers acquainted with every
" manœuvre, the reasons which occasion
" them, and the advantages that may be
" made use of. Should even the greatest
" part of them not learn by this to judge
" and to combine them; there will how-
" ever, always be a certain number, who
" will think and speculate. By this, a
" great deal would be already gained; be-
" cause from these, there may be formed
" in time able men, who, when they have
" attained a certain degree of knowledge
" of their profession, will be induced to
" read good books, and by this means
" en-

"enlarge their notions. Their eagerness
"will increase, in proportion, as they per-
"ceive themselves to advance in know-
"ledge. Because, one never labours in
"any profession whatever, with more plea-
"sure, than when one perceives in oneself
"the required capacity; it is then impossi-
"ble to withstand the desire of distinguish-
"ing oneself. It is to be wished, that
"such able officers, though they should
"not know how to draw plans, should
"understand them perfectly, with the ma-
"nœuvres of the troops, and the refer-
"ences marked upon them; and that they
"should endeavour to perform them; be-
"cause, this is the best method of exe-
"cuting them upon the ground. The ideas
"are formed much quicker upon a plan,
"than from the best relation without a
"drawing; because, the eye may follow
"the manœuvres, as if one was present
"at it. Those, who are deprived of this
"talent, must be contented with obtain-
"ing a general idea of the manœuvres, so
"as to be able to perform them directly,
"without a previous preparation.

"Ex-

"Experience has shewn, that with all
"the officers in general one may go far;
"and, when they have a certain degree of
"knowledge, one may proceed still fur-
"ther with them. For example; suppose
"a described position to be given of what
"is to be performed, and when they are
"well prepared for it, you then, when
"on the spot, perform unexpectedly, and
"without giving any notice, quite ano-
"ther thing than what they have been
"prepared for; in the beginning they will
"fail, but in time will be so used to this,
"that they will punctually execute what
"is commanded. This method sharpens
"their attention, and confirms that con-
"fidence which an officer should have of
"himself; it makes him bold and certain,
"and he will not seem embarrassed when
"any thing unexpected is to be performed."

His second remark is: "what further
"forms the officers, is this, to instil into
"their mind, those manoeuvres, which are
"seldom performed with large corps, be-
"cause in the field, they are more frequently
"done by only one or two battalions. For
"ex-

" example; you occupy villages; defiles
" of all forts: you force a paſſage through
" them, or over a bridge; you make your
" retreat over it, in the preſence of the
" enemy; and, for this purpoſe, ſingle
" men are taken to haraſs the battalion;
" you form an advanced guard, or a rear
" one, and you take different poſts accord-
" ing to the nature of the ground; this
" being done, you aſſemble the officers,
" and reaſon with them upon the poſitions
" which have been taken, ſo that they may
" learn to judge of them, and likewiſe of
" their ſtrength and weakneſs. At another
" time, you divide the battalion or regi-
" ment into platoons, and you repreſent
" the eſcort of a convoy; the platoons,
" are then to take poſts one after another,
" there, where it may be neceſſary; and
" are to be relieved by the following ones,
" as would be done in reality. Suppoſing
" the convoy is arrived and to be formed,
" the eſcorts are to aſſemble again, and go
" along with it, taking a convenient poſi-
" tion. In this poſition, the flanks are
" to be covered by detached platoons, which

" are

" are to be placed in favorable posts; you
" must crown the heights which the batta-
" lion occupies; and, when the reason of
" each position has been again explained
" to the officers, the march of the escort
" is to be continued; and several more of
" such like manœuvres. But it will be
" said: when shall this be performed, and
" where will you find time for it? when
" marching home from the spot of exercise,
" or from the environs where the manœu-
" vres were performed; and should they
" manœuvre till they come to the gate of
" the town, the little fatigue, and the short
" time employed in this practice, bears no
" comparison with the great utility arising
" from it to the officers and to the service
" in general; the road home will not ap-
" pear by this method too long to the
" soldier, and by this means, he will be
" ready for every thing that may really
" happen." This is the advice of the author of the above observations, which I think are of too great advantage not to be followed.

But

But the question is,

1. Who will take the trouble to instruct the officers, and to improve their knowledge? I think those who reap the benefit of it; and who, by the manœuvres in time of peace, will in time of service, receive much assistance from a corps of officers so well instructed. For, I believe every one will agree with me, that a commandant with a corps of well instructed officers, who understand the service, will execute a manœuvre with more order, than with another corps, whose knowledge is not equal to those above.

2. Who are those officers that one should endeavour to instruct?

All without exception, but the youngest most; because, it is the nursery from whence those subjects are taken, which are to succeed the old ones, who are supposed to understand the service; if they do not, it is a sure sign that they have been neglected in the lower rank of officers, as ensigns, or second lieutenants. A reason which must still further be a spur, not to suffer them to remain in ignorance; and it would be of no little advantage, if one was even to begin with the lance corporals, and bring them up for the rank of officers.

3. How are they to be taught?

With more patience than is commonly ufed.

A young, and in general every officer, who is not acquainted with what he is to be taught, muft be confidered as a recruit; and as this one has a right to claim the patience of the officer, who exercifes him; by the fame reafon, this officer may require the fame of his ftaff and commandants. Punifhment muft only take place with regard to thofe who are inattentive, and who fhew no inclination to learn. When reproaches are not accompanied with inftructions, they will be to no other ufe, than to let the officer know that he has committed a fault, but he will not know how to correct it in future. For example; if the officer of the 2d platoon after the firing of the 1ft, fhould not give the word as he ought to do; the telling him that he has given the word too foon or too late, and many reproofs, will not prevent him from falling

falling into the same error, or into some other. But, if the rules are told him, upon which word of command of his neighbouring platoon, he is to guide himself; this will certainly be of more utility.

4. In what manner must an officer be taught, and what method must be made use of for this purpose?

A very clear knowledge must be given to an officer, as well of the several words of command at exercise, as of the different evolutions which may occur; to what purpose they are, and why they are performed in such a particular manner, and not in any other. To this end, and that all the officers may be similarly taught, according to the same principles which have been given in the two first parts of this instruction, to which small plans have been annexed, which partly serve to make it intelligible, and partly to bring an officer, by degrees, to judge of the drawings of the manœuvres of a large plan, and to learn what their intention is. We must then go through this instruction with the officer, article by article, and converse with him on this subject. For example;

ample; when you intend to demonstrate, § 16. which treats of dressing in a line, then, all the advantages must be clearly shewn, that arise from a well performed dressing, and the inconveniences of a bad one; if this is done, the officer will see the necessity of dressing a single division in a right line, why that has been observed so scrupulously, and why in exercising a few men, so much attention has been paid to their not turning their shoulders; being convinced of all this, he will apply himself to the well performing the dressing; but, if this instruction is omitted, such an officer, who does not comprehend the use of it, will look upon his commandant as a capricious man, who cannot bear to see one or two men in a platoon, either a little forward or backward, for he will then think he stands upon trifles; but, when they are brought so far, as that one may suppose them to have sufficient knowledge, then let them give the demonstration themselves of some evolutions; an officer, who understands a little how to draw, may lay down on paper his ideas how he would perform

such

such things; if he cannot draw, small right-angled parallelograms made of wood or pasteboard, numbered and marked on the one side, by a strong line representing the first rank, may be made use of to represent platoons, or divisions; with which they are to shew on the table, the proportional evolutions; this method forms infinitely, and an officer, whose imagination has by this method been strengthened, will certainly when with his men at an evolution, commit fewer faults, than he who is not acquainted with such means. When an officer is faulty in the demonstration, you must set him right with gentleness; this will give him confidence, and encourage him to communicate his ideas to his commandant, or to any other officer, and to make questions upon things he does not understand. If on the contrary, reprimands are made use of, it will have no other effect than to intimidate him. These are the instructions, which, according to my opinion, are proper at a time, when exercise cannot take place, and when it will be convenient to go through it with the officers; and a commandant

mandant at exercise, will perceive the great benefit of it, if he has given himself this little trouble. He will see in a short time, that the staff officers and captains under his orders, will be excited to follow his example, and will so assist him, as to lighten his business; the emulation of becoming an useful member in a regiment, will induce them to teach the officers of their company, after the example of the commandant, who has it at heart to instruct himself, and all his officers.

When come to the place of exercise, and at the performance of the evolutions, we must not take from the officer what directly respects his duty. I shall give one example only.

Suppose you are to wheel up with a battalion, or after advancing, to halt; and the commandant gives the word: *dress!* then, proper time must be given to the officers to dress their platoons, according to the principles they have received; because, at the beginning of the exercise, the place of exercise must still be looked upon as being the school; and you are not to mind a little

loss

loss of time, which the officer occasions by his being somewhat slower in dressing. But when they are ready, then the commandant is to examine, and shew them where they have committed faults; but, it is common to proceed otherwise; for, the the commandant has scarcely given the word: *dress!* when he is the first himself who dresses, and orders the officers to return to their posts. It is partly from self-sufficiency that he is induced to this, because he thinks nothing can be well done, which is not done by himself; or, because he would make the spectators think so. Those, whose capacity is limited with regard to the knowledge of the service, will be imposed upon; but certainly, he will not deceive those who have more understanding; for these know very well, that it is not the business of one officer only to put a battalion in order, or to keep it so. He first of all, misses his end; and secondly, he prevents by this the experienced officers from shewing their talents, who are then so disgusted, as not to do any thing more than what is commonly required by him, who gives them no share of that honour, which a well exercised battalion has a right to claim. He will also, and to his prejudice, soon obtain the end of bearing himself alone the burden. He may likewise be brought to this, through the ignorance of his officers, and then he is the more to be pitied; because, the fault always reflects back again to him, for not having instructed them better; and when he does every thing himself, he obtains nothing further, than that he keeps his officers in ignorance, and prevents their ever making any progress in knowledge.

If it was even supposed, that the commandant did not want any assistance from his officers, and that for this reason he had no occasion to instruct them; I think however, that his affection for a rank, in which he himself has acquired glory, should induce him to form for the state he serves, useful members, and such as resemble himself. The glory of its being said in future, such, or such a man has commanded the regiment, and formed officers who do honour to himself, to the regiment in which

they

they are, and the state they serve; this is, in my opinion, another motive, which must incite him to set his heart upon the instruction of his officers.

The affection and reciprocal confidence of his officers, is the chief advantage he gains by their instruction and formation. The over looking their faults, and not correcting them; are certainly not the means by which their confidence is gained. They too easily see, that weakness, and a limited knowledge of the service, is the bottom of this. But, when a commandant endeavours to convince them, that his design is to enlarge their knowledge, to distinguish them from the common class, and to root out that prejudice which only allows to the soldier, very limited and moderate ideas, making him consider his condition, as being merely mechanical, and not a science; he has then a right to claim their affection and confidence, and he will only miss his end, with those who are ungrateful, and who will never do any honour to the profession to which they have devoted themselves.

Several

Several staff officers have another fault, which according to my opinion, is the greatest of all.

It is this, that when a battalion during the manœuvres, falls into any errors, whether it be by the fault of the commandant himself, or of the officers, who are but moderately or wrong instructed, they seldom confess that it is their fault; but throw it upon their inferiors, and pretend that every thing has been made clear to them. Why should I not confess a fault, which has been committed by myself, or through the indistinctness of my orders? There is less shame in confessing one's own faults, than in imputing them to those who are innocent; and, how can such a staff officer, gain the confidence of his officers, who always expect at every exercise to be reprimanded, not only for their own faults, but also for those committed by their commandant?

These few observations, in some manner, shew the advantages which are acquired by the instruction of a corps of officers, and the disadvantages that arise when this is omitted.

omitted. There are perhaps here and there, some ideas superfluous, and of such a nature as may be improved. But, when they are considered as advices, which are to guide us to further researches, how, and in what manner, we may form able and useful subjects for our profession; less rigour will be then used, in criticising such faults as may be found in them.

I now proceed to the evolutions in general, in order to shew the advantages which may be made use of, at the manœuvres; so as that they may be performed with order, and the trouble lessened, by making use of some expedients. But I suppose once for all, that the battalions are so exercised, as that no further care is wanted for their interior arrangement. But, as too frequent repetitions of the names, would make this instruction too diffuse; the battalions of the first line, will be marked and numbered by figures, according as they are arranged in natural order. The battalions of the 2d line, will be marked in another manner, and likewise numbered; and their numbers will begin, where the first line ended. But
the

the brigades will be marked by letters. I thought this necessary to be mentioned here, in order to instil it previously into the mind before I proceed further.

§ 31.

Of the March in Column.

As much as one is convinced, that in the march of a corps in column, nothing fatigues more than the irregularity of the march; that is to say, when the divisions stop or run, sometimes are obliged to halt, and step on again; yet however, it is very little considered how to remedy it. The introduction of an equal march, as well in regard to the length of paces, as the quickness; and an exact keeping of the distance by the officers, has greatly contributed to prevent this in some measure. But, it has not yet been brought so far, as to remedy it entirely. The reason of this, according to my opinion, is; that when a column, for example (Pl. 5. fig. 67), is to march from the point B towards A, it will seldom take

take the shortest line A B, to reach this point; and though even the 1st division does it, one may depend upon it that the rest will deviate from it, and either describe the curve line B E A, or a serpentine one, as B C D A; but both are longer than the right line A B; if then the divisions, which are of a sufficient number to fill up the distance A B, remain in an equality of march; they will not fail to lose their distance upon the lines B C D A and B E A; and as one suffices for this, it will follow, that all the divisions, reckoning by the 1st, who deviate from the line, will be obliged to step out more, and consequently must run. But, when the divisions perceive the fault they have committed, whether they are brought back again by the commandants of the battalions, or by the generals of the brigades, or perceive it themselves, and therefore come nearer again to the line A B; then there will necessarily happen, an opposite change in the march; for the divisions, which before were in the lines B C D A, or B E A, have not room enough in the short line A B; and as their distances

would

would be too short to be brought again into order, they must take shorter paces, and hence there will happen a stopping. From this, the following conclusions may be made: The faults of both stopping and running, arise partly from the changing of the march, from that of the direction, which the divisions should keep: now, to prevent the falling into this fault, no pains should be spared in keeping the direction; for this end, when the officers march at the flank, and if they do not so, the flank noncommissioned officers must be better practised to march after their leaders. It must be well understood here, that this means his leaders, and not leading man; because till now, no one has been without having had his leading man; but, whether he takes him as he should, this is another question. For example (fig. 68); the noncommissioned officer 3, will always believe he marches right, when he is in C or D, having his leader 2 before him: but, is this the real line A B upon which he is to march? certainly not! and the prolonged dotted lines C 2 F, and D 2 G will prove it.

What then are the means to be made use of, to keep constantly in the true line, or at least to deviate from it as little as possible? They are these, the officers and noncommissioned officers must be exercised to march in column, so as to have besides their next leader, several more, or at least one more, in a straight line with him. For example; the noncommissioned officer 3, must march after the one in 2, so as not to be able to see the first in 1, and both must appear to him to be only one person; he is then in a direct line with 2 and 1. The one in 4 must march so, as to be in the direction with the 3d, 2d and 1st, and when there are still more divisions before him, he must have them all in a line; he must, I repeat it again, at least have besides his leading man, one more; and I believe, that the stopping and pressing will then be prevented in the column, which is often falsely imputed to the captain, who marches at the head; the march into the alignment, will likewise be obtained with more certainty. To practise them to this, they must be placed at fixed

distances

distances from each other, and without their divisions must dress themselves in a line, and then march on in that direction. It will then appear, which of them judges right or wrong; independently of which, by the practice of this rule, this advantage will be also obtained, that on a march, the fatigue of the soldier will be lessened. It would be absurd to pretend, that in this march, the above rule should be kept to as scrupulously, as when marching into the alignment. No! this would be pedantic, and as to applying these means on a common march, it is only to be understood, that they are so to be made use of, as to save the men from those unnecessary windings, which greatly lengthen their march.

§ 32.

Of Marching into the Alignment.

It would be superfluous to mention here again, what is to be observed by the divisions of a column, at the wheeling-in point, and in general, at the marching into the alignment;

alignment; becaufe this has already been fufficiently explained in § 14: for, thofe rules which have been given for a fingle battalion, may likewife be made ufe of for a column, compofed of feveral battalions. It will be only fhewn here, how, and in what manner the ftaff officers are to proceed, not only to bring the column into the exact alignment, but likewife to keep it fo. For this purpofe, I fuppofe (fig. 69) four battalions, who having marched off from the left, are to march into the alignment A B; confequently, the point B will be the *point d'appui*, and A the point of alignment, where at the fame time the wheeling-in is to be performed. I further fuppofe, that the adjutants C and D have placed themfelves in the alignment; but as both are ftanding on rifing ground, in the valley G G, nothing elfe will be feen of the alignment, except the two adjutants C and D. Now the battalions are, as long as they march in the valley, in the fame cafe as if the alignment was not taken, confequently, always expofed to the danger of deviating one way or the other from the

O align-

alignment; and though in the end it may be obtained again, I think the faults that may be committed in this, have been sufficiently proved in § 31. Therefore, I shall here shew the means to be made use of in such a case to avoid them. It will be granted me, that at the wheeling-in point A, not only the opposite *point d'appui* B will be seen, towards which the march is; but likewise, the two adjutants C and D, between them; consequently, nothing is easier, than to march the battalion next to the point A, exactly into the alignment, when the commandant of it remains at the point A, and directs his divisions upon the point B, and the two adjutants C and D. This being granted, it will follow, that the battalion which is the nearest to the point A, will be the most consequential in the alignment, and that its eight divisions, may be looked upon as so many fixed points, by which to dress, and to come exactly into the alignment; if then these eight divisions can be considered as so many fixed points, then I think, nothing is so natural as to endeavour to get them; because,

cause, the more points there can be had in the alignment, the better and easier will the dressing be performed: Therefore it must be established, that the commandant of the battalion, is to remain at the wheeling-in point A, to dress his division in the alignment. He must not be fixed to his own battalion only, as commonly happens, or follow it when it marches ill; but he must consider that it is him who is to serve as a point of direction to those who precede, and that they are to dress by him, and not he by them. If then the commandant of the 2d battalion, or if he cannot leave the center of his battalion, his major, would be certain that his battalion marches truly in the alignment, he must then first dress himself in it, before he performs this with the divisions; what follows, will shew that this rule is well founded.

He must then,

1. Either near the 8th division when marched off from the left, or near the 1st when marched off from the right, dress himself by the divisions of the 1st battalion, which are supposed to march exactly; that is,

is, he muſt be in the direction with the wheeling-in point, or point of alignment, and with all the officers of the firſt battalion, as many as are wheeled in; ſecondly, the head of his horſe muſt be towards where the diviſions come from, otherwiſe he would obſtruct the march; and then he will judge, whether his diviſions march well or not. If ill, his officers muſt, to avoid the frequent calling to them, be accuſtomed by the ſignal of his ſword to paſs cloſe to the ſide of his horſe; as ſoon as his battalion is thus arranged, it will ſerve to direct the 3d battalion, to which it will give eight new eſtabliſhed points in the alignment; he will then be to the 3d, what the 1ſt was to him. To the 3d and 4th battalion, I ſhall ſhew the faults which have been frequently committed. For this reaſon, I ſuppoſe them to be on a low ground, where they cannot ſee the *points de vuës*; but the two adjutants who took the alignment, and the 2d battalion can; conſequently, the points of diviſion in the alignment are of no uſe to thoſe battalions. Therefore, when a commandant or major, will give a direction to

his

his battalion, he rides to any one of his divisions, and dresses from thence backwards by the two adjutants C and D, who are taken as *points de vues*. If this division has deviated from the alignment, as here in F, it naturally follows, that he will fall into this fault, and himself, as well as the 4th, will both dress according to an angle C F D, and by this will commit the fault of § 31. But when the 3d does not follow the faults committed by the 4th, who at first deviated from the alignment, but places himself first in H, in the direction of the eight divisions of the 2d battalion, and makes his battalion march towards him; he then will give an opportunity to the one of the 4th, to perceive the sooner his fault, who will endeavour to repair it again *.

---

* To avoid deviating from the alignment, when come into the valley G, I think a 3d adjutant might previously be placed in H, in the direction C A by the one in D, whereby then the 8th division of the 3d battalion, when arrived in C, would have the two points H and D to dress by; and if it was a pretty deep and wide valley, it would be necessary that two adjutants instead of one only, should be placed in I and K in the direction A B, either by the one in C, or by him in D.

These rules must be followed, though there were even no vallies or obstacles, that could obstruct the seeing the *points de vuës*; because by this means, the direction of the line will be obtained from one adjutant to the other.

It is of itself understood, that what has been prescribed to the commandants of battalions, is also to be observed by the brigadiers, that these likewise may assure themselves, whether their battalions march well dressed in a line.

§ 33.

Of Marching up to form the Line.

When a line is long, the marching up to form it, is commonly done by a given signal; this is in order, that they may all halt at the same time, and avoid thereby the losing any distance. When thus marched with proper distances, and with the abovementioned precautions, the irregularity of the falling-in of the divisions into the line, at the signal given, will be prevented; which
almost

almost unavoidably happens, though it cannot be said that the line was ill marched into the alignment. From whence then does this happen? I think, from a fault which is committed by most part of the commandants; which is, that when the signal is given, one gives the word to his battalion: *halt!* quite short; another: *battalion, halt!* a third: *the battalion, halt!* It must be understood, that the two last commandants, lengthen extremely their words; their intention being to give to their officers by this means, a little more time, that they may take their distances more accurately. But I believe, that this is rather the method to lose them the sooner; if not in one battalion, it certainly will happen in the next. To prove my assertion, I suppose three battalions, which march into the alignment. The 1st upon the signal, gives the word: *halt!* quite short; the 2d: *the battalion, halt!* I further suppose, that the extent of these words of command, amount only to one tenth of a minute; but, according to our adopted principles, seven paces and a half are made in this time. Where will there be ground enough to take thefe feven paces and a half, feeing that the firft of his divifions, have already ftood ftill fix feconds? No other anfwer can be given to this queftion, but, that the captain of the wing muft count the extenfion of the words of command of his commandant, and alfo take an interval of feven paces and a half more, which he may take in the mean time; or, he muft employ thefe fix feconds, when he has his exact interval only to lift up his feet, and bring them down again upon the fame place; for he cannot halt till the commandant has given the word for it, otherwife his word of command will be ufelefs. Both cafes will produce faults; this battalion in the firft cafe, will keep the 3d marching, and when there are feveral, all the reft; or it will occafion, that the whole, when they *halt* as the 1ft upon the fignal, muft begin to ftep on again to regain their intervals. In the fecond cafe, where the captain only lifts up his foot, and brings it down again on the fame place, all the officers will lofe their diftances, and have

their

their divisions too close, though they even had them before as exact as possible. I prove it thus: when the captain, for example, lifts up his left foot, the 2d officer lifts up his at the same time with him; but, he is not sure if the captain will take his pace or not; and he cannot perceive it in the last case, until the captain has brought down his foot; then he has already taken his pace, and will consequently have lost one pace of his distance. Though the 2d officer should perceive at the first pace, that the captain goes no further, the 3d officer is in the same case at the lifting up the right foot, as the 2d was before; and he will only perceive at the bringing down the right foot of the 2d, that he goes no further; he then has likewise already taken the pace, and consequently, his distance will be one pace too short. Thus there are then two paces lost, and alternately one pace after another is lost in the seven divisions: consequently, the whole battalion will have too short a distance by seven paces, which must be remedied by the whole line, whether they remain on the march, or step

on

on again. To avoid this fault, it must be once for all fixed, that the commandants, as soon as the signal is heard, never give the word: *battalion, halt!* but say quite short, only: *halt!* Here it is to be observed, that the commandant is not to look towards the signal given by the cannon; because it may happen that one perhaps will give the word upon the flash, which is seen sooner; and another upon hearing the report, which comes later; whence, another difference will still happen when such a signal is missed, and the word of command is given by the smoke from the vent.

Therefore it is a general rule, never to give the word of command but upon the report of the gun.

§ 34.

Of Dressing a Line.

The dressing with regard to the officers and majors in a battalion, has already been sufficiently explained in § 17. When all the

the battalions in a line, shall then obferve thofe rules, they all will be dreffed well, as to themfelves; but it will not follow, that the whole line will be fo; becaufe if a fingle battalion makes a fault, in marching into the alignment, and ftands either too forward or too backward upon it, this will directly make a great alteration in the line; and this fault has too much influence in advancing, not to require the utmoft attention to be paid to the remedying it. I believe every one who is convinced of the advantages, which are obtained by the different points, taken in the alignment, and which are endeavoured to be got by the adjutants, will agree with me, that the more of thofe points that can be taken in the line, the better it would be, on account of the feveral marks by which you are able to drefs; for this purpofe, nothing is better than the colours; becaufe, by them each battalion obtains its own fixed point, and the line will have as many of thefe points, as there are battalions in it. But how can the colours be dreft in a line, in the beft, eafieft, and quickeft manner? I think, by

following

following here the geometrical method of the engineer, when he traces a line on the ground, which line is traced out by banderols *, and performed in the following manner. For example; when a line is to be traced from A to B (Pl. 6, fig. 70), he sends forward an assistant with a banderol to a certain distance, C, taken at pleasure, and directs him by signs until he is in a straight line with B; then he is to fix his banderol as upright as possible. After that he goes towards D, where he likewise fixes a second banderol in a line with A B, directed by the engineer who remains at A. Now the assistant does not want to be directed any more; because he may at E fix a third banderol, and direct it himself in a line with C and D; then a fourth in F, and a fifth in G, will still direct the line with more facility, having now several points

* Banderol, or camp colour, is a little flag in form of a standard, extended more in length than breadth, fastned to a staff of about nine feet long, and one inch and a quarter thick at the foot; and it is tapered towards the top.

before him, two of which are sufficient to perform this exactly.

But an engineer well practised in this, will seldom place entire confidence in his assistant, but will himself see if the banderols are exactly in a line with the object B. He must never place his eye close to the banderol, but must stand some paces from it; because then the thickness of the staff, will not hinder him from seeing the others with the object; this must be also observed by his assistant. Now, I believe the application of this will not be difficult, by only substituting to the line A B, another a b, consisting of battalions. Let the point a be the right wing of the line a b; the colours c, d, e, f; the banderols C, D, E, F; and b the point of alignment: the general of the brigade must place himself in a, as the engineer did in A, and each commandant of the battalion, as his assistant; the first must also do what the engineer did before; that is, he must, at the right wing in a of the 1st battalion, direct the colours of his first commandant or assistant, to the point of alignment b, and without

proceeding

proceeding further, thofe of the commandant d; it will here be objected, that this one does not want to be directed, having before him, befides the colours of the 1ft battalion, the *point d'appui* a, by which he may direct himfelf; this is very true. But, as the *point d'appui* is fometimes fo fituated, that it cannot be well feen, or that you may be too near it; this might occafion fome fmall errors, which the nearnefs of the *point d'appui* makes imperceptible, and which may have a great influence upon the whole line. The beft way then will be, for the general of the brigade, to drefs the colours of the two firft battalions by the wing, to the point of alignment. The commandant e, as well as all the reft, are now in the fame cafe, as the affiftant to the engineer was, when he was at the point E; they want no more affiftance, than the one above who planted the banderol; they may now direct themfelves; becaufe the one in e, has for his direction, the colours of the battalions c and d, and fo on. Here likewife, what has been faid above is to be obferved, that is, not to be

too

too clofe with the eye to the banderol, in order to direct exactly in a line; the fame muft be obferved alfo by the general, and by every commandant. The firft one in c muft, when he will examine the colours e, place himfelf at the right flank of the colours in d, and not clofe to them, and the reft muft do the fame at the left flank; both will then judge with more exactnefs. When dreft by the left flank, you proceed in an oppofite fenfe; that is, the general of the brigade, who directs the line, places himfelf at the left wing b, and the commandants at the right of the colours. The rule § 25. (Pl. 3. fig. 51), which has been given to the officers, how to drefs themfelves by the colours; namely, that they muft drefs by the four, and not by a fingle one only, is alfo neceffary to be obferved here, in dreffing the colours, otherwife all this trouble would be ufelefs. When a line confifts of feveral brigades, the general of the fecond, would impede the quicknefs of the dreffing, if he was to wait till the firft had perfectly dreft his brigade.

To

To avoid this, he muſt begin to dreſs from the right wing of his brigade, and proceed the ſame as the firſt did, as ſoon as he is ſure that he himſelf is dreſſed in the line: Whether he has this line by the adjutants, or that he waits for the dreſſing of the colours of the two firſt battalions to dreſs himſelf by; and then the general in H, becomes the *point d'appui* from whence he dreſſes his colours to the alignment b, in the ſame manner, as the general of the firſt brigade dreſt his to the point a. The reaſons have been ſhewn § 17. why, the dreſſing is not quite in a direct line to the alignment, but the breadth of the officers added, who at the falling in, repreſent the true alignment; this muſt likewiſe be obſerved, at the dreſſing of the colours in a line after having marched into the alignment; when you are to dreſs by them, becauſe otherwiſe, you would bring forward all thoſe diviſions, which are already well poſted.

§ 35.

§ 35.

According to the preceding established principles, the colours may now be dressed in a right line, though upon no alignment: for example; when a line after having advanced, is to halt; or after retreating, is to front again; or, when it has passed through.

I shall (Pl. 6. fig. 71) again suppose nine battalions, who, by retreating, have lost the dressing, and consequently, would not make a right line when fronted again. I further suppose, that these battalions are to dress by the *center*; and shew, that according to these principles, the dressing in a curve line would be avoided, which generally happens by this method of dressing. The colours of the 5th battalion, would then be here the point of direction. When then the commanding general, or the general who has this battalion in his brigade, would give the line of direction to the colours of it, he begins by placing himself at the left A of those colours, and at a certain distance diftance from them, and confiders himfelf there as the *point d'appui*, from whence he dreffes the colours of the 4th battalion, by thofe of the 5th; and as foon as the colours 4 are dreffed in a line with thofe of the 5th, the commandants of the 3d, 2d and 1ft battalions, obferve what has been faid, when dreffing from the left wing; that is, they place themfelves at the right of their colours, and direct them by thofe of the two next battalions; namely, the one of the 3d, dreffes his colours by thofe of the 4th, in fuch a direction, as to cover thofe of the 5th; the one of the 2d by the 3d, and fo on.

The general, having finifhed the dreffing of the colours of the 4th battalion, places himfelf at a certain diftance, at the right of the colours of the 5th battalion, for example, in B; and then confiders himfelf there again as the *point d'appui*, from which he directs the colours of the 6th battalion, by thofe of the 5th; and all the commandants of the other battalions proceed in the fame manner, as was done when dreffing the right wing; that is, they place them-

themselves at the left flank, and dress by the preceding battalion. For example; the one of the 1st must go back, until he covers the colours of the 5th by those of the 6th, and so on. The prolonged lines of the 3d and 7th battalions, shew the errors into which one may fall, when dressed by the colours of the next battalion only, and not by those of two taken together; but the rules given for this being followed, there will be nine fixed points, each covering one another, and which will consequently, when connected, form a straight line.

§ 36.

The connection of certain fixed points, may happen to be made in different manners, either by a curve line or a straight one, which however, form an angle with that fixed point, or by other means, which are not liable to either of these two faults.

The manner of avoiding the first method, is shewn § 16. and how one may fall into this fault by the second method, is shewn § 25. (Pl. 3. fig. 50), when the platoons are diftinctly dreffed from the firft and beft point you ftand in to the colours. We have endeavoured to eftablifh rules, for avoiding thefe inconveniences, and to fhew what advantages are obtained, when you wait for the dreffing by the wing. But there it is neceffary, that the captain himfelf fhould be firft upon the true line, otherwife, all thefe advantages are loft; and to obtain this exactly, it has been fhewn (by the demonftration in Pl. 3. fig. 51), how, and in what manner, the captain fhould drefs himfelf by the colours of his battalion. The application of that rule, is alfo to be obferved here (Pl. 6. fig. 72), by the captain of the right wing of the 1ft battalion, and by the captain of the left wing of the 5th; to the other captains of wings I fhall propofe fome expedients, by which they will obtain a furer point in the line of alignment.

For this purpofe, I have fuppofed five battalions, every one of which has a different direction, though their colours be in an exact line; and the 3d battalion, is again to be the point of dreffing. See what has been

been said § 13. (Pl. 1. fig. 23) of the dressing of the adjutants, and endeavour to make use of the rules given there by the following method.

As soon as the colours of the 3d and 2d battalions are dressed, the captain in c, as the left wing captain of the 2d battalion, must dress himself by the one in d, in the direction of the colours of the 3d battalion, let him in d stand or move as he pleases; the one in d, on the contrary, looks to the right towards the one in c, and he will find that he has him in a line d c e, which being prolonged, will go behind the colours of the second battalion; whence the following conclusions may be made. My neighbour, who dressed himself with me and my colours, is upon the line which lies behind that, upon which his colours are dressed with mine.

2. As he did direct himself by me, I must likewise then be upon the line that lies behind. Therefore, to obtain the true line A B, I am obliged to advance.

3. My neighbour, who follows me with the same movement, and constantly remains

dressed

dreſſed with me and my colours, will always have me and my colours in a line; and as I advance from d to D, until I am covering the colours 2 by my neighbour C; it will follow, that both captains covering reciprocally each others colours, they will be upon the only ſtraight line, which can be drawn between thoſe colours. The following example, where I ſuppoſe the left flank captain f to ſtand before the alignment, will make this clear. According to the above method, by which the captain C has dreſſed himſelf by the one in D, and his colours 3; the captain g muſt dreſs himſelf by the one in f, and the colours 3; becauſe the 3d battalion has been given to dreſs by. As ſoon as he perceives, that his colours are dreſſed in a line with thoſe in 3; and the one in f, ſees the one in g in a line f g h, which paſſes before the colours of the 4th battalion, he then judges, that he himſelf is too much advanced; and for the ſame reaſon, that the captain d in the preceding example, did advance, the captain f here muſt go as far back, until he is in F, and ſees the colours of the 4th battalion

covered

covered by the one in G; the one in g, who follows the movements of the one in f, and remains dressed in a line with the colours 3, which he must do, will arrive at the same time, upon the line which may be drawn between the colours 3 and 4, when the other stops, and they reciprocally cover each others colours; they will then be in the required alignment A B. The flank captains of the other battalions, are to proceed in the same manner, as soon as their colours are in a line; namely, the one in k is to consider himself in the same case, as the one in c; and the one in i, as the one in d; and at the left wing, the one in m, in the same case as the one in g; and the one in l, as the one in f. But the captains N and O, at the extremities of the right and left wing, must only dress themselves by their own colours, or if possible, see two battalions together, to dress by their colours. The majors and adjutants, who can see best, being on horseback, must in this assist them. I believe there are now sufficient marks upon the line A B, by which the platoons may be easily dressed, according to § 25.

each right-flank captain, is now sure of being upon the true line, and dressing exactly to his colours; the officer of the 5th platoon, when he steps beyond the colours, and considers them as his *point d'appui*, may exactly dress to his left-flank captain, or as he cannot always see him, to the colours of the next battalion. This method of dressing, seems to be slow, and the reason which may be objected to it, is, that every one may not do his duty, and interfere with things that respect others; because, if a general should himself dress the colours of all the battalions in a line, he would certainly prevent a quick dressing. If on the contrary, the commandant of the battalion, will leave the dressing to his flank captain, the same thing will happen; and the dressing will be likewise very bad, or at least uncertain. But, when the general only dresses the colours of the three center battalions, and only examines those of the rest; when the commandants only attend to their own colours; the captains, after their colours are dressed, direct themselves without loss of time by them, and the other officers

are

are so instructed in this, as to be depended upon; then the whole will go together, and by degrees, the colours of each battalion will be dressed, in the same manner as the preceding ones have been.

N. B. The lance corporals and flag sergeants, must not be permitted to let either their halberds or colours over hang, but must keep them upright as much as possible, to which attention must be paid by the adjutants. I will suppose this method of dressing, to be somewhat slower than any other; but I think however, the time lost, is not to be compared with the advantages, which are obtained by these established principles.

1. I obtain a straight dressing of my colours, on which all depends in advancing.

2. In the intervals between one colour and another, I obtain through the captains, still more fixed points upon the line, which will serve not only to a more perfect dressing, but will likewise assist greatly in advancing, as will be seen hereafter.

3. I always avoid the dressing in form of an arc, when dressing from the wing or

center; and by this means, I do not fall into the faults, which in advancing refult from an ill dreffing.

4. The more evolutions I can put into practice by the fame principles, the better it is: and by thofe I have juft now given; I obtain not only the dreffing well in line, with or without an alignment, but what follows will fhew, that the dreffing likewife will be preferved in advancing.

5. The captains of the wings, may by thefe rules drefs without calling and hallooing, and it will always be known by whom the ill dreffing has been occafioned; for if (fig. 72) for example, the one in k is not in a line with the one in i, and the colours of the 2d battalion; it certainly is then the fault of the one in i, and not of him in k.

I leave it to the judgement of thofe, who are convinced of the juftnefs of thefe principles, whether it would not be advantageous, to practife the flag fergeants and lance corporals by themfelves, and without men; and to place them at the fame diftances, as the colours of the feveral battalions are from each other, and direct them firft in a line,

line, then the captains of the wings are to dreſs themſelves between them, with their proper intervals; this would better inſtruct the commandants, as well as the captains, and make them readier at this, becauſe being then not hindered by the men, their attention will be ſolely fixed upon themſelves.

§ 37.

Of Advancing.

In ſpeaking here of advancing, I refer firſt to what has already been ſaid upon this article, in the firſt and ſecond part of this inſtruction; and I ſuppoſe, ſuch battalions as have been perfectly exerciſed, according to thoſe given rules. Therefore, the advancing in particular of a battalion, will no longer be the queſtion, but thoſe rules only which relate to the whole advancing of a line.

But to be able to judge exactly if the rules given, or thoſe which will be given when made uſe of, are of greater advantage

in

in advancing, than those which have been hitherto followed: I shall again suppose two lines (Pl. 7. fig. 73 and 75), each composed of nine battalions, of which the one is to advance, according to the old system, and the other according to the new one; both are to dress by the center, because by that method, the faults committed at any one of the wings, may be perceived better; and both before they begin to step, must be dressed in a straight line. The comparison which will be made, will shew which of the two is to be preferred.

When thus a line is to advance, according to the old method, the first thing to be done, is, for the colours and flag sergeants of the first rank to step out six paces, and they are to be told to take a *point de vuë* in front, or it is given to them. The same is done by all the battalions, consequently, there are as many *points de vuës* as there are battalions; if it should fortunately happen, that the ground gave as many objects as would serve for such a purpose; but these *points de vuës* must all be supposed to be so many perpendiculars,

whether

whether they are so or not. But it has been proved § 21. (Pl. 3. fig. 41), that the exactness of these perpendiculars is only found by chance, and how easy it is to fall into errors; consequently, there will undoubtedly be obtained nine lines which are false, and not perpendicular. Each battalion however, believes itself in the right, and marches thus in the perpendicular; and notwithstanding, a battalion either from the right or left wing is given to dress by, as here for example, the 5th (Pl. 7. fig. 73), it is only understood that the intervals are to be taken, according to it, and there is seldom any attention paid if the same dressing, or the same line which this battalion has, is kept; from whence then the following faults will happen.

1. The flag sergeant who takes the *point de vuë*, pushes on forward; if he does not do so at his first stepping out, it will certainly happen in the course of his march, and when he comes near the *point de vuë*; if false, his position will also be false, in regard to his base.

2. The lance corporals and flag fergeants of the left wing, drefs themfelves by the one who has taken the *point de vuë*; if then his pofition is falfe, the others will have them likewife fo.

3. If the preceding flag fergeants have a falfe pofition, they will give thofe who march in the ranks, and who drefs by them, a falfe pofition alfo; and as thefe are to give the direction to the battalion, it follows,

4. That the whole battalion will have a falfe front; and by this means, one wing will be brought forward, and the other kept behind.

5. As all the nine battalions, have each their particular *point de vuë*, each will confequently fall into the above fault; it certainly will then happen, that each battalion will have its own front, confequently, there will be nine fronts quite different on the fame line.

6. If you would not march in the line, but without connected points, you then call to the wing captains to drefs themfelves; or, the commandants of the 2d and 3d battalions drefs their wings upon each other;

other; from whence it will happen, that the wings of the battalion will either be forward, or remain behind; and while marching thus, form a faliant or re-entering angle. Because, for example, the commandant of the 7th battalion, fees from his wing along the right of the 8th battalion, as the one of the 8th will fee from his right wing, along the left one of the 7th battalion, as may be feen by the produced lines a b, c d.

Both alfo believe that their wings are not exact, notwithftanding, both wings are exactly perpendicular to the line upon which the flag fergeants march. Both commandants then will call to their wings to ftep fhorter; and by this they effect nothing elfe than forming an angle towards the colours by their wings. But,

7. If a battalion marches either in the form of a faliant, or a re-entering angle, the men will not be able to keep in a direction with their colours; they fhould however, when the battalion is to advance well, be accuftomed to this; for this purpofe, they will be obliged fometimes to

ftep

step out, and sometimes to step short, from whence happens the waving. When,

8. In advancing, the battalions, as they have chosen their *points de vuës* by degrees, either open or crowd, as is shewn by the dotted lines of the wings, from whence happens the inclining towards that battalion, which has been given them to dress by; and where are then the established *points de vuës* and perpendiculars? All are lost: those who have them exactly, as here for example, the four battalions of the right wing, as well as those who have them not so, but kept to them; the same fault will be also committed at shorter distances. Besides which,

9. You are under the necessity of inclining with a false front; and, who does not know the bad consequence of this?

§ 38.

Endeavours have been made to remedy in some measure this fault, by permitting one of the battalions appointed for giving the direction, to take a *point de vuë*, and
ordering

ordering the others to drefs themfelves by it. But does this remedy the fault? By no means; as long as it is granted, that this battalion, appointed for giving the direction, may fall into the fame error, which has been committed above by the nine battalions, when choofing the *points de vuës*; and then, the evil indeed will not appear fo great as it has been. However, confider only the (74th figure), and you will find that the line, if not the whole, however the greateft part of it, will commit the fame fault as before; for, if the 5th battalion, which is again to be the directing battalion, takes a falfe *point de vuë*;

1. The inclining will be unavoidable.

2. The nearer the battalion approaches its *point de vuë*, the more it will change its pofition. But if it changes its pofition, the whole line which is to drefs by it, muft likewife change its pofition.

3. Should the line change its pofition; it naturally follows that one of the wings, as for example, here the left, muft run, and the other ftep fhort; and then all the battalions are again expofed to the waving.

4. If the dressing is given by one of the wings, the running or stopping of the opposite one will be the greater.

5. Suppose, for example, Y, Z (fig. 74) to be the enemy, opposite to whom I before stood parallel; I certainly expose too much the flank, with which I moved out. If it be objected, that when these faults are perceived, another position could be given to the dressing battalion and flag sergeants, I shall grant it. But it must likewise be granted, that the *points de vuës* which the flag sergeants had, are lost, and with it the whole system likewise. Would it not then be better to chuse another system, according to which one would not commit such faults, that occasion great confusion, or they would be however less? I shall therefore propose what follows, by which I believe that these faults, if not entirely, will however, as to the greatest part of them, be avoided.

§ 39.

The reason why perpendiculars have been taken in advancing, upon which the preceding

ceding flag fergeant is placed, is to endeavour to give a direction to the line, according to which, at each pace they make, it is to have a pofition parallel to the place it quitted; but that the line is not obtained by this, has been fufficiently proved in § 21. and in the two preceding fections.

Now, the end of giving a direction to the battalion will be fooner obtained, by placing the advancing flag fergeant upon a line parallel to that upon which the battalion ftands; when, by placing the advanced colours, the rules are obferved which have been propofed § 36. for by this method, I obtain the ftraight line C D (fig. 75) by given now to this line two or three points, as a, b, c, at equal diftances from the bafe E F, it will be evident, that the prolongation of this line, drawn through thefe three points a, b, c, will be in all its parts equally diftant from its bafe E F, and confequently will be parallel to it. The greateft difficulty then, is, to obtain exactly thefe three points, by taking the colours of the 5th battalion, as the dreffing battalion; and thofe of the 4th and 6th, for thefe three

points

points a, b, c; and making them step out six equal paces, a part of this difficulty will be removed; but the least turning of the shoulders of the flag sergeant or lance corporal, may in regard to the dressing, occasion a great difference in the rest of the line: for this reason, one of the generals, either the brigadier of the three next battalions, or the commanding general himself, must give the dressing in the same manner, as was performed in § 36. when dressing the line. His eye here in respect to the parallel, will not much deceive him; because, in case he should dress the colours of the 5th battalion ill, as for example, upon the line A B, those of the 6th battalion will be further, and those of the 4th will be nearer than six paces from the line; but, should the fault at this battalion be ever so little perceptible, it will certainly appear still more in the 3d and 7th battalion, and then it will be very easy to remedy it.

It is the business of the commandants to dress the other flag sergeants who advance, and nothing will be easier to place them exactly,

exactly, than to follow all the rules of § 36. namely, the one of the 3d, places himself in d, at the right flank of his flag sergeant, upon those of the 4th and 5th taken together; and the one of the 7th in e at his left flank, upon those of the 6th and 5th taken together; the one of the 8th in f at the left flank of his flag sergeant, upon those of the 7th and 6th taken together.

Now here is a line established, which may serve as a direction to another line; namely, that upon which the battalions stand. It must be considered as a base, which has not any longer need to be dressed by another; but the one that follows it, must dress itself according to all its movements; and as all the parts of this line C a b c D, must be at the distance of six paces from the line of the battalions E F, in order to be parallel to it; therefore, when the battalions are to follow it, they likewise must remain six paces from it; and as the flag sergeants who precede the march, so as to serve as a direction to those of the center, and to the battalion; it follows, that when the whole line in all its parts, is at the distance of six paces from the above established base, the points according to which they are to dress, must then be exactly at the distance of six paces also. Therefore, it must be established as an unalterable rule, that the center colours constantly keep the distance of six paces, and dress themselves always by the preceding flag sergeants, as has already been said § 21. (fig. 44), and to avoid prolixity, I refer to the other rules given there, respecting the dressing of the shoulders and heads of the flag sergeants and lance corporals; as well as to the cadence of their march, and length of their paces. When the preceding marching flag sergeants and colours, do not chuse any object which is to serve to direct them in their march, they will run less hazard of changing their position, upon which the whole depends; if these do not change their position, those of the center who dress by them, will likewise not change theirs, and still less the battalion which dresses by them.

The preceding marching colours of the nine battalions, keeping the same cadence and length of paces; and those of the center

their

their diſtance of ſix paces; the battalions at each pace they are performing, will ſtand upon a new line, which will be perfectly parallel to that they left. But it would be hazarding too much, to affirm, that a line can without any further aſſiſtance, advance well, according to theſe principles. I ſhall therefore ſhew the faults, which may be committed by the preceding colours, and how to prevent them.

1. The preceding marching colours, may remain behind with regard to the reſt, though they are in a ſtraight poſition, (A) by the fault of their commandant who marches too cloſe before them, or with regard to his own perſon, ſtands back, and by this hinders them from keeping the ſame adopted length of pace.

To avoid this fault it is fixed as a rule, that all the commandants muſt conſtantly keep four paces before their colours. If they come nearer, they muſt permit thoſe who carry their colours, to deſire them without any danger of being reprimanded, to ſtep out further. They may alſo avoid it themſelves, if they endeavour to dreſs by each

each other. For example; the one of the 3d battalion will remain in the line, when he dresses himself in it, with those of the 4th and 5th; the one of the 2d, with the 3d and 4th taken together. At the left wing, on the contrary, the one of the 7th by those of the 6th and 5th, and so on.

However, a commandant must constantly remain dressed in a line, with two others taken together, (B) on account of the uneveness of the ground; because, when a battalion marches over a rising ground, or through a valley, more time will be wanted for a line to pass through, than for those battalions who march on even ground; if then they keep an equal length of paces, it naturally follows, that they will remain back, (C) by breaking off, particularly when the colours must break off at the same time. But all these faults may be easily remedied, partly by the generals; because, when they ride, for example (fig. 75), at the right flank c of the preceding colours of the 6th battalion, they will see if the preceding colours of the 8th and 7th, are in a line behind those of the 6th. They may do the same, by placing themselves at the left flank of the preceding colours of the 5th, when they see those of the 3d behind those of the 4th, and at the left flank of the colours of the 4th, they will see them of the 3d behind those of the 2d and 1st. On the other hand, the closing majors and adjutants, may when they are practised to it, remedy these faults with little trouble; because for example, when the major or adjutant of the 7th and 3d battalions, which are behind in respect to the line G H, rides close to his colours at the 3d rank, he will then see the back of all the other battalions. He then will easily judge if his battalion is behind, and therefore must give notice to his preceding colours, or to the commandant, to step out further, till he sees that his center colours at the 3d are again in a line, either with the center ones of those of the 2d and 1st, or with the center ones of those of the 4th and 5th taken together; the one of the 7th is to do the same with those of the 6th and 5th, or with the 8th and 9th. When a battalion has come forward out of the line L M, as here for example the 4th has, with regard to the 3d; there is, I believe,

lieve, no need of establishing in this case other rules; because by observing the above, the general will perceive the advancing out of the preceding colours, so will the major and adjutant by the same rules; for they will see along the front of the other battalions, and therefore, he must call to his flag serjeant to step shorter.

2. The preceding marching colours of a battalion may take a false position, and by this may give the same to the battalion; the generals will likewise perceive this fault, if they now and then ride close to the line; because, when for example, in the line N O (fig. 75) the left wing of the 4th battalion comes out, it naturally follows, that the right will be behind; the general being then at the line, for example, at the 3d battalion, he will see the whole front of this battalion; and, he will also see that the prolonged line from the 3d to the 8th battalion would cross it. On the contrary, when the general is at the 5th battalion, he then sees this 4th in its rear. In both cases, he will judge that this battalion is out of the line; the closing majors and adjutants

jutants may, by making use of the above rules, namely, when they ride near their colours close to the 3d rank, perceive this fault much sooner; there, they will see their left wing i in a line i g, which will pass before, and deviate from the battalions of the left wing; and, on the contrary, its right h will pass behind, and deviate from those of the right wing as h f. But the loss of the intervals, will make it sooner perceptible, when a battalion has thrown itself to the right, as here the 7th has done; then the interval between it and the 8th will be too great, and that between it and the 6th too little; but when the intervals between the 6th and 5th, and between the 8th and 9th are exact, one may conclude for certain, that the 7th has thrown itself out.

But if it is objected by the major or adjutant, that he cannot know whether the intervals between the 5th and 6th, and 8th and 9th battalions are exact or not, because he cannot stir from his post; my answer is, that he certainly may know it; because, if the 6th has too great an interval with
the

the 5th, he will confequently think that it comes upon him, and will then be fooner obliged to incline than his will; and the 8th would alfo be fooner obliged to incline than his, having too narrow an interval with the 9th; for which reafon, the rule has been given, that one muft not incline directly after the lofs of three or four paces in front, but examine the matter firft. An experienced major or adjutant, will directly perceive this, when one wing is obliged to ftep fhort, and the other, on the contrary, to ftep out; as for example, here the right wing of the 7th battalion muft ftep out, and the left ftep fhort. All thefe faults muft be remedied, by the direction of the colours, and their exact pofition; and by fuch means, the due intervals will be regained, without any neceffity of inclining. Might not general rules be drawn from this with regard to the dreffing by the colours? Thefe are,

1. For the generals of the brigades.

A. To preferve the colours in a line, they muft diligently ride fometimes to the right flank, then to the left; fometimes to one, and then to another battalion; and

direct

direct themselves by as many colours as they can see in the line, in order to correct those which are too forward, or remain behind.

B. The commandants of all the battalions, must look upon the dressing battalion as being infallible; (but not so the general), therefore they must not lose sight of it; and with regard to the dressing, proceed the same as with any other battalion.

C. To observe the position of the flag sergeants, they must often ride close to the line, and proceed according to the rules which have been given upon this head.

D. As soon as they see that a battalion begins to incline, they must directly ride to the preceding colours, and place themselves at one of the flanks; there they will directly perceive if the flag sergeants deviate; if they have done so, they are certainly not in the direction with any one in the line L M (fig. 75).

2. For the closing majors and adjutants.

A. These must often ride near their colours, and close to the 3d rank, to see if they

they are dreffed with their battalion, and with the next to it, or whether they are forward or behind.

B. They muft often look at the flag fergeants and colours, to fee that they do not look back and turn their heads; and that thofe of the center, conftantly keep their exact diftance of fix paces, otherwife, they never will be fure to perform what has been prefcribed to them.

C. They muft exactly obferve the intervals, but not make them incline for the fake of three or four paces; but wait till the battalion, which firft begun, fhall be in its proper pofition. For example; when the dreffing of the line L M, is made by the 5th battalion (fig. 75), the intervals with it muft likewife be obferved; but the 7th battalion lofes its interval at the right wing, confequently, the interval of the 8th will be too great. If this fhould then directly incline to the right, they both will meet; becaufe, the 7th will at the fame time incline to the left, and the 8th muft again give way; this needlefs inclining of

the

the 8th, will then occafion a waving in the other battalions, which are below it.

§ 40.

Of the Dressing the Wings in a Line.

A line may be confidered as to its whole to advance very well, but the contrary *in detail*; that is, the center of the battalions may be very well dreffed in a line with one another, but their wings may fometimes prefs out, and fometimes ftop. One ill dreffed foldier may occafion this, and it has been already fhown in Part II. § 23. (Pl. 3. fig. 45), how to remedy this fault. It may however, on the other hand, be eafier done by the clofing majors and adjutants. For this purpofe, certain marks muft be given to them, by which they may drefs again the preft out, or remaining back platoons. Thefe marks muft then be the wing captains, who muft drefs by one another. It is to be underftood, that this is to be performed by them at all advancings. But,
the

the method of dressing themselves in a line, in order to draw an advantage from it, is unknown to most of them. They think they have done enough, and imagine they are well dressed in line, when one looks at the other, and remains dressed with him; and so long as no other rules are given them upon this, it cannot, in my opinion, be imputed to them, that they have committed any faults; because they can constantly give for excuse, that both are upon the same line, and consequently dressed in it. But let two persons stand wherever they please, and there may be always a right line drawn from one to the other. What results from these perplexed conceptions, which the flank captains form to themselves of the dressing? Nothing else, than that the fault of one battalion, will have an influence upon the other; thus when (Pl. 7. fig. 76) the captain b of the right wing of the 2d battalion B, remains behind; the left wing captain a of the 1st battalion A, will certainly follow him: thus both are behind: they will then call to their battalions to keep back, and consequently, they will

will lead them into the same fault. The commandants, the closing majors and adjutants, will by this be deceived; and as they take it for granted, that their captains are dressed in the line; those of the 2d battalion imagine, that their 4th, 3d and 2d divisions have stept out too far; and those of the 1st will imagine, that their 5th, 6th and 7th have done the same; both then keep their divisions back, and dress by the lines c a and d b, consequently make an angle, and by this fall into that waving, to which a battalion is exposed, as soon as it marches in the form of an angle; and until it pleases the captains to take another position, either more advanced or farther back. But, by giving to these captains certain fixed points, upon which they are alternately to direct themselves, no faults will happen, but there will be a true alignment. The colours are taken again for this purpose, which the lance corporals are to consider as *points*, and dress themselves between them, as they did when standing. § 36. (Pl. 6. fig. 72); namely, that the 3d battalion (Pl. 7. fig. 77), having been

given

given to dreſs by the captains f and l, dreſs in a line with thoſe in d and e, by the colours of the 3d battalion, and place themſelves in a line with them; thoſe in d and e ſtep out or go back, until the one in e ſees the one in f, who is to follow him in all his motions, ſo as not to let him paſs his alignment with the colours of the 2d battalion; and the one in l ſees the one in d in the direction of the colours of the 4th battalion; the captain in h dreſſes by the one in g upon his colours, and proceeds in like manner, as the one in e did with him in f. The ſame is performed by the captain in a, who dreſſes by the one in b, and his colours 4; and this one b advances or goes back, until he has the one a in the direction of his colours 5*. They are to continue this operation, as long as they advance; the only difference between the dreſſing in a line of the captains when advancing, with that when ſtanding, conſiſts in this, that in one caſe the *points de vuës* are fixed, and in the other they are moving.

* Here it is ſuppoſed, that the colours during the advancing, are preſerved dreſſed in a line.

I obtain however here, as when ſtanding, two intermediate points by the direction of one colour to the other, which, I am ſure, are in as exact a ſtraight line, as can be drawn from one to the other. If theſe colours are kept in a ſtraight line, it will follow, that all the wing captains will be in the ſame ſtraight line; now to ſucceed in the preſerving of the colours and wing captains in a ſtraight line, I believe it would be advantageous, if the colours as well as the wing captains, were to practiſe the advancing without men, keeping the ſame diſtance, as if they were actually marching with the battalion; by this means, the majors, the adjutants, and captains, not having their attention divided, will perfect themſelves better in what they have to do. But, when the wing captains dreſs by their own colours, as many files of their diviſions as they can call to without hallooing, ſhould they even be only ſix or eight files, I obtain from each wing of the battalions, the beginning of the line, which my colours have with the next battalion. The colours of the center, with the colour files (for

which

which purpose, the best, most dexterous, and well dressed men are chosen), will give me another part of the line. Will it now be difficult for the closing majors and adjutants, to keep the rest of the battalion dressed between these parts of the line, whether they step out too far, or remain behind, as the figure shews? I believe not, unless they entirely neglect the established rules given about dressing.

§ 41.

When a LINE halts, after ADVANCING.

Notwithstanding, all the trouble that may be taken to keep a line straight in advancing, it will seldom happen that at the signal, or upon the word: *halt!* it will stand in a perfect right line. It must however, be as well dressed in a line as possible; because otherwise, a good retreat cannot take place. The interval between the signal, upon which the line halts, and that upon which it must go to the right about, is commonly very short;

short; but let it be ever so short, it must however be dressed in a line, as quick as time will permit it to be performed. The shortest and surest method, is, as has been said § 35. (Pl. 6. fig. 71), first to give to the colours of the battalions you are to dress by, and to the next battalions at the right and left, the position the line is to have; and if the commandants of the other battalions, proceed upon the same principles, and the wing captains, according to what has been prescribed in § 36. (fig. 72), dress by the colours of the next battalions, and the officers dress their platoons, according to § 15. by their colours; there will be then obtained a line, if not very straight, however, considering the short time given, better than it could be performed according to other rules. The commandants, as when marching into the alignment, give the word: *halt!* short and loud; and not: *battalion, halt!* upon the report, and not upon seeing the smoke of the gun; the same is to be likewise done in future, when a line halts after advancing.

§ 42.

Of Retreating.

It has been said in the preceding §, that the interval between: *halt!* and: *to the right about!* is very short. It would be hazarding too much, to pretend that in so short a space of time, the line could be made so straight, as a well performed retreat would require; yet less must it be imagined, that there will be time enough to bring it in a right line, after it has gone to the right about, and before it begins to step on. Therefore, some other means must be procured to dress it, so that during that time, it may keep itself in a proper direction. I shall then again suppose, a line C D composed of nine battalions (Pl. 8. fig. 78), the four first of which in advancing remained behind, and the four last, on the contrary, have stept out too far, in respect to the line E F; and, that there is no time remaining to bring these battalions again into a right line. When this line has gone to the right about, then the four firſt battalions will be advanced and form a falſe front, and the others will then be behind with a falſe front likewiſe. If now the advanced flag ſergeants, were to march upon perpendiculars, according to the old method made uſe of, they would naturally take falſe ones; becauſe, the baſe of their battalion will itſelf be falſe, in regard to that of the other battalion; what ſort of retreating then will reſult from this? certainly not a good one. This proves, that the ſyſtem of marching upon perpendiculars in retreating, is not at all admiſſible. But, let us try the application of the ſame rules to a line retreating, which in § 39. has been given to one advancing; if by this method we ſhall find the ſame advantages, which have been obtained by it when advancing; then, I believe, this method will be preferred, without heſitation to the old one; and that ſo much the more, becauſe I am able to make uſe of theſe rules in ſeveral caſes. Let there be given to a line advancing, another line by the advancing flag ſergeants and colours, which is to ſerve as a direction to the advancing line; this one is firft dreffed parallel to the bafe upon which the battalions ftand. An advantage, which I cannot have in a line, which after going to the right about, ftands falfely dreffed, as (fig 78), confequently, we muft try to eftablifh a right line by the advanced colours, to which thofe colours that march in the ranks, muft endeavour during the retreat to keep parallel.

So foon as the line has gone to the right about, all the adjutants difmount directly from their horfes, and drefs their colours; the one of the 5th battalion as the directing battalion, is now to take the poft of the general, and give to his colours, as has been fhewn § 39. (Pl. 7. fig. 75), the pofition the line is to have, that is, parallel to his battalion; the other adjutants, take the poft of their commandants, and proceed in the fame manner, as has been done § 39. that is, the one of the 4th battalion, places himfelf at the flank of his colours, and directs them by thofe of the 5th; and muft by the left flank, for example, in f (fig. 78) of his colours, correct thefe faults of thofe of the 6th; the adjutants of the 3d, 2d and 1st battalions, likewise those of the 7th, 8th and 9th, will thus find the dressing of the colours in a line, to be as easy to them, as that performed by their commandants when advancing, when those of the right wing dress their colours from their left flank; and those of the left wing dress their colours from the right flank, by those of the two next battalions taken together; as for example, the one of the 3d dresses his colours, by those of the 4th and 5th taken together; the one of the 2d, by those of the 3d and 4th; the one of the 8th, by those of the 7th and 6th, and so on.

By this operation, the advanced colours, will indeed be some of them nearer, and some further off, than six paces from their battalions; but this is a natural consequence of all straight lines, when drawn opposite curve ones. Therefore, the adjutants must not be embarrassed, but continue their operation, even though their colours should come close to their battalion, or be at the distance of 10, 15 or 20 paces from it. By this method a line A B is obtained

(Pl.

(Pl. 8. fig. 78), and another C D which is the real base; that the battalions C D must endeavour to get during the line of retreating. That is to say, the advanced colour upon the signal or word of command, begin to step on; and, as they are to serve as a line of direction to the battalions, it consequently is not their business to dress, according to the battalions; but these are to dress by them; the center colours are not to be further off from the preceding ones than six paces. As these continue their march, there is nothing else to be observed except the stepping further out, when they are at a distance of more than six paces, or stepping shorter when the distance is less. When thus the colours in the battalion, are first at the distance of six paces from the line A B, the battalions which dress by them, will likewise obtain it, consequently, will mark the line C D which is parallel to A B.

Thus, as the line during the advancing, may, by the care of the preceding flag sergeants, be kept in its proper direction, the same must be endeavoured to be obtained

when

when retreating. But the flag fergeants may during the retreat, commit the fame fault as when advancing § 39. remarks 1 and 2. But faults of the fame kind, muft likewife be remedied by the fame fort of means; and as they have been fhewn in the fame §, I believe, it will be fuperfluous to give a longer detail. It will be fufficient to fay, that the clofing majors and adjutants, now perform what the generals did before, in order to keep the colours dreffed in a line; namely, thofe of the right wing, muft often ride at the left flank of their preceding marching colours; and thofe of the left wing at the right flank of their preceding colours, and keep them in a line with the firft preceding colours of the two next battalions; they muft not take up much time in performing this, otherwife they would, by being in the line of direction, obftruct their next neighbour in the dreffing; and for the fame reafon, the majors and adjutants muft for their own fake, give their whole attention, that all thofe who clofe the rear of the battalion, whether officer, noncommiffioned officer, or drummer, may

each

each remain refpectively dreffed. They will by this means, be partly kept from obftructing the reft, and the noncommiffioned officers, will likewife partly procure means of keeping the men in a better line. At the end of § 39. A, B and C, there have been rules prefcribed for the majors and adjutants, the defign of which is to perform the advancing well; thefe rules are likewife to be obferved when retreating, and as it was them who before affifted the line in the rear, here this muft be done by the brigade generals and commandants of the battalions, who being on foot are able to execute it. The dreffing of the wing captains upon the colours, remains the fame as when advancing—an effential article; where it is further to be obferved, that the captains muft remain at their firft rank; becaufe, if one is at the 1ft, and the other at the 3d rank, the dreffing in a line can never be performed.

§ 43.

§ 43.

When a LINE in RETREATING, fronts again.

The pace in regard to the cadence, as well as to the length, which the flag fergeants ought to have, has been fixed in the firſt part of this inſtruction.

When charging with platoons or battalions, in advancing or when in retreating, the troop is beat; both are to be performed with the ſame ſtep, that is, with a cadence of 75 paces in a minute, which are not to be made longer or ſhorter than uſual, only the heel of the one foot muſt be placed at the joint of the great toe of the other; both conduce to the ſame end, namely, that the battalions of a line by this equality of ſtep, keep themſelves better dreſſed in a line. Notwithſtanding all theſe precautions, the battalions may yet, during the retreat, loſe their dreſſing; and when they have fronted, form a line which is not ſufficiently ſtraight, to produce a good advancing when beginning

ning to ftep on again; and as little time as
there remained to drefs, when after advancing
they have gone to the right about, there
will be alfo as little time when they front
after retreating; the line will then be in
the fame cafe, as it was when it went to
the right about; for thefe equal cafes, rules
of the fame kind may be made ufe of. When
thus the line fronts again, the colours are
likewife to advance again, as they are not
fure if the line is not to ftep on again. If
now the commandants place them again, as
the adjutants did before, in a ftraight line;
there will be obtained a line of direction by
which the center colours, and by thefe again
the battalions, may place themfelves parallel during the advancing.

In Pl. 8 (fig. 79) will make this § clear:
when this line after having fronted is to halt,
the word is given: *drefs!* then the flag fergeants and colours ftep into their ranks again;
and in order to drefs in a right line, you
proceed according to the rules given in § 35
(fig. 71) and § 36 (fig. 72).

REMARK.

Remark.

If hitherto, in dreſſing, advancing, or retreating, the dreſſing has been given by the center, it does not follow that it ought to be conſtantly ſo. It has only been done with the deſign of ſhewing the faults which might be committed at both wings, and to make the means to remedy it clearer.

Moſt commonly, and almoſt always, a battalion of the wing is given to dreſs by. But it would be ſuperfluous to give ſtill further rules upon this, which would be nothing elſe than a repetition of the preceding ones. The change of poſition of a battalion makes the only difference; for example, the dreſſing being given from the right wing, the commandant of this battalion is in all the three caſes, only to place himſelf in the center of thoſe of the 6th, 7th, 8th and 9th; if on the contrary, the dreſſing is given from the left wing, the commandant of the battalion of the left wing puts himſelf into the place of the one of

the

the 5th battalion, and all the rest in the places of the commandants of the 4th, 3d, 2d and 1st.

§ 44.

Of Inclining with a Line.

Several causes may occasion this movement; and it would be here too prolix to detail them all, particularly as it is not laid down, why such or such evolutions are performed, but how and in what manner they are to be executed. One single example will be sufficient to make this clear: for example, suppose the line A B (Pl. 8. fig. 80), was marched up obliquely towards that of the enemy C D, so that its right wing joins the river, and by this position out-flanks the enemy. If it is now to march in this position, without inclining, it will not only when it comes to be in E F, be out-flanked by the enemy's line and taken in flank; but it would likewise lose the advantage of the support of the river. In this case, the dressing should naturally be given from the right

right wing, which will be ordered not to leave the river; this battalion is then continually to incline, sometimes to the right, then again sometimes to the left, according to the different bendings of the river; and its movements must be followed by the line. It has been shewn § 4, what faults may be committed by a division when inclining; the men follow the natural leaning of their body, and bring back their shoulders to that side towards which they direct their march; or by too frequent calling to them, they are thrown into the opposite fault: and likewise, the means have been shewn, how to prevent this fault; this will now become essential in a line: because, if for example, the wing battalion when inclining to the right, should bring forward the left shoulder, it will occasion not only the running of the rest of the line, because it dresses by it; but the line will likewise, the nearer it approaches, have its left wing the more exposed to the enemy, as may be seen by the line G H, which however should be refused; if on the contrary, the wing battalion brings the right shoulders too far out, it will oc-

casion

casion a stopping in the rest of the line, which will then have the river behind it, when in the direction I K. This will be to its prejudice in case of a retreat, as it before had the advantage of having it for its support.

By this may be seen, how necessary it is to pay particular attention, that the men do not twist their shoulders, but keep them constantly in the same position, as they had them at first. You will here still further find, the utility of the rules given upon this head in § 39. (fig. 75) (see D for the generals of the brigades), namely, how to keep the colours dressed in a line; if then the general of the wing, or the commandant of the battalion applies them, and takes care not to lose sight of the colours of the 1st battalion, he will dress the line again; because he knows, according to what principles he is to proceed with the preceding marching colours, whenever the colours deviate from this line, either in H or K, and make an angle with it. If these colours then are kept in their position, the commandants of the other battalions, will

likewise

likewife be able to perform the fame, when from the left flank of their colours, they keep them dreffed with the others; and when the preceding marching colours are in a like pofition. I believe what has been faid, will fufficiently prove, that it will be an eafy matter to keep the reft of the line in an equal direction.

§ 45.

Of the ATTACK *en Echellon*.

It has been feen in the preceding 80th figure, that by an oblique march towards the enemy, the advantage will be obtained of refufing the left wing, fo as not to expofe all the troops at once to the fire of the enemy. But it is likewife at the fame time proved, that the attack cannot be begun without expofing the right flank to the enemy, when in this pofition advancing towards him, even though he had already been out-flanked, unlefs the line inclines to this purpofe. This movement, is on ferious occafions particularly, fubject to very

very dangerous confequences; therefore, the means of attacking *en echellon* has been tried, by which the faults that might be committed by inclining, will be avoided, without lofing the advantages which may be gained by an oblique marching up. If thus (Pl. 8. fig. 81) the line A B, is marched up towards the enemy X Y, in an oblique pofition; it is then previoufly determined, how many battalions each attack is to confift of. I fuppofe here, that the nine battalions are to be divided into four attacks, the firft of which to be of three, and the others of two battalions each; this being done, the 1ft divifion of the right wing battalion wheels as much to the right, as will make it ftand parallel to the enemy, which I fuppofe to amount to two paces. This wheeling, and the number of paces it amounts to, muft directly be told to all the other battalions by the adjutants. The wing battalions of all the other attacks, as foon as they have got the *point d'appui*, muft with their 1ft divifion, alfo perform the wheeling of two paces. By this is obtained the beginning

of

of four lines, which will be parallel among themselves, and also to that of the 1st; and, as this last is parallel to the enemy, it follows, that they all are so; and to bring the rest of the line likewise into the same position, the other battalions of each attack, must in the same manner as when wheeled with battalions, wheel-in in the prolonged line of their wing divisions, as A C, D E, F G, H I; but to prevent the divisions from an erroneous dressing by deviating from the line, as it commonly happens; as for example, in the position A K, by which the attack of the wing is exposed to the enfilade fire of the enemy's battery; we must then endeavour to give them a mark, by which they may direct themselves, and which they are to look upon as their *point de vuë*, and the right wing division as the *point d'appui*; and, as I have supposed, that the right wing division has wheeled two paces with its left flank, the 2d division will likewise be obliged to wheel with its right flank two paces, and with the left four paces, to obtain the line which has been formed by the prolongation of the wing division: thus, the progression from one division to the other is two paces. Now to determine the *points de vuës* of each attack, multiply the number of divisions that compose it, plus the intervals between the battalions, which is each equal to the distance of a division, by 2, the product will be the number of paces which the left wing of each attack is to perform, to come into the alignment of the wing division.

If now the number of paces is taken from D to C in a right line, by the left wing captain of the attack, he will serve as a *point de vuë* to all the divisions of this attack, as has been said § 16. and will be able to dress without fear of missing the alignment. For example; the first attack consists of 24 divisions and two intervals, which taken together, makes 26 division distances; these 26 being multiplied by 2, gives 52 paces, which the left wing captain D of the 3d battalion is to perform from D to C, to serve to the other divisions as a *point de vuë*. The second attack, consists of 16 divisions and one interval; consequently, of 17 division distances, which being multiplied by

2,

2, gives 34 paces from F to E, for the *point de vuë* E of the second attack, and so on

By this operation, there will be a parallel line broken towards the enemy, whose left wing if the whole line was to wheel, would have been obliged to make 160 paces from B to L; but by the above movement, the left wing makes only 34 paces from B to I; consequently, there are gained 1st, 126 paces, by which I remain further distant from the enemy; and 2dly, the great movement of the line, which it would have been obliged to make by the whole wheeling, will be saved. The object of refusing the wing, is however yet too small; because at the second attack, it is only at 52 paces from the first, and the others 34 paces from their preceding attacks. There is also a determined number of paces fixed upon, how far one attack is to be from the other, which is seldom less than 100 paces, but rather more. If then, the attacks are to keep at the distance of 100 paces from each other, and the 1st begins to step, the 2d waits until the 1st has made 46 paces more, besides the 54 paces distance, which the 1st already was from the 2d, and then begins to march. The 3d and also all the rest are to remain, until their preceding attacks have made 66 paces more, besides the 34 paces distance they already were from each other, before they begin to march; consequently, the 4th attack will arrive 300 paces later to the enemy than the 1st, which is sufficient for refusing the wing of a line of nine battalions. But every precaution that may be made use of, to give to the attacks such a position, as shall not expose them to the enemy's enfilade, will be of little use, if the attacks in advancing, do not keep the same position, which at their first setting out had been given to them. But, it is more difficult to preserve the colours of two battalions in their proper position, than those of a whole line, where they may be connected with several others. Therefore, more attention must be here paid to the colours and flag sergeants; the majors and adjutants, particularly those of the wing battalion of each attack, by whom the dressing is performed, must constantly

have

have their eyes fixed upon them. For example; the closing major E of the 6th battalion (fig. 82) (which represents the 3d attack of the preceding figure), must, from the right of his colours, constantly look at those of the 7th battalion; if then he perceives that his left wing should step further out, and that his left wing captain F, by following the movements of the right wing captain A of the 7th battalion, keeps on the same pace, he may be sure that his colours have an exact position, and that the fault lies in the divisions. But if his wing captain F should also step further out, it is a sign that the colours of the 7th battalion do the same, it being supposed that they keep dressed in a line with those of the 6th; because the wing captains follow the movements of the colours; but if the colours of the 7th battalion are obliged to step further out than those of the 6th, you may depend upon it, that those of the 6th bring their left shoulders forward, and by this means, bring their left wing out. But should these colours fall into the opposite fault, and bring their right shoulders too

far

far out, they will produce the opposite effect; and all those who are below them, and who before were obliged to step out, will now be brought to a stopping. This is what the colours of the wing battalion are to observe at each attack; and it would be needless to enter here into a longer detail, on what is to be observed by the colours of the 2d battalion; because, I suppose, that the rules given in § 39. having been well instilled into the mind, relative to the dressing of the colours, it will be very easy when practised accordingly, to keep the colours dressed in a line with the wing battalion; but as they cannot be connected with several more, so greater attention must be paid to dress them from their left flank, upon the four preceding colours taken together, according to the rules given § 25. (fig. 51). The preservation of the intervals at the attacks *en echellon*, is likewise as essential an article, as at the attack of a line; because, the same causes exist in both cases, which makes this necessary; the greatest fault in the attack *en echellon* arises, when the attack halts, and the others next to it

form

form the line, that is, when near enough to the enemy to fire at him, commonly the flank is then given to the enemy, which however should be refused; and this arises for want of attention, in giving the same dressing to the falling-in attack, as the other attack has. But, I think, this fault may easily be avoided, when the rules upon dressing the colours, which have been given in § 35. are made use of. By following them, it will be very easy to the commandants of the falling-in battalions, to bring their colours in a line with those already fallen-in; because, they can connect them in the dressing with the line. It also depends solely on the general, who leads the first attack, to give it that dressing in a right line, whose prolongation passes before the enemy's front (fig. 81). The 2d line, when there is one, must in every respect follow the movements of the 1st; the battalions of it must wheel in the same manner as the 1st, and keep an equal position with it; and as the 2d line is to support the 1st, it follows, that the attacks of the 2d line,

line, muſt ſtep on at the ſame time with thoſe they are to ſupport.

§ 46.

Of what is called, throwing one-ſelf upon the ENEMY's FLANK.

We ſhall not here ſpeak of the means, which may be made uſe of to deceive the enemy's attention, in order to gain his flank; theſe are things which belong to the more ſublime ſcience of tactics. The caſe which will be treated of here, is, that evolution which is made uſe of, not only to with-draw the line from the enemy, but alſo to take him in flank with the ſame line, and with the quickeſt method poſſible, though it had been already marched up parallel towards him, and had in this poſition advanced to ſuch a diſtance, as to be expoſed to his fire, at leaſt to a cannonade.

For this purpoſe, I ſuppoſe (Pl. 9. fig. 83), a line of ſix battalions in the poſition A B, which is already expoſed to the cannonade of the enemy C D; with this line, I am,

I am, for some reason or other, obliged to fall on the enemy's flank, which however, cannot be performed otherwise than by divisions, marched off in a line from the right, in order to turn his flank; this will then be the first movement required to be done with the line. If now these divisions march on in the direction A B E to gain the alignment F G, they would be needlessly exposed to the enfilade fire of the cannon from the whole front of the enemy; the line must then be withdrawn from this fire as fast as possible, and this is performed by the means of wheeling with divisions, as described by the arcs B L I H, A M K G; this wheeling may be performed by several methods, either with divisions, or by marching to the right by files. In the first case, when the divisions begin to step on, they are ordered to incline to the right, and follow the direction of the first division in B, and keep distance accordingly. In the second case, the divisions are commanded after having first wheeled: *to the right!* and at the stepping on, they are also ordered to keep to the right, and to follow the direction

tion of the 1ſt diviſion. I believe, this laſt method is to be preferred to the firſt. 1ſt, becauſe its execution is by this means eaſier; 2d, becauſe a diviſion which marches to the right by files, is able to march faſter, than one that inclines; particularly when performed with the lock ſtep. In both caſes, the following rules are to be obſerved.

1. He who leads the 1ſt diviſion, muſt not make it march too faſt, nor let it ſtep out too much; becauſe otherwiſe, the nearer it comes to the left wing, the more impoſſible it would be for that part of the line to follow; becauſe the arc A M K G, which the left wing diviſion deſcribes, is much greater than the one B L I H, deſcribed by the 1ſt diviſion. Therefore, if this was omitted, the line would undoubtedly break; conſequently, the general muſt meaſure the extent by paces, without however loſing his time, by making them too ſhort, or ſtepping out too flow.

2. During the march, ſuch a direction muſt be given to the 1ſt diviſion, as that when arrived upon the line F G, it may ſtand perpendicular upon it; but it muſt not

not have this position, until it is just upon the line; because, if the divisions are brought about too soon or too quick, in order to be in the position I; the last division A will describe the arc A K, during the time the 1st division B describes only the arc B I, which may be seen by the figure to be out of proportion; consequently, the last division A when it comes in K, will nearly have performed the whole arc A G, when the 1st B has made only about one half of the arc B H. But, if on the contrary, a proper direction is given to the 1st division as in L, the last division being then in M, will always describe in the same time any arc, as A M proportional to that B L described by the 1st. Whence it follows, that the direction of the 1st division, must constantly be such, as that when it has described a part of the arc B H; the last division must have in the same time, described a part of the arc A G, proportional to the 1st.

3. All the divisions, as many as there may be, must follow the direction of the first; that is, the wings, as here for example,

ample; the right one, muſt remain all in the ſame direction, let this evolution be performed either by inclining, or by to the right by files.

4. To ſave time to the diviſions, particularly to the laſt ones, which they are obliged to uſe in deſcribing the extent of their arcs, they muſt be permitted to take their diſtances ſomewhat ſhorter, it being known, that having reached the alignment, they muſt neceſſarily march forward, to gain the enemy's flank; and alſo becauſe they are ſure, that in this there is no danger; for ſuch an evolution is conſtantly covered by ſome other part of the troops.

5. In caſe the laſt diviſions ſhould not be in the alignment, when the 1ſt has already reached it, it muſt not be corrected, but they muſt march on with a good and ſtrong ſtep; becauſe, thoſe who ſucceed will gain time enough by having ſhorter diſtances to follow, and reach them, without being obliged to run.

6. As in ſuch evolutions, an alignment can ſeldom be given, becauſe it depends ſolely on ſuch movements as the enemy may

may make, during the time I am performing my movement, the march is then only directed upon the leader. Now if the general, or he who leads the 1st battalion, gives to the 1st division, after the officers have placed themselves at their left wing, the direction the line is to have; the officers who follow, must here apply the rules which have been given in § 31. (Pl. 5. fig. 67), relative to the march in a column; that is, they must march so, that the one before them covers the preceding one. For example; the 4th marches so, that he keeps the 2d covered by the 3d; and the 5th in the same manner, keeps the 3d covered by the 4th, and so on.

§ 47.

When a CORPS, which is not yet formed, is to MARCH into the FLANK of the ENEMY.

This movement is similar to the preceding one, with this difference only, that one is performed by inclining, and in this the diſtance between the diviſions muſt be obſerved. For example; a corps of 12 battalions in two lines A B, C D (Pl. 9. fig. 84), is marched off from the left, in order to fall upon the enemy's right flank E; the alignment of this corps muſt be in the direction H I and K L; if then, the commanding general was to direct his march ſo as to wheel in at the points I, L into the alignment by diviſions; the enemy would not only directly gueſs his deſign, but would alſo have an opportunity through the great diſtance, to make an oppoſite movement, which would occaſion the miſcarriage of his deſign. He then will chuſe another method, which the ridge G G between him and the enemy affords him, by which he will be covered in his march: he will direct his march along it in the direction A B, the enemy till then will always imagine that he is marching up parallel to him; and partly for theſe reaſons, and partly from the ſmall diſtance, will be obliged to remain in his poſition. But to gain the enemy's flank, he who leads the 1ſt diviſion

sion must, as has been said in § 46. turn it gradually, so that when arrived at H as the *point d'appui*, he stands perpendicular upon the line H I. If now the other divisions observing an accurate distance, endeavour (§ 31. fig. 68) to march in the direction of their leaders; the direction of march of the line A B will be according to the dotted lines A H and B A N; the 2d line C D must as soon as the 1st moves, perform a like movement, and by turning its divisions must give the direction of the march expressed by the dotted lines C K, D C P. But these divisions have a longer march than those who form the 1st line; consequently, the 2d line must step out further, and the 1st on the contrary must slacken its pace, so as not to oblige the 2d to run. It has been seen in the preceding §, that to keep a proportionate march amongst the divisions, it is necessary not to permit the first division to turn suddenly; but it must be done gradually, that he may not get the perpendicular position till he is just upon the line, which has been chosen for the alignment. The application of this rule is here of abſolute neceſſity; becauſe 1ſt, if in this caſe there is not given a proportionate turning to the 1ſt diviſion, which is to ſerve as a direction to the reſt; the diviſions of the 1ſt line will be thrown into the 2d, which in reſpect to the greater diſtance it has to march, cannot perform the movement ſo quick as the 1ſt. By theſe evolutions, I not only obtain the enemy's flank ſooner, but he likewiſe will not perceive my deſign, until my right wing is come nearly into the alignment, and the whole corps formed ready to wheel into it, where it will be then very difficult for him to oppoſe a counter movement. A general rule, and which never muſt be neglected at theſe manœuvres, is, that the 2d line K P is to outflank the 1ſt H N, by half a battalion at leaſt; and it is ſtill better when done with a whole one: the reaſon is, becauſe by this means not only the wing of the 1ſt line is covered, but I may likewiſe in caſe of neceſſity, fall with a greater power on the flank of the enemy, or even on its rear. There are commonly made on ſuch occaſions,

occasions, an attack by the advanced guard which precedes that of the wing, with which the attack is intended; if so, the 1st line must likewise outflank the attack, as the 2d line did in respect to the 1st.

§ 48.

Of Passing Through.

The several methods of passing through, as also how, and why one passes through, have already been mentioned in § 26. The same rules which have been given there for one battalion, are applicable for all the battalions of a line, however strong it be: particularly that rule, by which a certain number of paces have been fixed upon for the divisions, which they are to take from the 3d rank of the 2d line, in order that when passed through, they may again form a position which is parallel or nearly so. If this rule is omitted, one may be sure that the least false position of one single division, will mislead all the rest, and make them run beyond the proposed alignment;

the

the bringing them back again to which will be attended with a great deal of trouble; but the determinate number of paces, will not alone produce the parallel which I intend to form again behind the 2d line; unless this last was to relieve the post of the 1st line, or meet it when it retreats, joining all the battalions, and this in advancing; in this case, all the divisions at the passing through, must make equal paces; it will be difficult however in both cases to succeed in this, and consequently, a straight line will never be obtained by a determinate number of paces only; however, the giving of them must not be omitted, in consideration of the expedient it procures for obtaining sooner the end proposed, and facilitating the dressing in a line, which as may be seen is very necessary here. I shall therefore suppose (Pl. 10. fig. 85), that the six battalions of the 1st line have passed through the 2d with 150 paces, and is to form up again behind it in a straight line; but that by this, the opposite battalions would meet unequally, an equal length of paces not having been observed amongst

the

the divisions, some having gained more, and some less ground, and therefore would not have formed such a straight position as when first drawn up: in this case, to obtain it, a battalion must be given them to dress by, as for example here the 1st; then as soon as the divisions have fronted, and the officers have stept to their left flank, the general of the 1st brigade, or the commandant of the 1st battalion must from the point A, give to the two or three first divisions, that dressing which the line ought to have.

When this is done, he then orders the other officers to proceed, as has been said § 31. (fig. 68) that is, to dress by their leading men; but the commandant remains at the 1st division, who is then to be considered as the *point d'appui*, from whence he may see if his officers remain in the proposed line, and are exactly dressed in it. The 1st battalion being thus placed, the commandant of the 2d battalion, rides between the 6th and 7th division of the 1st in C, to see if his 1st division is in a line with the 7th and 8th division of the 1st battalion; and his 2d with his 1st division and the 8th of the preceding battalion. If so, he will then be able to dress in the same line his other divisions by his 1st; as soon as the 2d battalion is fixed, the commandant of the 3d in D, proceeds in the same manner as the 2d did in C, and so on. It must be observed as a general rule, that an officer must never begin to dress the line, until his preceding division stands fast; and this is still more to be observed by the commandant of the battalion, who must wait till his preceding battalion also stands fast; because, the hurrying of this operation, will always occasion a tossing here and there in the line; likewise, no officer must busy himself with his division: If he does, he will not only hinder a quick dressing with regard to himself, but will likewise by turning his body to look at his division, impede the rest from taking an exact direction. He must therefore, pay attention to the dressing of himself only; and when this is done must stand still, so that the next may be able to do the same. The men of his division must be so practised,

that

that without being told, they may dress themselves by him.

If the 1st line passes through retreating with to the right by files, so that it would then stand as when marched off from the left *, then the 6th battalion is the one to dress by, and the direction of the line must then be given by the three last divisions of that battalion; as to the rest, the same is to be performed by the left wing, as has been done before by the right one.

§ 49.

Of Dressing a Line from the Center, after having Passed Through.

On such occasions where it is necessary to pass through, and required to form again quickly; the dressing from the wing, particularly in an extensive line, would take

---

* Here it is to be understood, that after being thus dressed in the line, they are to wheel to the left into the alignment A B.

up

up too much time. It will then be better to take a battalion at the center to dreſs by, and to perform the quickeſt and eaſieſt dreſſing, one may, I believe, apply with advantage the following rules. The line A B (fig. 86) has paſſed through with to the left by files, it will conſequently ſtand as marched off from the right; with regard to the diſtances, every thing elſe is done the ſame as in the preceding §, that is, by the *point d'appui* A, which has been taken at the right wing: But the dreſſing is to be by the 3d battalion; it is therefore the diviſions of this battalion, which are to proceed the ſame as in § 48. the 1ſt battalion did; and thoſe of the 4th, 5th and 6th, perform likewiſe the dreſſing by the 3d, as has been alſo done in the preceding § by the 1ſt battalion. The officers of the 2d and 1ſt battalions, are not able to direct themſelves, becauſe the alignment upon which they are to dreſs lies behind them; they muſt then be aſſiſted, and this is done, when the commandant or major of the 2d battalion, rides between the 2d and 3d diviſion of the 3d battalion; and

from

from thence by calling only, dresses first his 8th and 7th, and then the other divisions of his battalion by the 8th.

When this battalion stands placed, the commandant of the 1st battalion proceeds in the same manner with his, as the commandant of the 2d did. But if the line in retreating, was passed through to the right by files, so as to stand marched off from the left; then the 2d and 1st would be in the same case, as before the 4th, 5th and 6th have been; and these three last battalions, in the same case, as those of the 2d and 1st: that is, the commandant of the 4th must ride between the 6th and 7th division of the 3d battalion; and when this battalion stands placed, he then dresses in the line the two first divisions of his battalion, and by these the other divisions. By this method of dressing in a line from the center, as soon as the dressing battalion stands formed, you obtain at the same time the dressing of the two wings, and consequently the whole line much sooner. The only inconvenience here, is, that the commandants or majors are obliged to bring each
division

division to its place by calling to them; because the officers have no alignment before them, upon which they could direct each other; as at the taking distance backwards. There will in this case be a constant noise until the line is formed; which however may be avoided, when the line is passed through in two several methods (this is to be understood in retreating) (Pl. 11. fig. 87). The three battalions of the right wing go off to the right by files, and the three battalions of the left, to the left by files; and then the *point d'appui* of the left wing will be the 1st division of the 4th battalion: consequently, the distance and dressing is taken at the same time by it. If now the commandant of the 3d battalion, places himself behind the 3d rank of the 1st division of the 4th battalion, from hence he will very easily dress in a line his 7th division upon his 8th, and the 1st of the 4th battalion, (to which the position which is to be taken must have been given).

The commandant of the 4th battalion, dresses in a line from behind the 3d rank of the 8th division of the 3d battalion, his 2d upon
his

his own 1st and the 8th of the 3d battalion: when these four divisions are placed, it will be easy to the rest of the right and left wing to dress by their leaders, according to § 31. (fig. 68), and the commandants will then by signs only, as the officers are facing them, be able to finish the dressing in a line. But by this it may be seen, that the lines must pass in two different methods, which however might not always be practicable, partly because a variety of evolutions in a line, which are to conduce to the same end, must be avoided as much as possible; because it occasions too much confusion. The first method then must be kept to, where the whole line passes through in the same manner: but to effect the dressing, according to the other method, is in my opinion better, because it prevents the calling and noise; I shall suppose the line A B (fig. 88) which in retreating, has passed through to the left by files, and which is to dress by the center. The *appui* will then be the division of the right wing of the 4th battalion, according to which the distances must be taken; when all is placed, the

the officer, who is to direct himself by the diviſions behind him, has nothing farther to obſerve forward. Then, thoſe who are beyond the directing point, may be ordered, as ſoon as they have placed themſelves at the left flank of their diviſions, to turn about, and to face towards the direction they are to dreſs by. Thoſe of the three firſt battalions are then ſo poſted, as if they ſtood marched off from the left, notwithſtanding, their diviſions ſtand as marched off from the right; and now the ſtaff officers and officers are in the above caſe, where the line paſſed through in two different manners, and all may now dreſs according to that preſcribed method. As ſoon as each officer of the three firſt battalions has dreſſed himſelf in line, he again turns about upon the ſame ſpot, ſo as to face towards where he ought to front, and then his diviſion is to dreſs by him.

§ 50.

§ 50.

Of Refusing a Wing of a Line that has Passed Through.

The refusing the wing of a line passed through, is done in order to render the enemy's design upon the flanks to no effect; or at least to oblige him to take a great detour to perform it; or also to force him to form his wing upon a possessed rising ground G, from whence he may be exposed to your fire. Thus let the line be A B D (fig. 89), which again is composed of six battalions, and which is to refuse with three battalions, so that its right wing may come to be in the position B D; and suppose the line was passed through in retreating to the left by files, as being the case the most difficult *. There is nothing farther to be

---

* The passing through to the left by files is here only supposed. The figure 89 relative to this §, shews the passing through to be to the right by files.

be observed by the three battalions of the left, than what already has been said § 48. (fig. 85), for those three first battalions. The 1st division of the 4th battalion, will then be the *point d'appui* for these three battalions, and this battalion proceeds here with the dressing, as the 1st did above; the 5th as the 2d, and the 6th as the 3d. The three battalions of the right wing, have a very difficult manœuvre to perform: their *point d'appui* is the angle B, where the line begins to break, and where the captain of the right wing of the 4th battalion is, after his division has wheeled-in; they are then not only obliged to take distance backwards, but likewise to dress backwards. Both should be performed with the left wing of the divisions, because the line stands marched off from the right; but this will be very difficult to the officers, because being obliged to be at the

The author at the end of this §, says, that when refusing the right wing, the passing through should be performed to the right by files; and when refusing the left wing, the passing through is to be performed to the left by files.

right wing of their divisions to lead them, they consequently will seldom have their proper distance with the left wing, though even they had it exactly with the right one; because the least irregularity in the position of their divisions, will occasion the loss of it. Still less will they be able to know, when their left wing is in the alignment, and when they should give the word: *halt!* therefore they must be assisted, which may be done in the following manner: The commandant or major of the 3d battalion, after he has given to his officers nearly the direction which they ought to take with their divisions, rides to B, as being the point where the captain of the right wing of the 4th battalion is to be posted, after he has wheeled in; where he is to give the word: *halt!* to the 8th division of his battalion, as soon as he sees that its left wing is in the given alignment. If now the officer of the 8th division, upon the word *halt* of his major, steps to his left wing, and places himself so as to face towards him, he will then be able to direct him so, as that he may be duly and exactly

U placed

placed in the direction of the point of alignment D. This 8th division is now to serve for the *point d'appui*, from whence the major is to direct the 7th, proceeding in the same manner as before with the 8th; and the officer of it, as well as all the other officers of the right wing of their divisions, must be occupied with nothing else than the taking distance by those behind them. When these two divisions are placed, the forming in respect to the alignment, will then be easier to the rest, having by the right wings of these two divisions two fixed points, upon which they will be able (according to § 31. fig. 68) to dress their own right wing. But it must not be imagined, that by the alignment of the right wing, the dressing of the left can be accurately performed, which however it ought to be. It will serve to prevent the divisions from going too far, or perhaps from halting too soon, and before they are in the alignment. This is only to effect the dressing nearly; and, I shall suppose this case, that, for example, the 5th division of the 3d battalion, was come somewhat

beyond

beyond the alignment of the three laſt ones; this fault however would not be of ſuch great conſequence, as if there were no rules fixed, according to which the diviſions might proceed, ſince you would be able to recover it very ſoon: By degrees as the diviſions halt, that is, when their right wing is dreſſed in line with the one behind it, the officer then ſteps to his left wing, and directly faces with his front towards the *point d'appui,* and he as well as all the ſtaff officers proceed as to the reſt, in the ſame manner, as has been ſaid § 49. (fig. 86) reſpecting the three battalions of the right wing. If the left wing was to be refuſed, this would then rather be eaſier than difficult to the officers, becauſe they are then already fronting towards where they are to direct themſelves and take their diſtance, and are then obliged, as in the preceding caſe, to turn about again, after having dreſſed themſelves. It would then be better, if the paſſing through could always be performed thus, according as either of the two wings is to be refuſed. For example; in retreating to paſs through to the left by files,

files, is consequently to stand as when marched off from the right, when refusing the left wing; the contrary would take place when the right wing was to be refused, being marched off from the right by files, and standing as marched off from the left. What has been said § 26. (fig. 55) of a battalion that has passed through, and is to crown a rising ground, is quite sufficient for applying the same to a whole line; it would therefore be superfluous here to add any thing more.

§ 51.

Of the RETREAT, *en Echiquier*.

This position is named from the resemblance it has to what is signified by that expression. When such a position is given to a corps, so that the battalions of it are placed in the same manner, as the squares of a chess board, the corps is said to be *en echiquier*; which position is given to it, that a part of this corps may be quicker withdrawn from the enemy, than by any other

other method; while at the same time the other part covers this retreat. To give to this corps, which (Pl. 13. fig. 90) consists of nine battalions, such a position, that every other battalion, as for example, here the 2d, 4th, 6th and 8th, are to go to the right about, and are to retreat as many paces as are contained within the reach of musket shot. When they have attained this distance they front, dress in a line with each other, and observe at the same time to be exactly opposite to the intervals they left, in case they should have deviated from them; which however must be avoided as much as possible. The observation of this rule takes place, only as long as the retreat is performed in a straight line, and that the ground is of such a nature, that no advantages can be taken from it, otherwise, an exception would be made. The two extreme wing divisions a and b of the four battalions D, E, F, G, 2d section, are to form *en flanc*; and, as soon as they are gone to the right about, to retire also *en flanc*; the two other battalions E, F form no flanks.

All the battalions, 1, 3, 5, 7 and 9 of the 1ſt ſection I K, are to form flanks with their wing diviſions, as ſoon as the 2d ſection goes to the right about; and that the flanks when retreating, may be able to march ſo as not to hinder their battalion, they muſt always be perpendicular to thoſe battalions, and by only preſenting to the right and left, cover the intervals of their next battalions, as the reſt of it is to cover by its platoon fire, the whole front, until the 2d ſection fronts again. As ſoon as theſe give the word: *front!* the battalions of the 1ſt ſection muſt go to the right about, ſtep on, and retire through the intervals which are left open of the 2d ſection, behind which it is to halt at the ſame diſtance, as the 2d did behind the 1ſt, front again, and you proceed in the ſame manner with regard to the intervals and dreſſing, as long as the retreat is going on in a ſtraight poſition; and that theſe battalions may better cover the intervals of the 2d ſection, they muſt as ſoon as they have fronted, wheel-in their flanks; except the extreme wing diviſions, which remain *en flanc*. As foon as the 1ft fection comes near the 2d, it begins the firing by platoons upon the fpot, and proceeds the fame as the 1ft did before. The wing divifions of all the battalions form flanks, as foon as the 1ft fection has gone through it, and when they have fronted at their proper diftance, their flanks are to wheel in again, and are thus to wait for the 2d fection.

But if in the purfuit of a retreat, fome heights or favorable ground offers which could be made ufe of, it would then be a great fault to neglect the advantages arifing from fuch a ground, by obferving the direction of the intervals, and confining one-felf to the given diftance, which one fection is to have from another; or, to attend to the exact dreffing of the fection in a line. For example; in the pofition A H, the 8th battalion would be very ill pofted if it placed itfelf in B, behind the interval it left, and was not to take poffeffion of the rifing ground L; from whence it will be able to command the whole ground abandoned by the 1ft fection; the 4th battalion would likewife commit a fault, if it was to confine itself to the 150, or 200 given paces in C, and not occupy the rising ground before it, at 30 or 40 paces from c to d, which otherwise would be given up to the disposition of the enemy. In both cases these heights must be occupied; but the battalions which are to occupy a rising ground, must observe to bring their wings back and dress by their next battalions, so as to be flanked by them. But it will be said that the 7th battalion, by the position of the 8th, which partly stands behind it, will when retreating meet it, and consequently, part of it will be obliged to pass through it; this however when done, would likewise be a great fault, because the 7th when retreating, would then not be covered by the 8th. What is then to be done? Each battalion must go through the intervals by which it is to retreat; as for example, here the 7th must pass between the 6th and the 8th; but this interval being now more to the left than it would have been, if this battalion did not occupy the rising ground; it must then incline accordingly as soon as it

begins

begins to retreat; and should the interval be even too narrow, it must endeavour to pass it, breaking off one division more, and joining it to the flank; be it as it will, it must pass through the interval, that the other battalions may not be obliged to alter their distances; because by this, the defence of the preceding interval would be lost; but as soon as it is passed through, it is to incline again to the right, so as to obtain the proper interval between it and the 9th battalion; the 8th by continuing the retreat, is then in the same case as the 7th was; and as it must pass between the 7th and 9th, it must incline so as to be able to pass it, and then both are again in their first order.

§ 52.

Of the same RETREAT, when a WING is to be REFUSED.

In the same manner, as in the passing through a line, any one of the two wings may be refused; the like may be performed at the retreat *en echiquier*. For example
(Pl.

(Pl. 13. fig. 91); when the 7th and 9th battalion of the 1st section A B is to refuse, these two battalions when the three others 1, 3 and 5 halt and front in E C, keep on marching; and their flag sergeants are to turn them so, as when fronting they may be posted in the given position C D, in which the battalions are to refuse; that is, they must be dressed in a line between the left wing C of the next battalion, which they consider as their *point d'appui*, and the real or imaginary *point* of alignment D. The battalions 2, 4, 6 and 8 of the 2d section have to observe, 1st, to march through their respective intervals; and 2d, that at the same time, when they are behind the battalions of the 1st section E C D, and at the given distance they are to cover, they must during the march, and before they arrive at these intervals, take by their flag sergeants the given position which they ought to have, so as to be able to protect the intervals by their fire.

§ 53.

§ 53.

Of the Retreat *en Echiquier* in Two Lines.

When (Pl. 13. fig. 92) a corps composed of 18 battalions in two lines A B, C D, is to form *en echiquier*, each line proceeds by itself, according to what has been said § 51. of one line; that is, the 2d section of each line is to retreat, and if the 2d line should be more than 300 paces from the 1st; then to divide this distance, 150 paces must be given to each section for their retreat.

If then the 1st section 1, 3, 5, 7, 9 of the 1st line A B, performs its retreat through the 2d section E F, it is then always in the same case as it was in § 51. it must also proceed according to the rules which have been prescribed there, and conformable to the position which the battalions of this 2d section have taken. But when past through the 2d section E F, they will exactly meet the battalions of the 1st section

tion of the 2d line C D; they therefore must pass through, according to the usual method as has been shewn § 26. for which purpose they must also know what battalion of the 2d line is standing behind them; and as they have nothing further to fear, being covered by two sections, they march by divisions through the intervals of the 2d section of the 2d line, and wheel at 150 paces behind it, see § 48. The 2d section of the 1st line forms flanks, and as soon as the 1st goes to the right about, the 2d performs the same, and begins its retreat; as soon as it perceives that its 1st section has passed through the 1st section of the 2d line, it is to consider this section as if it was that of the 1st line; that is, it passes through their intervals; and as in continuing its retreat, their battalions meet those of the 2d section of the 2d line, they pass through them by divisions, and proceed to all the rest as the 1st section did before. The 1st and 2d sections of the 2d line, are now in the same case as the 1st and 2d of the 1st line; whence it follows, that these also are to proceed in the same manner

in

in their retreat. If now the 1ft line confiders itfelf as the 2d, and the 2d as the 1ft; this laft will eafily perform the retreat, according to the rules which have been prefcribed to the battalions of the 1ſt line, and which rules they muſt obſerve in their retreat: from thefe three fections, the following general rules may be eftablifhed.

1. The battalions which are removed back and far diftant from the enemy, have never flanks, except the extreme ones at the right and left of the fections; the reafon of which is, that the whole front of the battalions can cover better the intervals which are before them.

2. The battalions of thefe fections which are the neareft to the enemy, form flanks as foon as there is nothing before them.

3. The battalions muft conftantly paſs through their refpective intervals, let the battalions which are behind them ftand as they will; and no miftake will be made when it is obferved as a rule, that all the battalions in their retreat muſt always paſs with their left wing, clofe to the right one of the next battalion.

4. If the ground offers any advantages, it muſt be made uſe of; and one is not to confine oneſelf to a ſtrict obſervance of the orders which determine the diſtance of each retreat, and the exact poſition behind the intervals of the preceding ſection.

5. As long as there is no ſection behind, there is no need of paſſing through by diviſions; but you muſt always paſs through the middle of the interval, and if it is not directly behind the battalion, the battalion muſt incline.

6. All thoſe who retreat muſt march quick, and take juſt as much time as will avoid confuſion. For the defence of ſuch a retreat, it is neceſſary, 1ſt, that the battalions of that ſection, whoſe front is neareſt to the enemy, ſhould charge with ſix platoons upon the ſpot, to cover the retreat of the 2d ſection. 2d, The flanks of each battalion of this ſection, are only to fire when the enemy endeavours to penetrate the intervals, in order to fall upon the retreating battalions; and here the flanks muſt preſent to the right or left, according as they ſtand: 3d, upon thoſe who only
ſkirmiſh

skirmish single men are to fire, upon small troops the parapet fire must be used, and upon large troops the platoon firing; the same is to be done in retreating: 4th, when retreating with parapet firing, the flag sergeants keep always their usual march, because otherwise, besides the time lost by the files who fired, you would also obstruct the falling-in, and put them into confusion. But when firing by platoons, should it even be with one only, the flag sergeants must take the charging step, to which they must be very attentive when any officer shall give the word of command; but in case they should not hear it, it must be made known to them: 5th, should the enemy attempt to penetrate an interval, not only the flanks, as has been said, are to fire, but likewise the platoons of the battalions of the section standing behind; which they may do without exposing to any danger, the battalions retreating before them.

§ 54.

§ 54.

Of the Square and Oblong.

As the subject here will be that of a square or oblong, consisting of several battalions, it will be easily understood that for the forming of it, no fixed rules can be given, when it is considered that it depends on the nature of the ground, the position of the troops, the movements of the enemy, and several other circumstances; so that it would be too prolix, if one was to establish for such instructions, rules for all the different cases. Besides which, the formation of the square, is the business of the general who is to cammand it. Some general rules therefore given to the battalions which are to form it, will suffice to enable them to execute the orders of the general with expedition and accuracy, and to facilitate his intentions. For this purpose, the movements of the parts that compose the square, should be well instilled into their minds, so as they may be able

to

to combine them with those which have been mentioned § 29. of the formation of a square with a single battalion. The head A of a square or oblong (Pl. 14. fig. 93), is that battalion which marches towards the object you intend to go to; from this head a grand division B is taken out, called the advanced guard; the 1st platoon of this advanced guard, forms a right flank, and the 4th platoon a left flank; this advanced guard marches constantly before the center of the head, at the distance of 8 to 12 paces from the head to the flanks. The right flank C C, are the battalions, who with their left wing join behind the one of the head. The left flank D D, are the battalions, who with their right wing join behind the left one of the head. The battalion E, which shuts in the square or oblong, is called the tail; and as the head A covers the flanks C C, D D, the tail E is to do the same. To cover any thing, is, when by my front, I prevent the enemy from enfilading my flanks. The rear guard F is a grand division, placed in the center of the tail, which is formed in the same

manner

manner as the advanced guard, that is forming flanks on both sides with platoons, whose distance from the tail ought not to exceed 12 paces. The side patrols G, are sub-divisions taken out of the flanks; two of them are taken from each battalion, which commonly are the 2d and 7th. Those who are next to the head and tail, are in the form of a carpenter's square; that is, one platoon is to front with the distance of eight paces from the wings of the head or tail, and dress in a line with them; the other, with to the right or left by files, joins in a right angle the files which march in front, according to the flanks where they are to be: The side patrols march simply to the right or left by files, towards the center of their battalions, and with a distance not exceeding 16 paces from the flanks, and are broken off by an officer. When a square or oblong is to be formed, it commonly happens that it is closed with a great deal of trouble and loss of time, and consequently not quick enough. But whence happens this fault? it is because the proper dressing is seldom

given

given to the flanks; one imagines one is well dreſſed in the line, when placed in the prolongation of the diviſion which is next to the head, without paying attention whether that diviſion itſelf has the proper dreſſing it ought to have to anſwer that purpoſe; when this diviſion has not its proper poſition, it follows, that the flank will alſo not obtain it, and will inſtead of being perpendicular, ſtand obliquely to the head. If now to remedy this fault, we join one wing of the tail to this left flank, and dreſs in a line the 2d flank by the oppoſite wing of the tail; there is indeed gained by this, that inſtead of two, there is only one flank to be dreſſed. But there reſults a ſecond, and at the ſame time, a greater fault; for then inſtead of a ſquare *, which it ſhould be, it will be a rhomboides, which will not be able to march 20 paces without breaking.

But all theſe faults may be remedied, when the following few rules are made

* Inſtead of a ſquare, it ſhould be here called a right angled parallelogram.

ufe of, which if they do not intirely remedy them, will however at leaſt ſerve to avoid great errors.

1. The tail muſt be ſo placed behind the head, as in no manner to out-flank it. Becauſe otherwiſe, it would form if intended for a ſquare, a rhombus, and if for an oblong, a rhomboides.

2. It muſt as much as poſſible, have the ſame poſition given to it as the head has.

3. The wings of the head muſt be conſidered by the flanks, as the *points d'appui*, from which, and from no where elſe, the dreſſing is to begin.

4. The wings of the tail are the points of alignment to the flanks; conſequently, the dreſſing muſt be performed by them. But to dreſs truly, according to the adopted rules, one or more battalions upon a given line, it is neceſſary that the beginning of this line ſhould be exactly taken. This beginning is the diviſion next the head, which the major who commands it will dreſs in the ſureſt and beſt manner, by placing himſelf according to § 29. (Pl. 4. fig.

fig. 59) before the flank files of the head; and he then dreſſes the 1ſt rank of this diviſion by the flank files of the oppoſite tail. When this diviſion is properly dreſſed, it will be very eaſy to the reſt of the flanks to obtain their proper poſition.

5. To be certain that the wings of the tail ſtand accurately with thoſe of the head; for otherwiſe, a rhombus or rhomboides would unavoidably happen. The general who commands the ſquare, may make uſe of this laſt rule; that is, place himſelf ſideways, at a ſmall diſtance from the flank files of the head, which files muſt be well dreſſed upon their leaders, from whence he will better remedy any error, in caſe the flank men of the tail do not ſquare well with the flank files of the head.

§ 55.

Of the MARCH of a SQUARE or OB-LONG, and how the Movements which may be made with it, are to be executed with Order.

The trouble taken to form a ſquare, and to make it as much as poſſible rectangular, is with the intention of performing its march well. But this trouble would be loft, if every attention during the march was not paid for keeping it in order; and for this purpose, the following rules muſt be obſerved.

1. The head muſt be preceded by the flag ſergeants by whom they dreſs, as when advancing; theſe muſt obſerve the cadence of the uſual march, without taking too long paces, ſo that the flanks may obtain more time to keep themſelves in good order.

2. The tail is likewiſe to be preceded by the flag ſergeants, who are to march ſtraight on upon thoſe of the head: their march muſt be ſo regulated by the major or adjutant, that they do not crowd the flanks, nor remain too far off.

3. But the main attention reſts upon the march of the flanks; if theſe do not march well, it will be impoſſible for the tail to cover them properly. Some examples will prove the truth of this: ſuppoſe (Pl. 14. fig. 94), that the right flank H E, does not keep its proper diſtance, but open their files too much; that flank will naturally

turally be longer by all the part E D, than the left one G C which keeps its proper diftance: whence it follows, that the right wing of the tail will be preffed back to it, which by this muft neceffarily be fo much the more in confufion; becaufe, the men and all thofe who form the tail, look towards the center, and not towards thofe files who are preffed. If the major or adjutant, would remedy this by changing the pofition of the flag fergeants, fo as to bring the tail in the direction C D, there would arife a much greater fault; becaufe, 1ft, the battalion or tail which completes the line C E, will not fill up the line C D, which is longer than C E; confequently, an opening muft happen between the tail and the flank. 2dly. The tail in this direction, cannot keep the fame march which the head takes; but, as it is abfolutely neceffary it fhould keep it, the tail will conftantly be expofed to an inclining, which muft above all things be avoided. To prevent thefe faults there is no other means, than to be careful that the diftance between the files are preferved; which however,

cannot

cannot be effected otherwife, than by following exactly the rules of the 2d §; namely, that the whole flank fteps on at the fame time, and with equal length of paces: for this reafon, the officers of the flanks are permitted to march along the fide of their divifions, fo that the men may not only keep the pace with them; but likewife, that the officers may be enabled to take better care of their men.

4. It is not fufficient to imagine all is done, when the men preferve the ftep, and are kept at proper diftances. One muft likewife endeavour to maintain the flanks perpendicular to the head, otherwife the above fault will happen, or another as dangerous. Suppofe for example, the flank C G to march in a ferpentine form C B G; it will be feen by what has been faid § 2, that the men who filled the ftraight line C G, will only come in a curve line to F: This flank G F will confequently be fhorter than G C, and the tail will alfo be obliged to march in the direction E F, to cover the angles of the fquare; it is then in the fame cafe as it was when before in the

the position C D, and consequently, will be exposed to all imaginable inconveniences. If the flank marches on in the direction E K or E A, there will happen, besides the above fault, where the tail was brought into an oblique position, because, both the lines E K and E A are longer than E H, that in the first case, the tail in E when come into H, will make an opening equal to H K, and the tail will then not be able to cover the flank, without breaking at its center: and in the second case, the part in E when come into A, will be pressed out: whence it may be seen, that it is necessary to keep the flanks perpendicular to the head; which may easily be done, when the flank men who join the head are practised to march straight upon the flank files of the head, and these must constantly be kept so by the flank officers. If the flank men march well and perpendicularly, it will be easy, according to what has been said § 2 and 3, to keep the rest of the flanks likewise in this position.

§ 56.

§ 56.

Of Wheeling with a Square or Oblong.

This evolution is certainly one of the most difficult in tactics; it is however not impossible to be performed, and with a few rules it may be made very easy: suppose for example, the oblong A B C D is during the march, for some reason or other, to take the position a b c d. In doing this, the greatest care must be taken, not to give too quickly to the head the position a b, but rather slowly; proceeding in the same manner as has been done § 22. (fig. 45), in order to give to a battalion when advancing, another position; that is, you wheel with both wings at the same time, with this difference only, that the left wing of the head steps shorter, and describes the arc B b, at the same time that the right wing describes the arc A a; by this is gained that the flanks are not brought about at once,

once, which would otherwise as well as the tail unavoidably break; and, as the flanks and tail are obliged to incline to the right, and to advance at the same time, their march is extremely difficult; for this reason, the head must march very slow, until the whole square has again obtained its preceding form: the flanks must regulate themselves by the slow march of the head: they must as quick as possible, but however so as not to fall into confusion, form again perpendicular to the head.

§ 57.

Of the Breaking off a SQUARE, and forming an OBLONG.

1. When a square A B C D (fig. 96), is obliged to break off, in order to pass a defile; the first rule to be observed here, is, to break off as many files from one wing of the head, as from the other; because, if it was not done so, one of the flanks would necessarily become longer than the other.

2. As many divisions as break off from the head A B, so many must likewise, and at the same time, break off from the tail; otherwise, the flanks would be obliged to march obliquely, which as has already been proved is very dangerous, and cannot be long maintained.

3. As necessary and as useful as notices are on all occasions, so much the more necessary are they to the square, particularly when it is to break off; because, if a square is to break off in good order, the movements which each part of the square is to perform must be done at the same time: but if they are to be performed at the same time, the officers who are to execute them, must also be quickly informed what is to be done. If then (fig. 96) the 1st and 8th division of the head A B of the square is to break off, the commandant of that head is to command it with a loud voice, so that the adjutants of the battalions which join the head, and are at the angles of the square, may hear it; these are to acquaint their next adjutants, and those again the other officers, that a division at the

the head breaks off; the other adjutants give notice further, and so on as far as the tail C D, which is to be informed of it by the adjutant of the last battalion of the flank. Upon the word being given by the commandant: *break off from the head!* the officer of the 1st division gives the word: *to the left!* and joins behind the right wing of the 2d, and the one of the 8th, orders his division: *to the right!* and joins behind the left wing of the 7th division; the rest of the head must step on with them at the same time, so that the divisions may readily join behind, and not interrupt the flanks in their march, which continue their proper pace; as soon as these divisions have thus joined, the flag sergeants resume their usual pace. The flanks after being informed that the divisions at the head break off, give the word, namely the right flank A D: *incline to the left!* and the left B C: *incline to the right!* till they are again in a right line with the broken-off divisions (which are now to keep perpendicularly to the head) after this they give again the word: *forward!* the officers to avoid inclining either too much or too little into the oblong a b c d, may here be greatly affisted by judging how many paces they should incline. For example; a division of grenadiers, of which the head is commonly formed, confifts of 20 files, which make about 16 paces. Wherefore, when a division breaks off, each fide of the fquare will be 16 paces lefs; which number of paces the flanks A D, B C, are obliged to incline either to the right or left. In all thefe movements, what has been faid § 5. upon inclining to the right or left by files, will be very ufeful; becaufe by obferving that rule, you will not fall into the fault of changing the direction of the flanks which fhould fcrupuloufly be preferved, in order not to fall into the greater faults mentioned there. As the head by ftepping out further, will facilitate the breaking off of its divifions, the tail on being informed of this, muft concur to the fame effect by taking fhorter paces; and, as foon as the commandant of the tail gives the word to the divifions, who are to break off: *break off!* the flag fergeants, and with them the whole

tail

tail muſt immediately fall into a very ſhort pace, until the diviſions have joined the flanks. But the officers of thoſe diviſions which break off, muſt command the one of the 1ſt diviſion: *to the right!* and thus joins the right flank, and the one of the 8th: *to the left!* and join the left flank. The broken-off diviſions of the head, and alſo thoſe of the tail, muſt conſider themſelves as belonging to the flanks; conſequently, they muſt obſerve what theſe have to perform, in caſe it ſhould be neceſſary to break off more diviſions from the head.

§ 58.

Of forming again a broken-off Square.

When the oblong a b c d (Pl. 14. fig. 97), is to form again the ſquare A B C D, the commandant of the head gives to the broken-off diviſions which are to form-up, the word: *form-up!* the flag ſergeants, and the head at the ſame time with them take ſhort paces, inſtead of ſtepping out as above

when

when they broke off, until the broken-off divifions are formed again, and then they take their ufual pace. The divifions which are to form-up, are to proceed according to what has been faid § 11. (fig. 18), and drefs themfelves with the head; the flanks which before inclined to the right and left, towards the infide of the fquare, now incline according to the fame rule, but however in an oppofite fenfe, that is outwardly. For example; the flank a d inclines to the right towards A D, and the flank b c to the left towards B C; and are to march up fo as the length may be compleated. The tail upon notice, are to ftep out a little more; which, as well in breaking off as in forming again, muft be given by the adjutants, fo that no opening may happen between the marching-up divifion, and the reft of the tail: the divifions which march, remain joined to the flanks with their right or left flank files, according as they ftand, and march up with the rank which faces towards the infide of the fquare. If for example, the fquare is fo formed, that the 1ft rank ftands on the infide of the fquare,

then

then they march up with the 3d rank. As long as the divisions are marching up, they cast their eyes to their next flanks; but as soon as they are marched up, they cast their eyes again towards their flag serjeants. Should it happen, that one or more divisions from the flanks are to march up towards the head or tail, they have only to consider themselves as if they were divisions broken off from the head or tail, and proceed according to the same rules as given above. The following few rules, are also to be observed to preserve order in the march of a square.

1. In the turning of a square, the movement must be performed very slowly.

2. The breaking off and forming up again, should be done successively by one division after the other; because otherwise, the movement of the flanks would be too violent. It will however be objected, that when marching through a defile, this is not practicable; because then the breaking off begins from the center: but I believe, that in this case, it would be better to begin by breaking off sooner, and before you come

near

near to the defile; that by this, the flanks at the tail may not be expofed to too violent a movement.

3. To keep the flanks well dreffed in a line, the major of the battalion next to the head, fhould place himfelf at the angle formed by the flank and head, from whence he may drefs his battalion with the wing of the tail, much better than from any where elfe; in the fame manner, the major of the neareft battalion, muft often place himfelf at the wing of the preceding battalion, and from thence alfo drefs his battalion by the wing of the tail.

4. There is but little to be faid with regard to the defence of the fquare, as this depends folely upon the attack. It muft only be obferved as a general rule, that two divifions joining each other; muft not fire, nor prefent at the fame time. Upon fkirmifhers, fingle men are only to fire; upon fmall bodies the fide patrols fire; and the parapet fire is for large troops: but thefe muft be fupported by the flanks.

5. The flanks of the advanced and rear guards, never fire by parapet fire, but by

the

the whole platoon which form them; because otherwise, they would obstruct the fire of the head and tail.

§ 59.

Of Marching into the Alignment, in order to Deploy with close Battalions.

A corps which is to deploy, is usually marched off by wings, as for example, the battalions in (Pl. 15. fig. 98). These battalions may according as circumstances require, march into several alignments. Are they to march forwards into the alignment— the battalions then incline from about 100 to 200 paces from each other behind the alignment A B, in the following manner: The battalions 1, 2, in the column E F which are to deploy, receive the word from their respective commandants: *to the right, march!* the 2d battalion marches to the right by files, till it has passed the 3d, preserving its proper intervals; and observing as much distance, as will enable its odd divisions to form up near the even ones, when the grand divisions are to be formed; then the word is given: *halt, front!* The 1st battalion continues marching until it has passed the 2d, observing likewise the distance for its even divisions, and then gives as the 2d did, the word: *halt, front!* and *march*. A battalion of each column is called the head, and is always that which with one of its wings fixes at the *point d'appui* marked by the adjutant. Here for example it is the 3d; this battalion remains fronted, the 4th on the contrary gives the word: *to the left!* and marches after having fronted so far, as that it may not only be able to pass along the 3d, but likewise march to the distance of one division further; so that the even divisions of the 3d battalion may have room to march up at the forming of the grand divisions. As soon as each battalion has room enough to march forwards, the word is given: *march!* without paying any attention to the rest, and so it marches into the alignment. The 3d as the head, fixes its right wing close to the adjutant

at

at D; and the commandant of it dresses by this point D his 1st division, in the direction of the *point de vuë* B. The commandant of the 4th battalion, rides before his battalion comes into the alignment, to some files beyond the left wing of the 1st division of the 3d battalion, which is already dressed in the line, and considers this as his *point d'appui*; from whence he will perceive much better, the moment his battalion enters into the alignment, than if he remained with his own battalion; and then he proceeds as the one of the 3d. In the same manner, the commandant of the 2d battalion rides to some files beyond the right wing of the 3d battalion before his own comes up; from whence he dresses the left wing of his 1st division, in the direction towards the *point de vuë* A. The commandant of the 1st battalion, proceeds in the same manner, and considers the battalion already dressed in the line as his *point d'appui*, from whence he is to dress his own battalion in the alignment. The battalions of the 2d column, proceed in the same manner as the 1st, with this difference only, that the head battalion is to fix the left wing of its 1ſt diviſion to the *point d'appui* marked by the adjntant in G; however, at ſuch a diſtance from it, that his 2d diviſion between him and the adjutant, may have room enough to march up; unleſs the 1ſt diviſions were drawn out of the grand diviſions; in that caſe, he is to place himſelf cloſe to the adjutant. For this reaſon, the columns muſt before they incline from each other have already marched ſo, that no needleſs inclining of the head may happen; thus the 1ſt column marches with the right wing of their diviſions towards their adjutants in D, and the 2d with the left wing of their diviſions towards the one in G.

It muſt however be adopted as a general rule, that all the battalions which are to deploy to the right, are likewiſe to incline to the right by files; and all thoſe which deploy to the left, incline to the left by files; except the head which marches ſtraight forwards, however the columns be marched off.

Should

Should this same corps (Pl. 16. fig. 99), which is marched off from the right, take a position sideways in the alignment A B, at its left flank; then the divisions of the 2d column, which hitherto have marched with half distances, are to begin to march up as if they were in close order for deploying; care must only be taken, that there remains between each battalion, as much distance, as to permit a division to wheel into it; at the same time the 1st column gains ground as quick as possible, but without running; inclines to the left, and endeavours to obtain the direction E F of the march of the 2d column. This being done, the divisions of this column march up to deploy, in the same manner as those of the 2d; both columns are then to march, until the 3d battalion (as the head of the 1st column), is with its 1st division, within the distance of a division from the adjutant D; and till the 6th battalion (as the head of the 2d column) is with its 1st division, within the distance of a division from the adjutant C. By degrees as the columns have reached their points,

points, they halt; and all the 1st divisions of the battalions of both columns, wheel at the same time to the left, march forwards into the alignment, and proceed as to the rest as in (Pl. 15. fig. 98). When the 1st divisions of the battalions have wheeled, it has always till now been endeavoured to bring the seven others as quick as possible behind them; therefore, they must then as it is commonly said, throw themselves behind; but this movement is, in my opinion, unnecessary; because they are obliged to come back again, and no ground is gained by it; for, the 1st division must either march slow, or be obliged to halt, till the seven other divisions are behind them. I therefore, would rather chuse that the 1st division, as soon as they are about, should step out briskly; and, that all the other divisions should wheel upon the same spot where the 1st did; by which all the above unnecessary movements would be avoided.

If this corps is marched off from the left, and is to take a position in the alignment of its left flank, I believe it will be
needless

needless to enter here into a further detail, because there is nothing more to be observed than what has been said above (Pl. 16. fig. 99), and *vice verfa*.

The 2d column is now to perform to the right, what before the 1st did to the left; likewife the divifions are now to wheel to the right, whereas before they wheeled to the left.

But when this corps (Pl. 17. fig. 100) is marched off from the right, and is likewife to take a pofition in the direction of the given alignment A B which is at its right flank, you begin here to perform what has been faid (Pl. 16. fig. 99); that is, the divifions are to clofe, in order to deploy; at the fame time the 2d column is to ftep on brifkly, and incline to the right, to gain the direction C E of the march of the 1ft column. As foon as the 1st battalion of the 1ft column is as far from the point E, as about the length of four divifions and one interval, which point E is oppofite to the point F as the *point d'appui* of the 1ft column; then the 1ft divifion of this is to wheel to the right, and march directly

with

with a strong pace into the alignment: the seven other divisions of this battalion, as well as all the rest of the 1st column, continue marching straight on without the least inclining, or throwing themselves behind their 1st division; as otherwise, the whole column would be forced to an unnecessary movement; and these seven divisions wheel upon the spot where the 1st has wheeled and follow it. The 2d battalion continues in the direction of its march, until it comes to the distance of two divisions and one interval from the point E, it then likewise wheels to the right with its 1st division as the 1st did; this is followed by the other divisions, and so enters into the alignment. The 3d proceeds in the same manner; and when in its march it comes with its right wing to the point E, it wheels as the two first did. The 4th wheels when it has passed behind the 8th division of the 3d battalion, and has marched to the distance of one division further off from its left wing, where it is to proceed as the three first did, and so enters into the alignment. The 5th battalion, as the

1st

1st of the 2d column, is to proceed in the same manner as the 1st did; when it is come to the diſtance of four diviſions, without adding any interval from the point H, which is oppoſite to the point G, and which is the *point d'appui* of this column. The 6th which is the head of this column, proceeds as the 2d of the 1st did; that is, when come to the diſtance of two diviſions from the point H; the 1st diviſion of the 7th is to wheel, after it has paſſed the point H about eight paces, or as many as are given for an interval; and the 8th is to perform its wheel in the ſame manner, as the 4th of the 1st column did when it paſſed behind the 7th, and marched to the diſtance of one diviſion more.

If this corps is marched off from the left, and is to take a poſition in the alignment at its left flank, it is to proceed according to the rules given for it (fig. 100), but however in the oppoſite ſenſe; the 1st column inclines forward to the left, and marches in the direction of the 2d column, in the ſame manner, as was before performed to the right by the 2d column; and now

the

the battalions wheel to the left with their 8th divisions, in the same manner as they wheeled before with their 1st divisions to the right; that is, the 8th division of the 8th battalion of the 2d column, begins to wheel to the left, when it is at the distance of four divisions and one interval from the point, which is opposite to its *point d'appui*; the 8th division of the 4th battalion of the 1st column wheels, when it is also within four divisions without adding an interval, from the point which is opposite to the *point d'appui*.

Suppose again that this corps was marched off from the right, and is to take a position in the alignment A B, which is in its rear (Pl. 18. fig. 101), keeping at the same time its order of battle: for this purpose, you must begin by changing the wings; that is, you must endeavour to bring the right wing to where the left stood, and *vice versa*. To perform this, all the divisions of the 1st column go to the left by files, and those of the 2d column to the right by files, and march thus through one another, until the 2d column has reached the position the 1st had,

had, and this laft, the pofition the 2d column had; for this purpofe before both columns march, the pofition where they ftand muft be marked by the adjutants; at this paffing through, the divifions of the 2d column muft obferve to march in fuch a manner, that the divifions of the 1ft column to which they correfpond may have the right; on the contrary, thofe of the 1ft march ftraight on, as may be feen by the figure 101. When the 1ft column is arrived at the place where the 2d was, it is directly and without fronting, to perform firft the countermarch as follows: The divifions wheel to the left about with their left flank files: The 2d column performs the fame, by wheeling to the right about with their right flank files and countermarch. Then both columns: *halt, front!* and thus, the divifions of the 1ft column will juft be upon the fpot, where thofe of the 2d ftood; and thefe of the 2d, upon the fpot where the 1ft ftood: by this countermarch, both columns are ftanding as when marched off from the left; and in this order of march they go back again, until they are at a

proper

proper diftance from the alignment, which has been given them to enter into the firft one. When arrived there, the battalions incline from each other, as has been fhewn by the explanation of (Pl. 15. fig. 98); and by what has been faid above, it will be feen how neceffary it is, that the divifions when marching to deploy, fhould march exactly with half diftances, and not lefs; becaufe the preceding movement is already very difficult to execute, and it is not known whether one may not be obliged to perform it.

F I N I S.

ERRATA.

Page	Line	for	read
2	3	known by	known that by
8	4	is obliged	is then obliged
8	8	prevent	prevent it
10	6	muſt be	muſt not be
18	13	loading	firing
27	3	by	are led by
37	8	it	this
40	10	men	man
53	2	movement	command
86	8	ſuppoſing	and ſuppoſing
96	7	diviſions march	diviſions may march
107	19	diviſions, towards	diviſions to the left, towards
117	1	could	might
122	laſt	though	through
126	laſt	are of	are at
130	5	or	for
132	20	and	or
134	4	endeavour	endeavours
135	21	be thus corrected	be corrected
138	8	break	breaks
141	18	the battalion	the battalion is this
152	20	converge	tend
166	14	come	came
173	22	it	them
227	16	given	giving
250	5	colour	colours

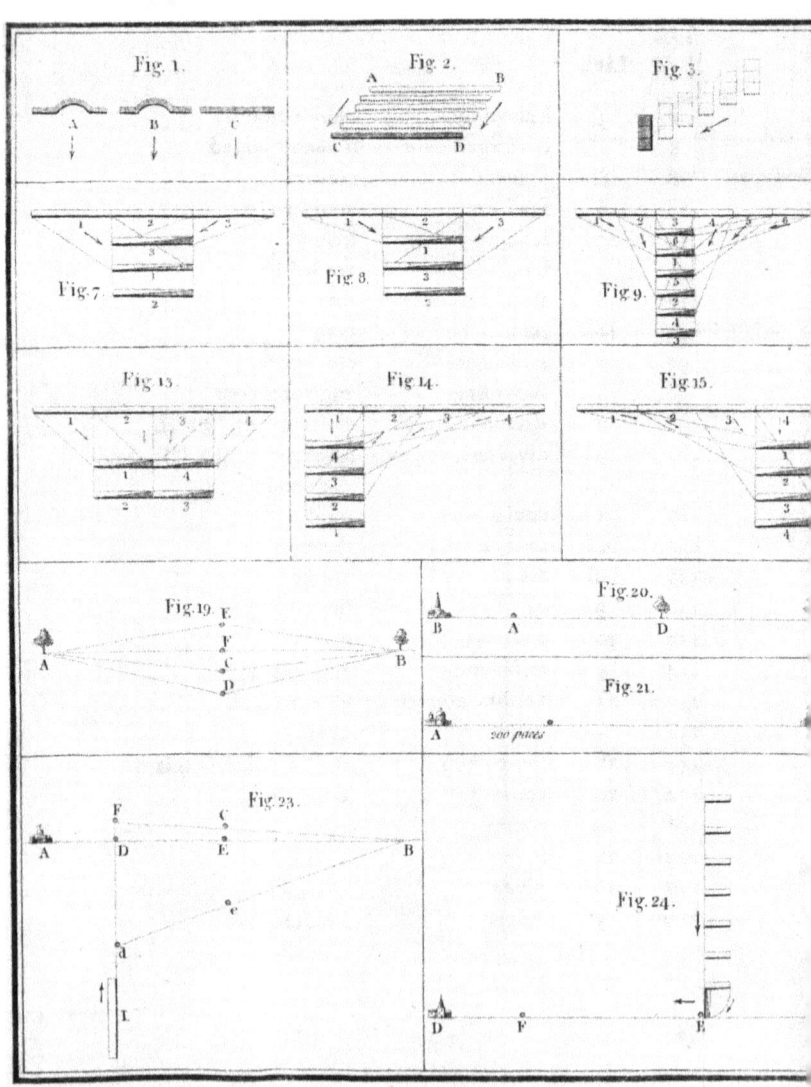

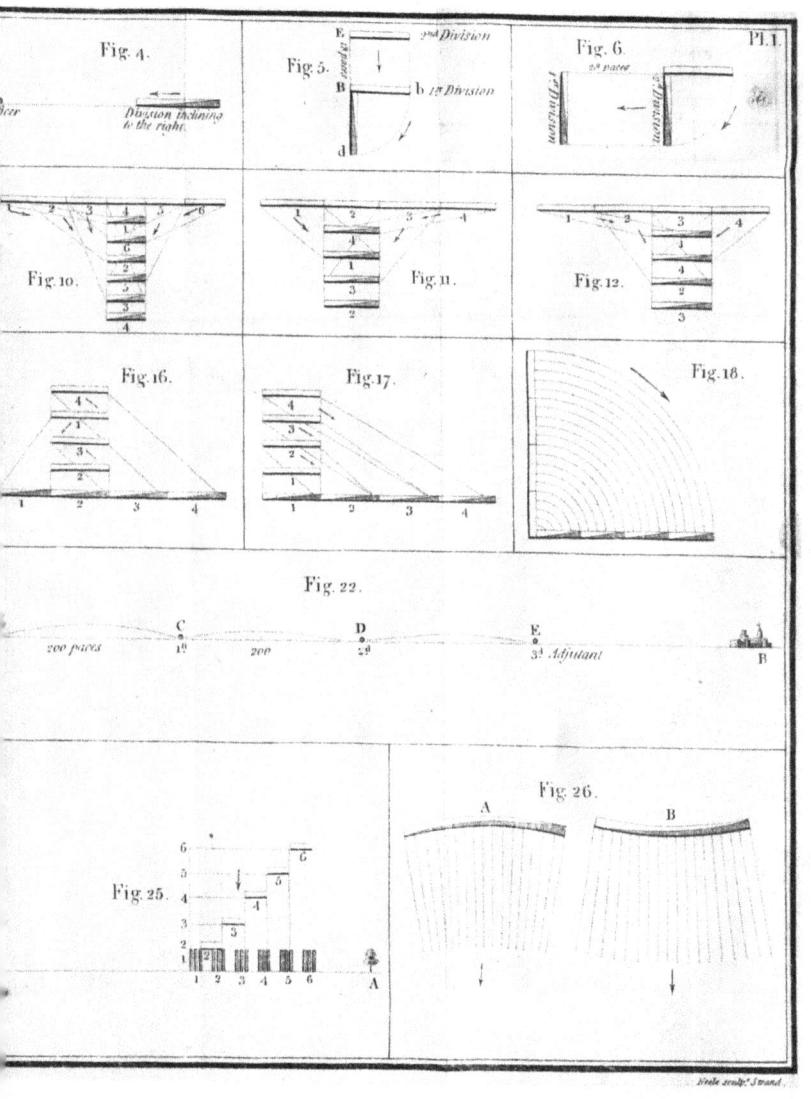

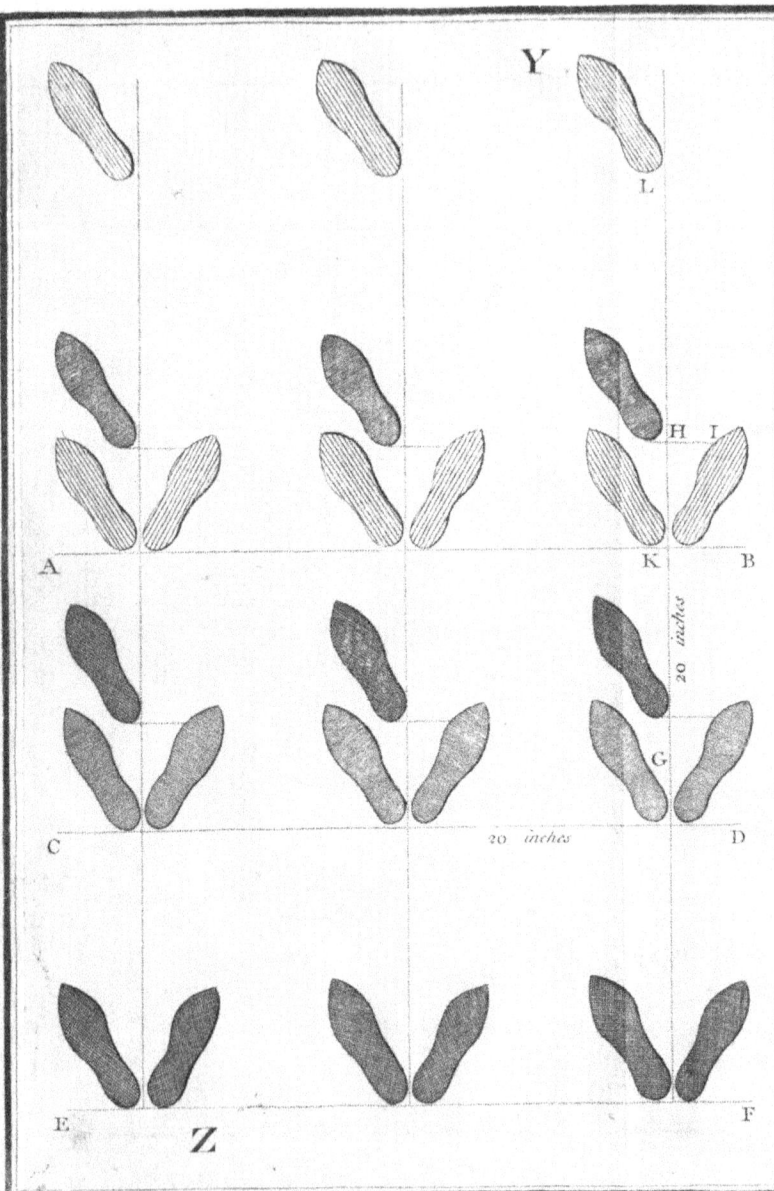

Pl. 2

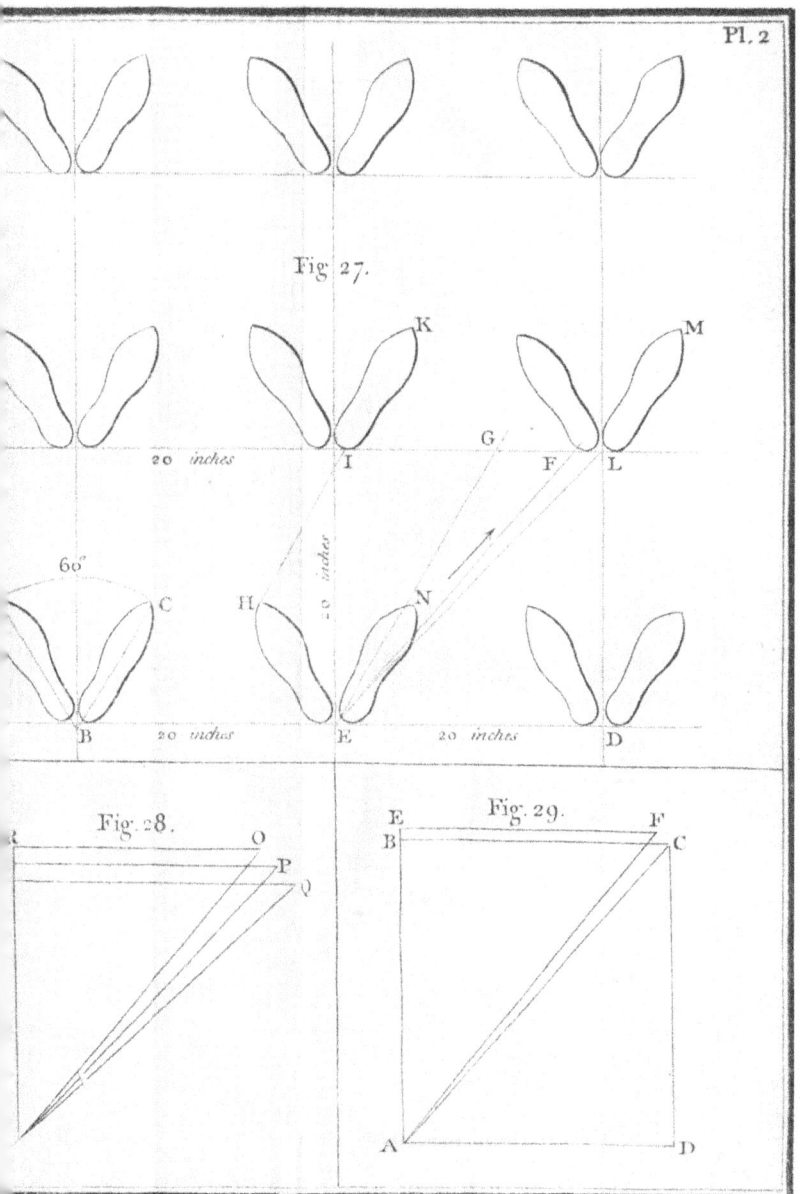

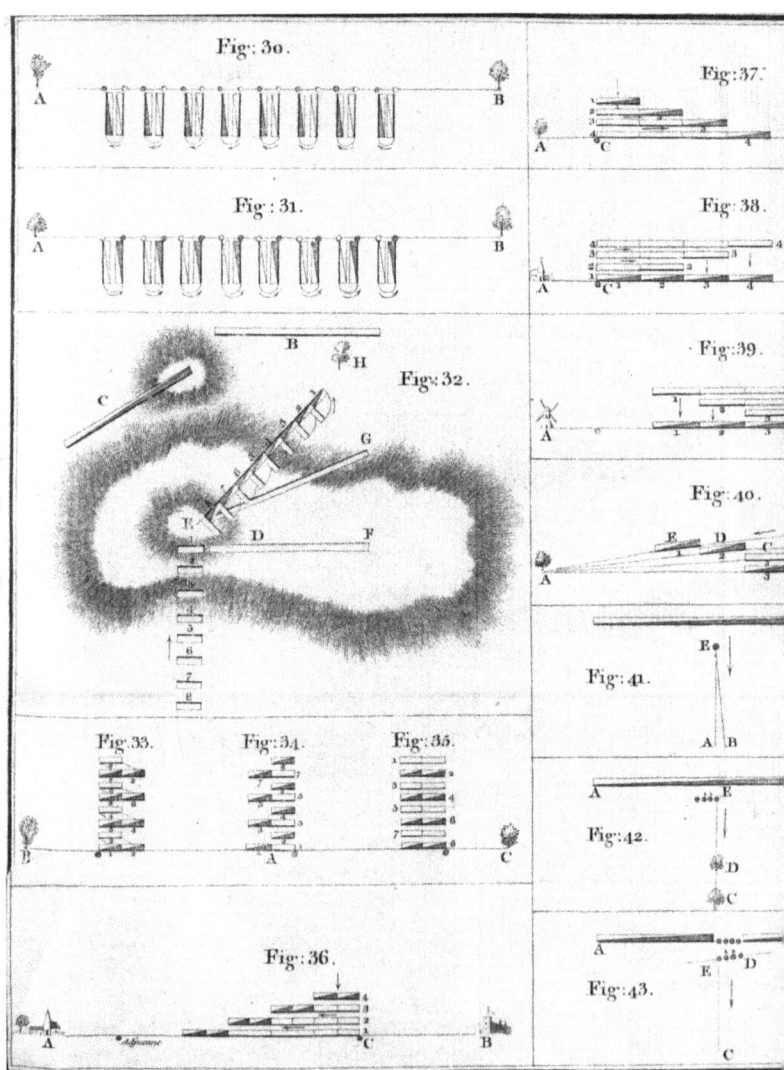

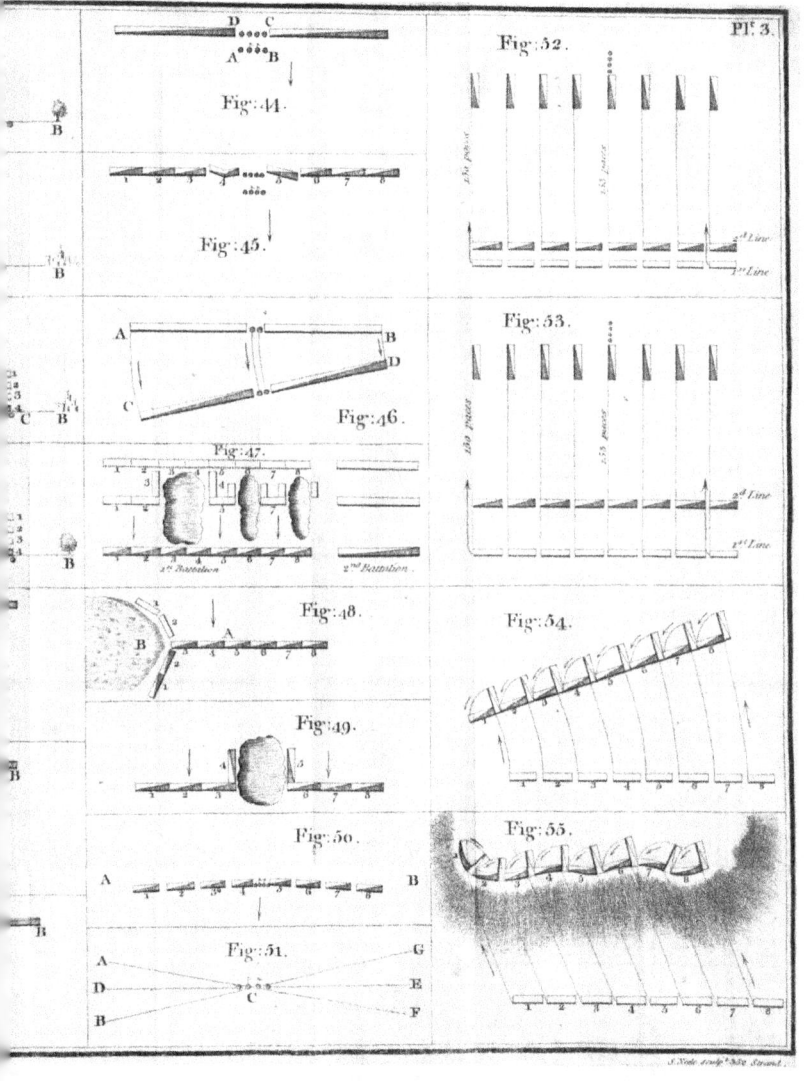

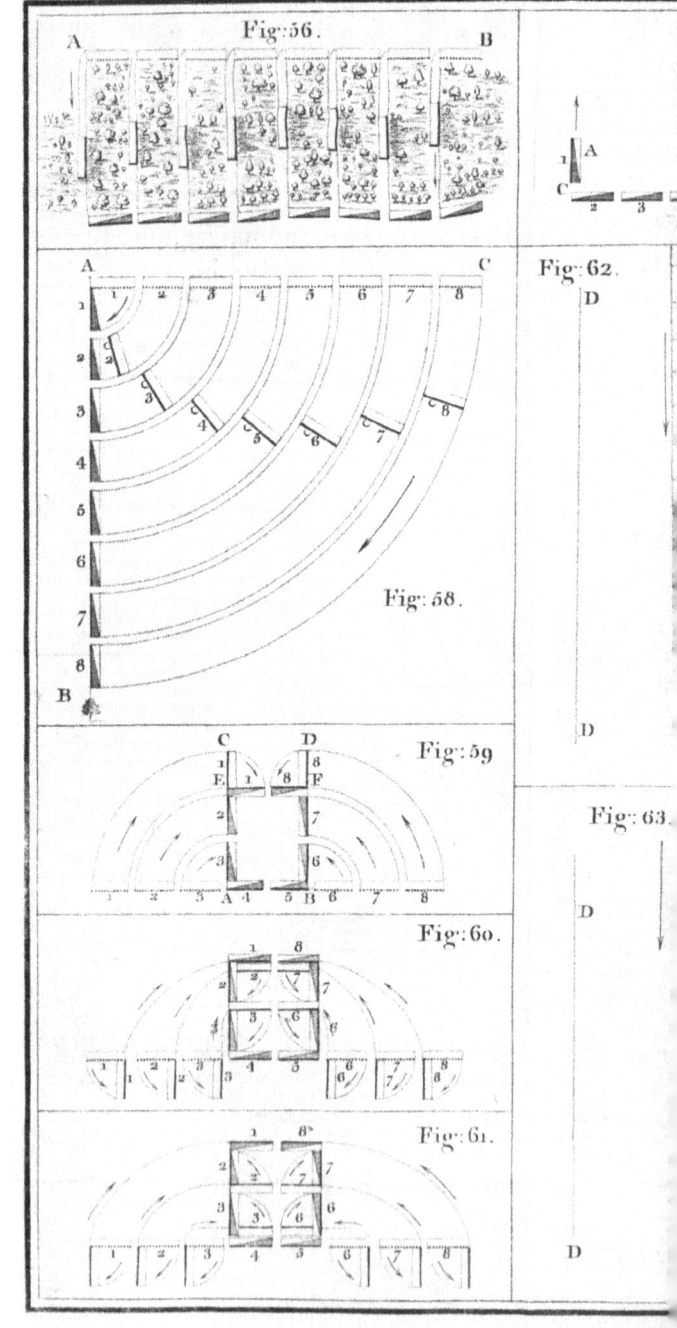

Pl. 4

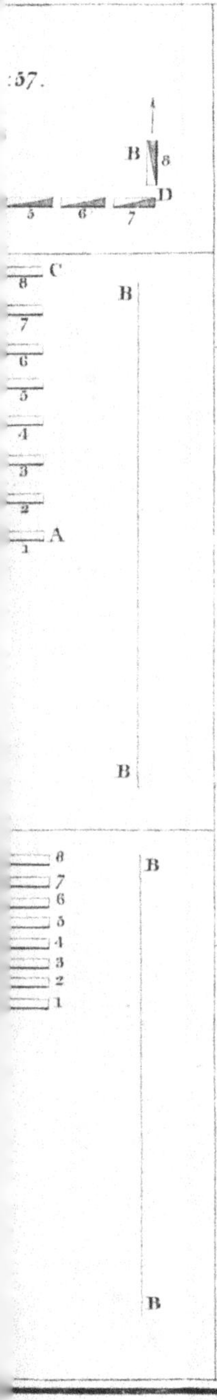

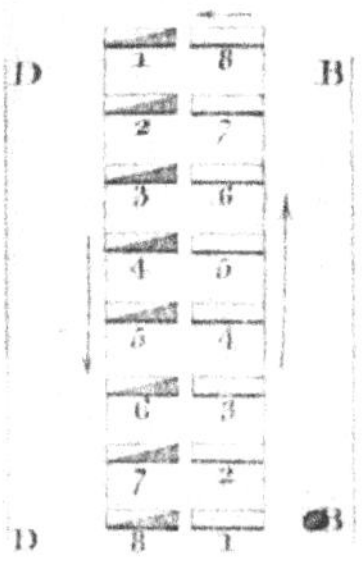

Fig: 64.

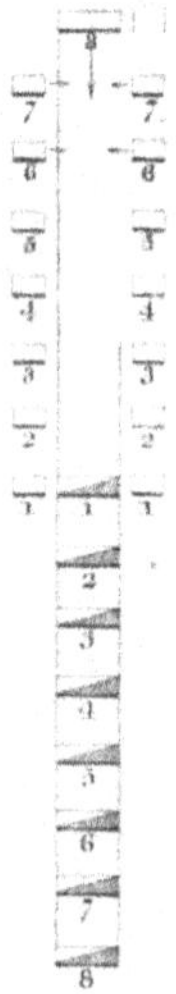

Fig: 65.

Fig: 66

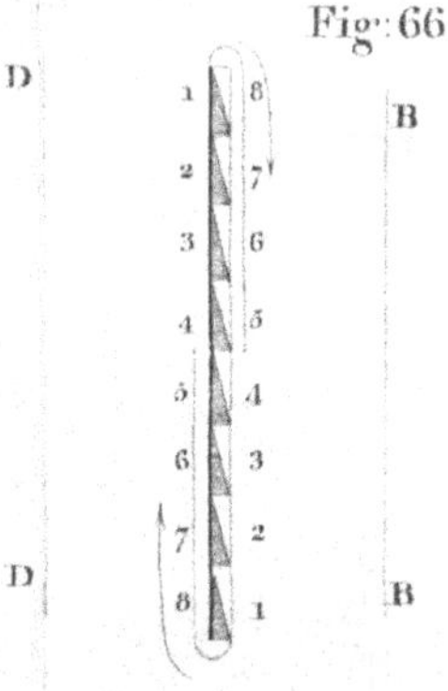

Neele sculp.

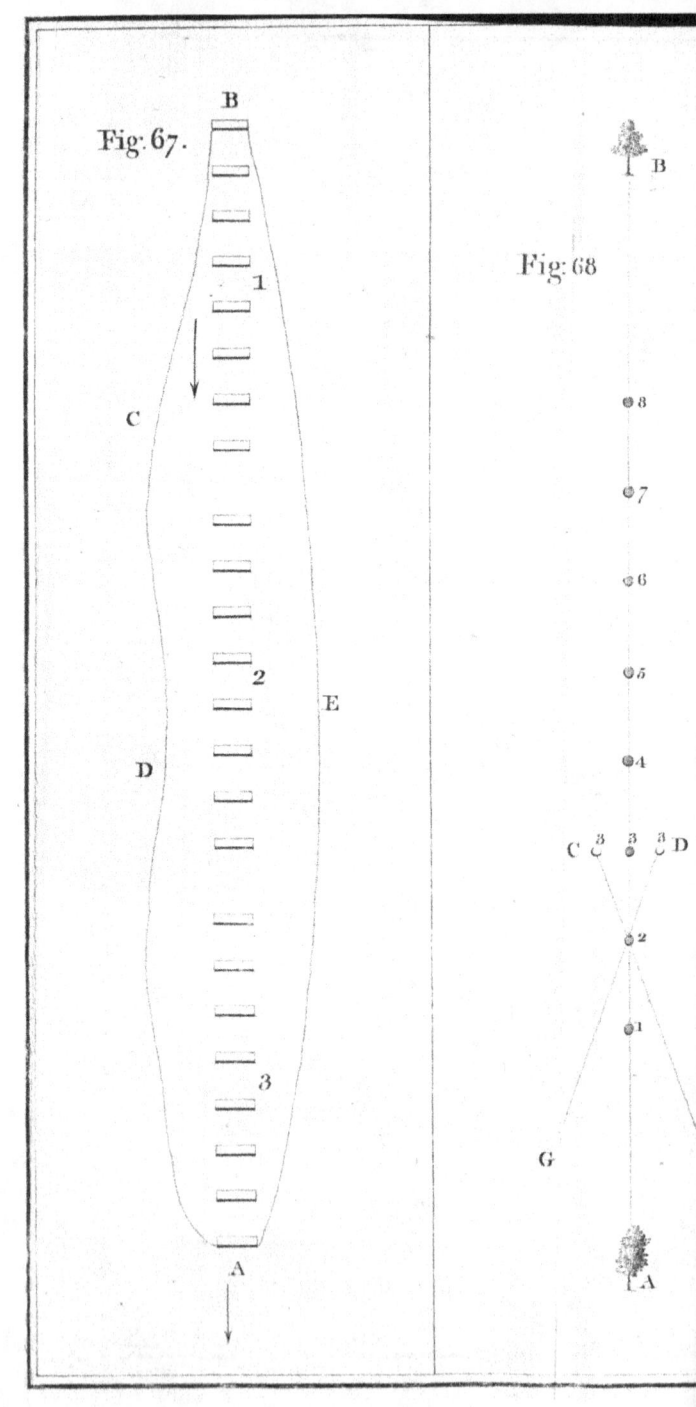

Fig. 67.

Fig. 68

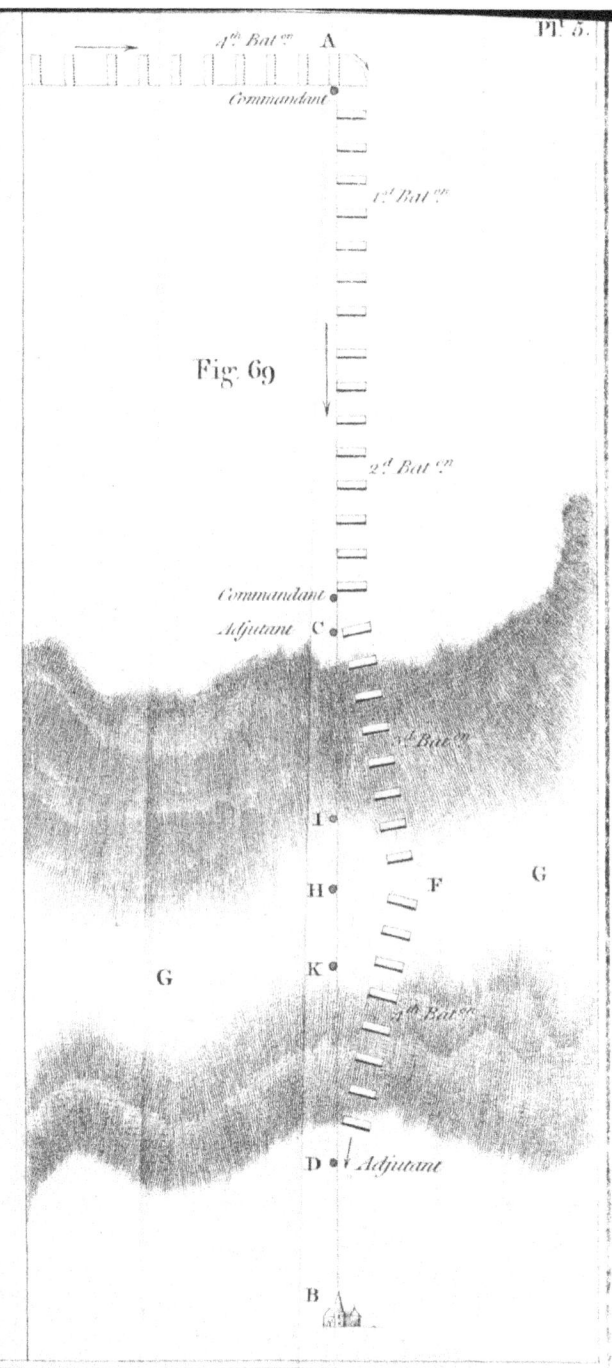

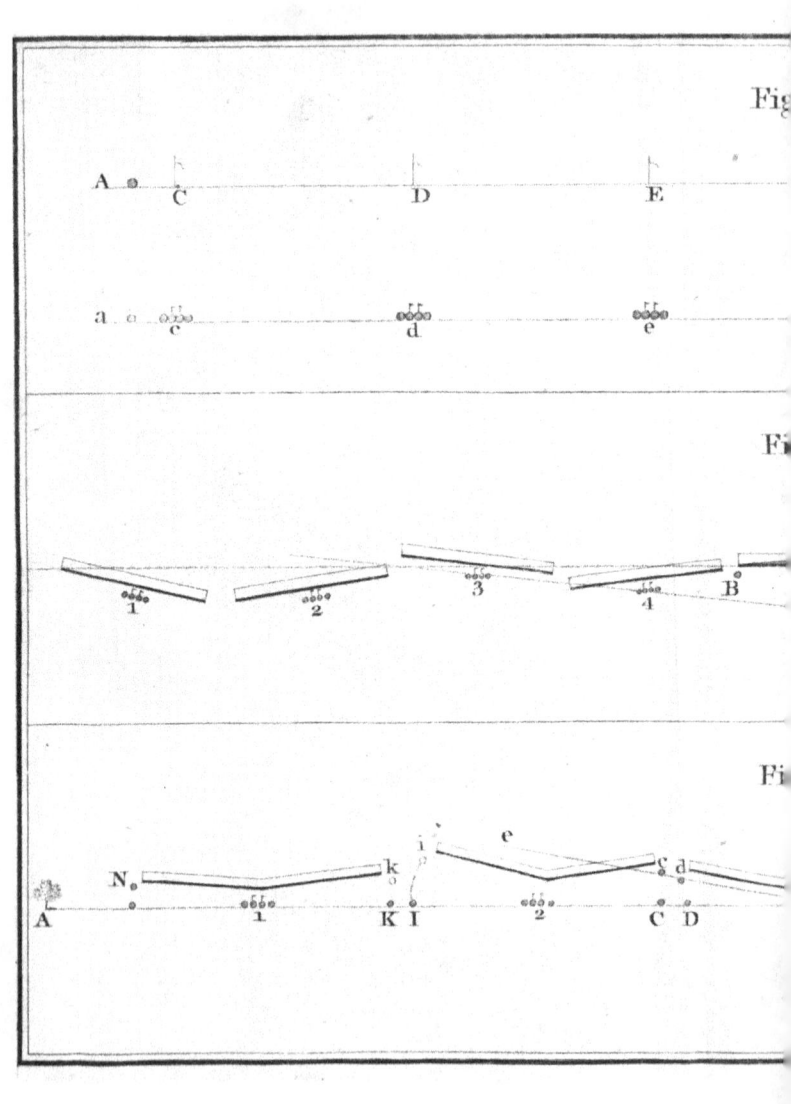

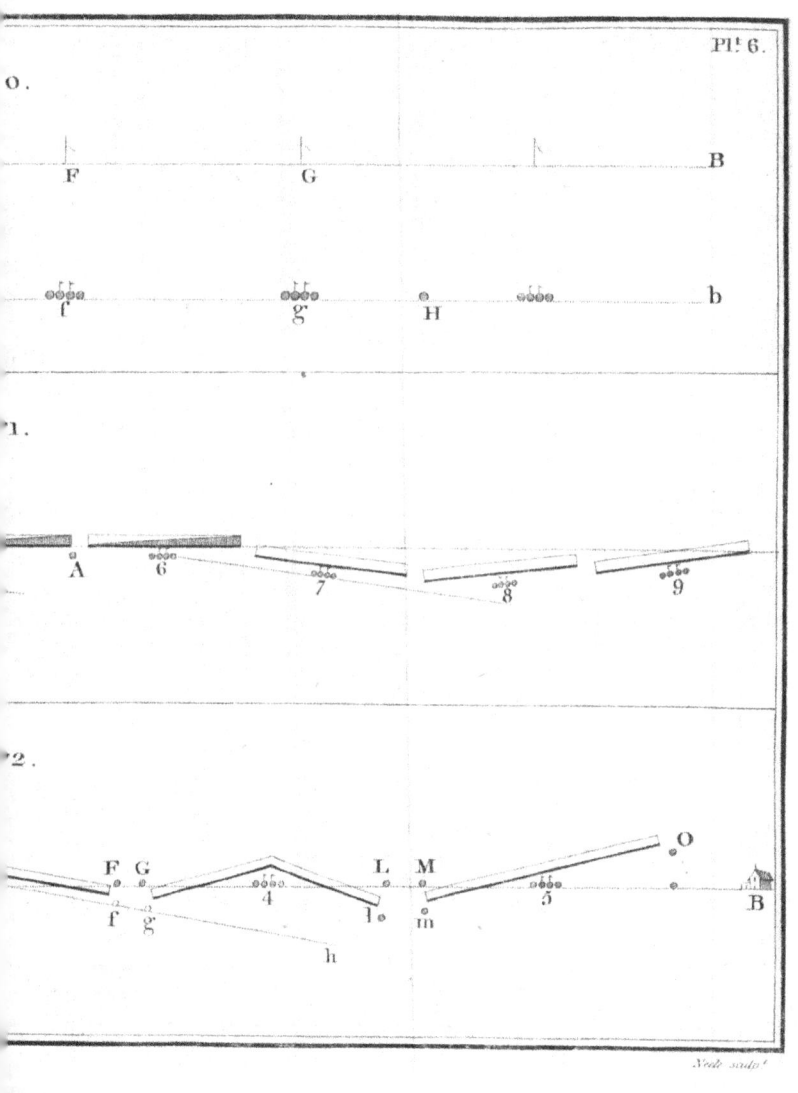

Pl. 6.

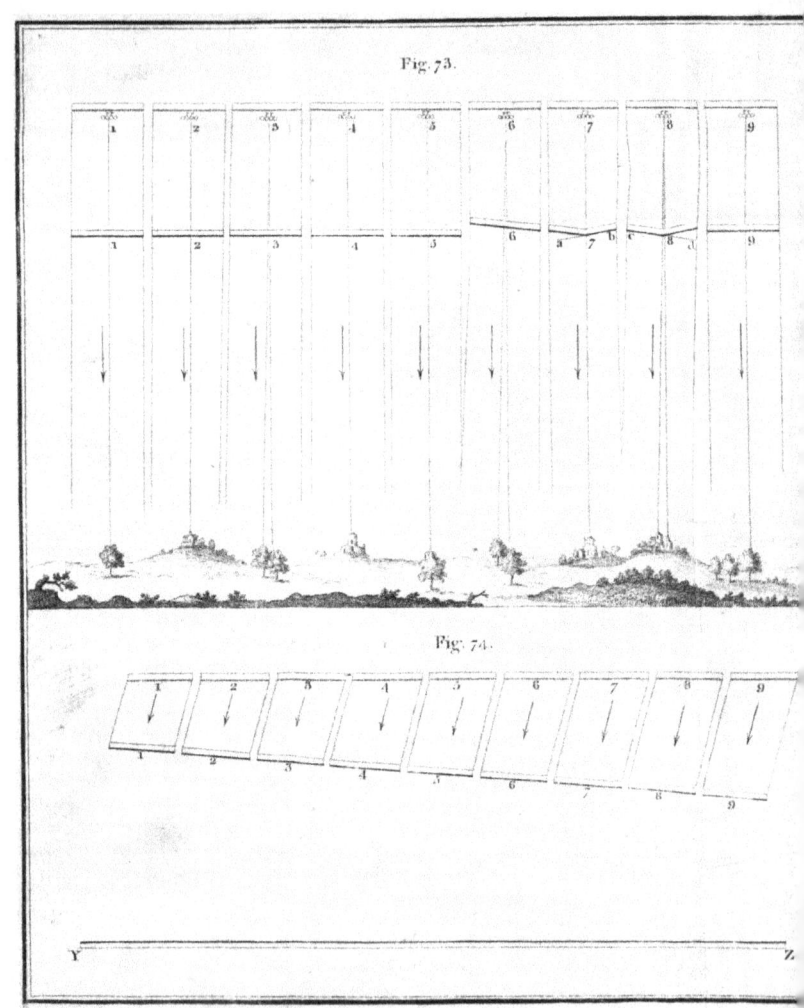

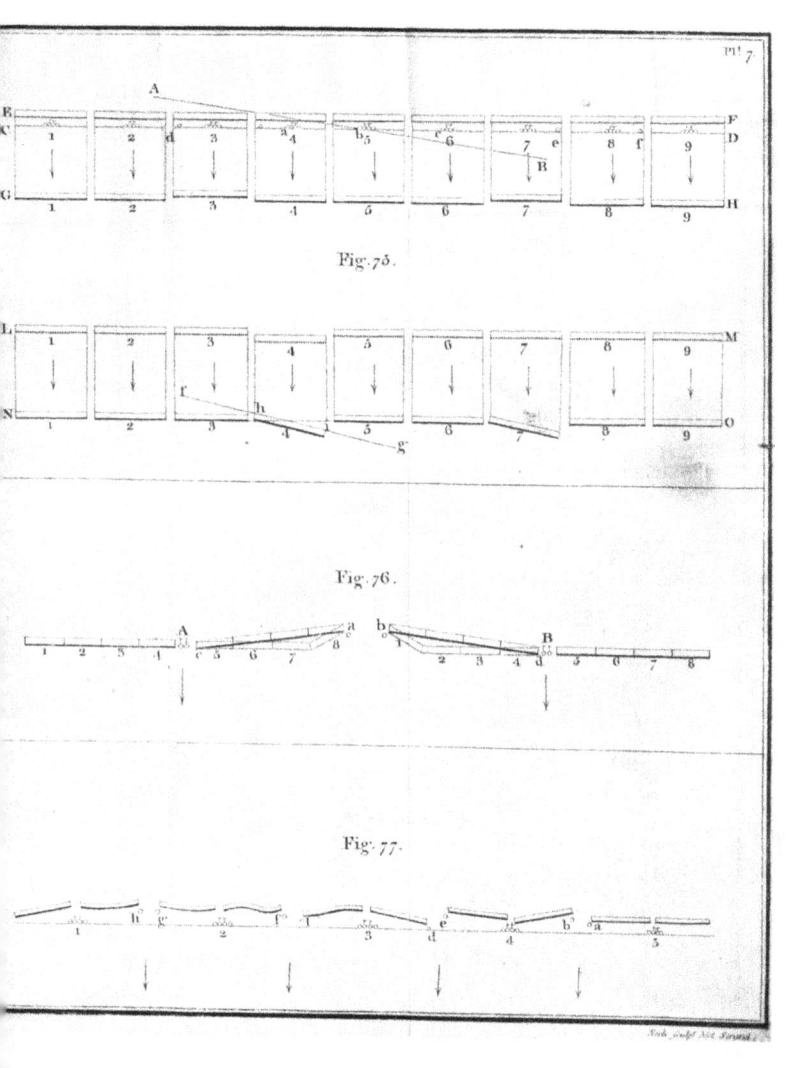

Fig. 75.

Fig. 76.

Fig. 77.

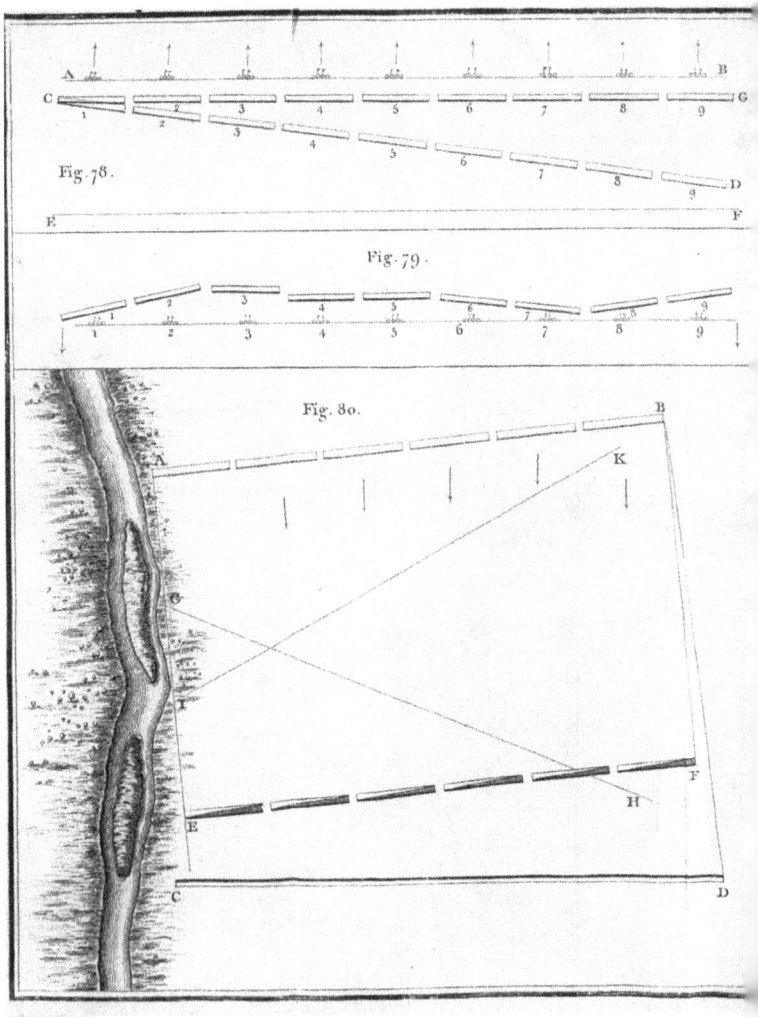

Fig. 78.

Fig. 79.

Fig. 80.

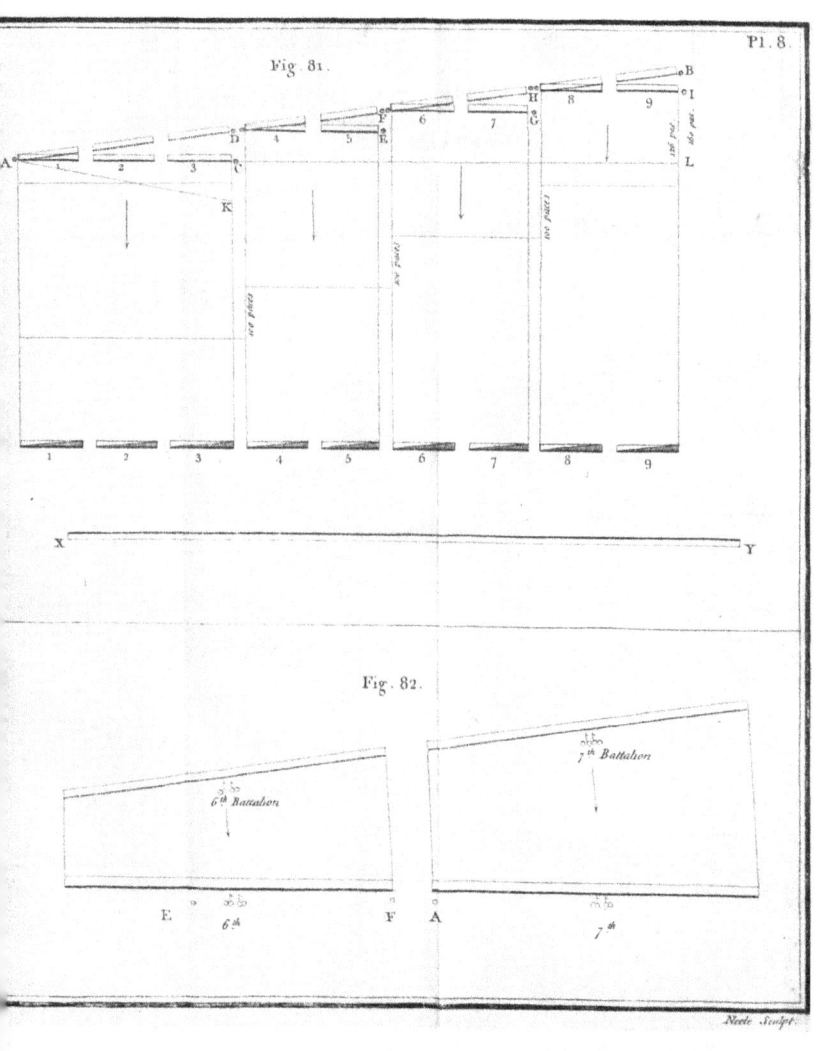

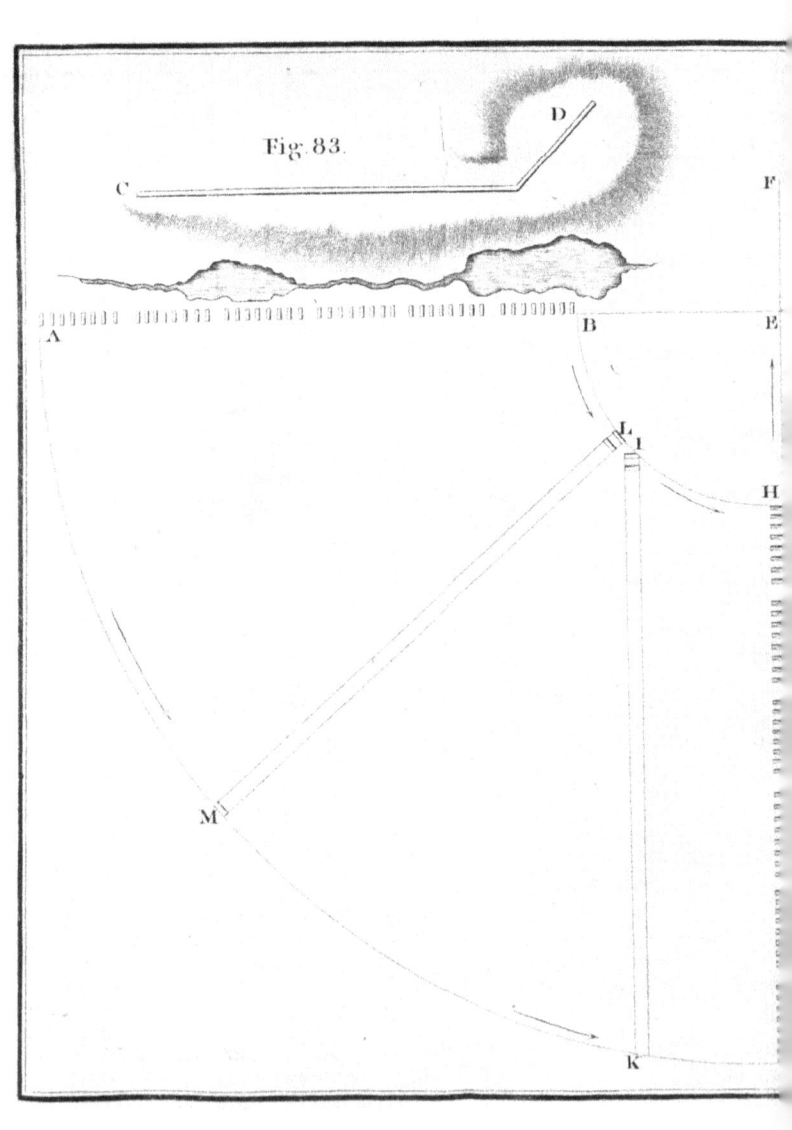

Fig. 83.

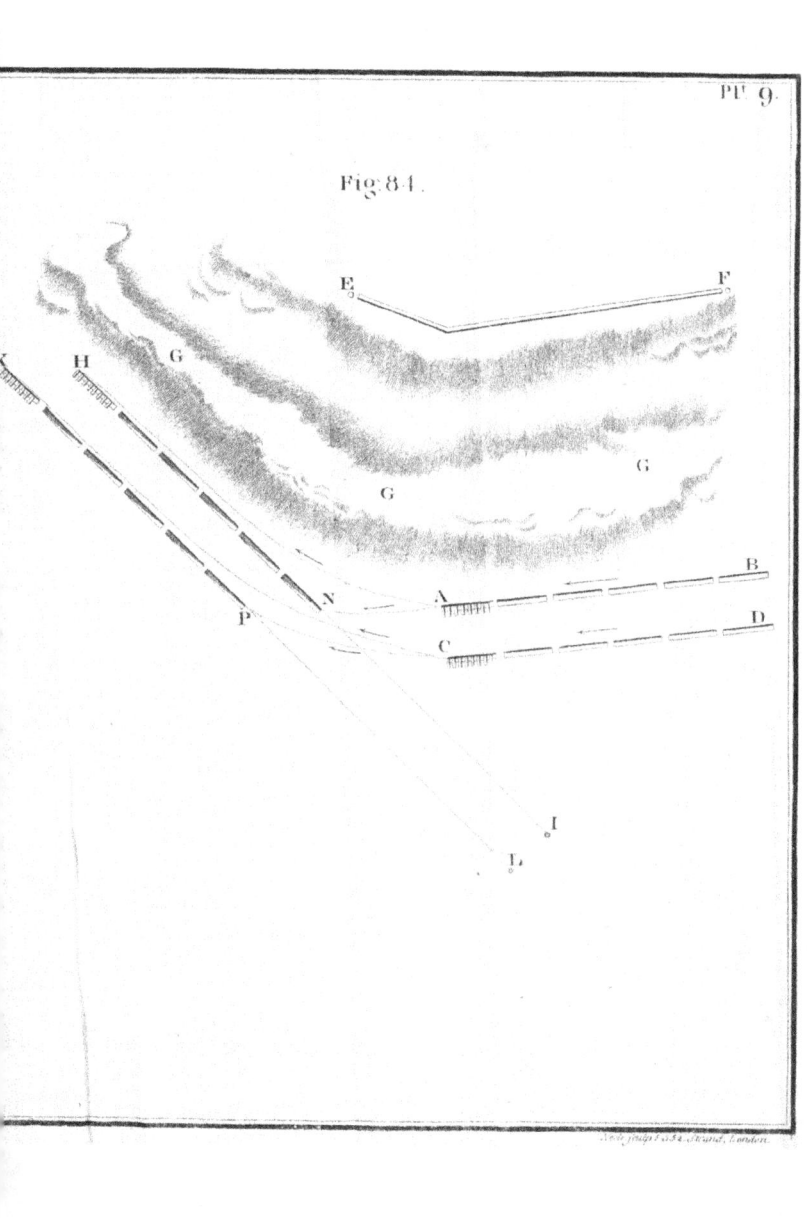

Fig. 84.

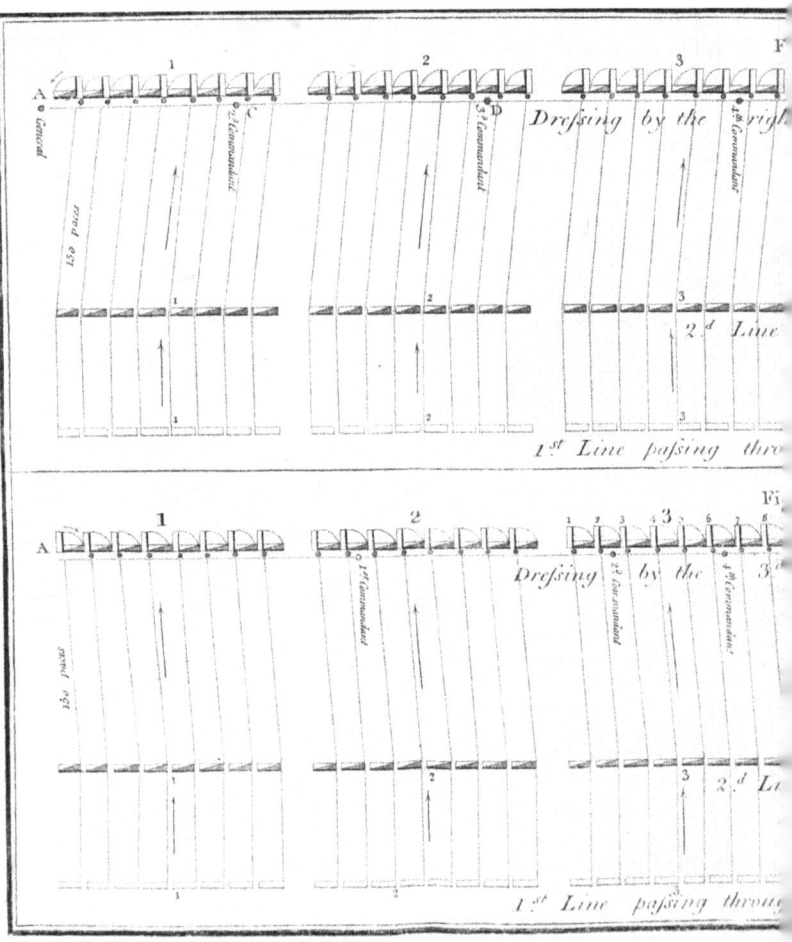

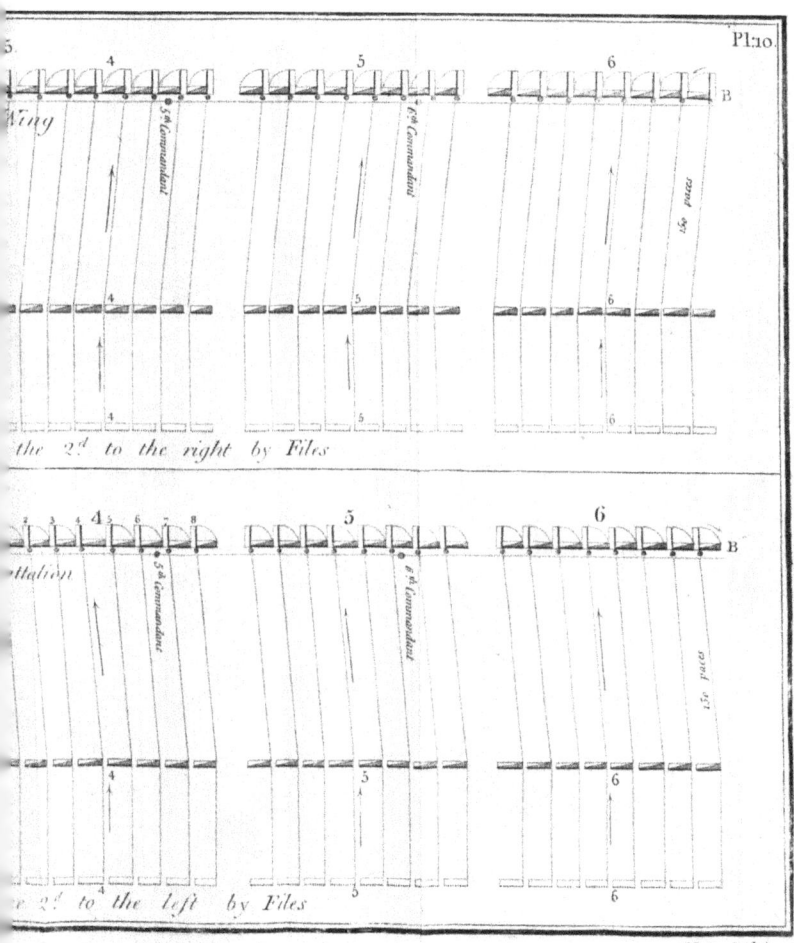

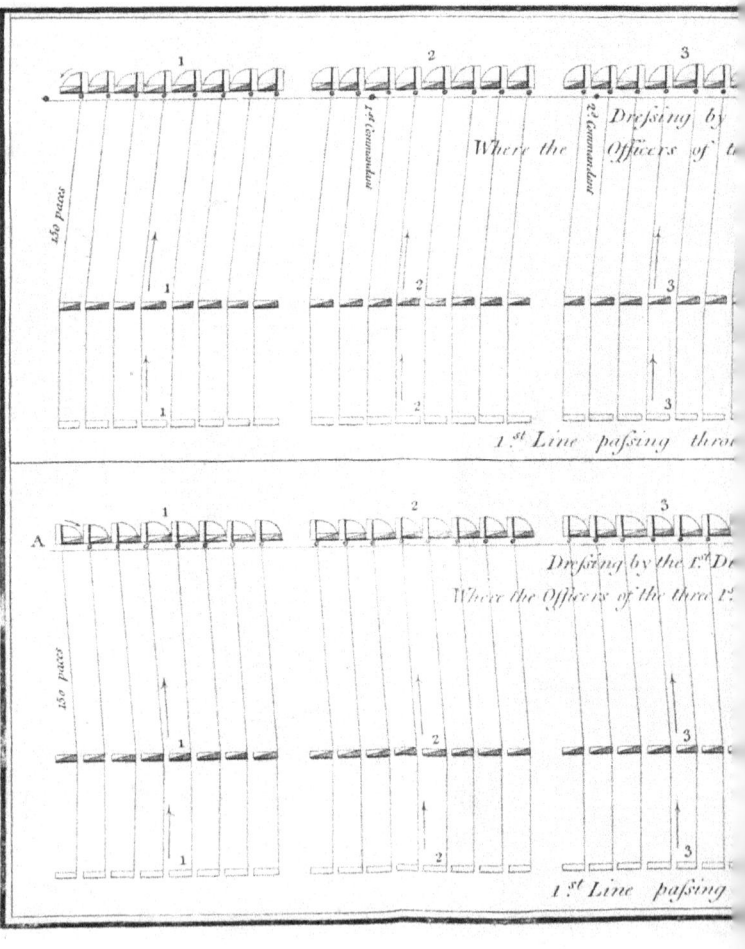

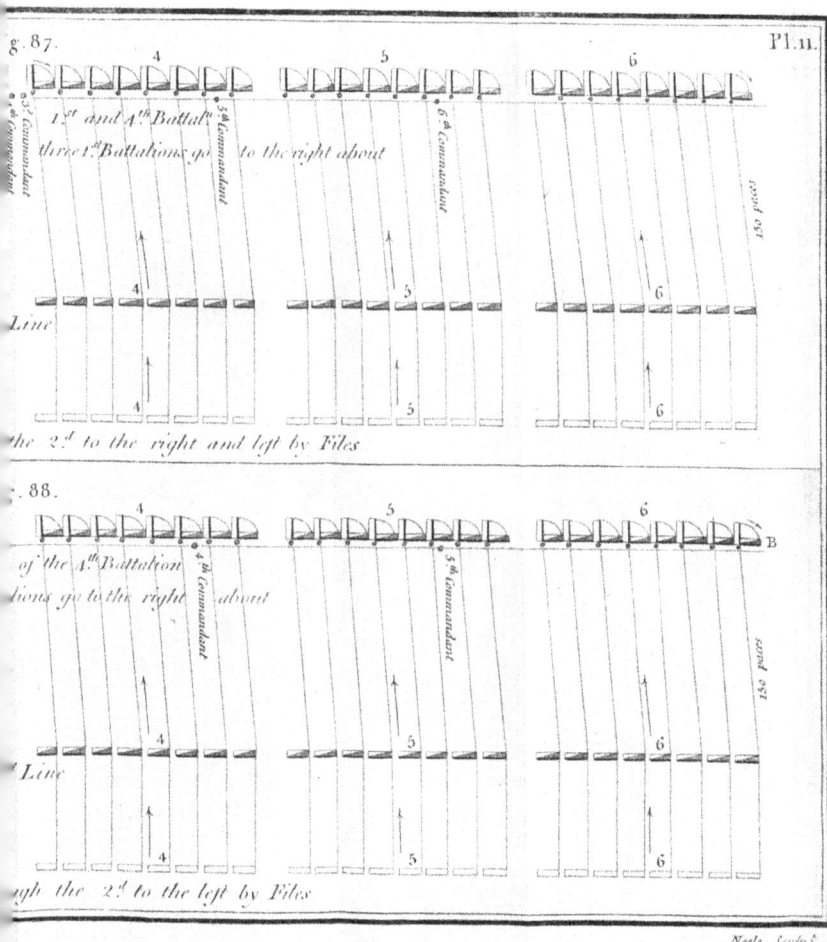

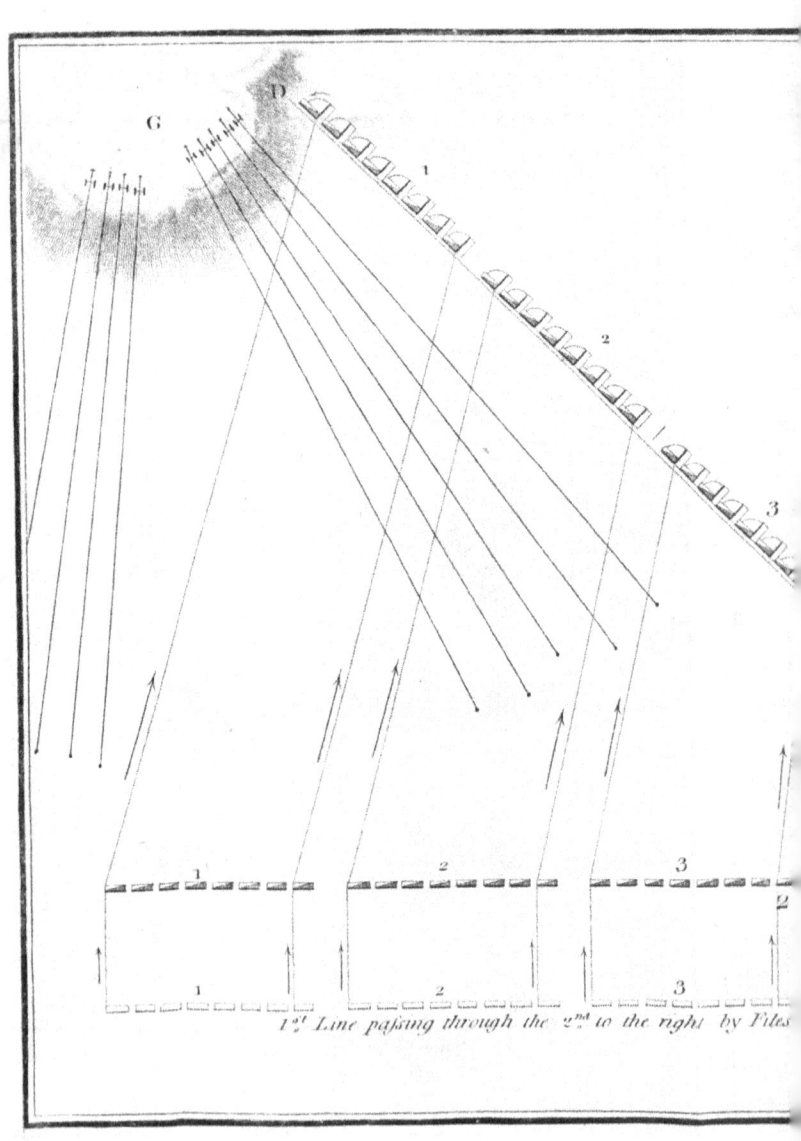

1st Line passing through the 2nd to the right by Files

Pl. 12.

Fig. 89.

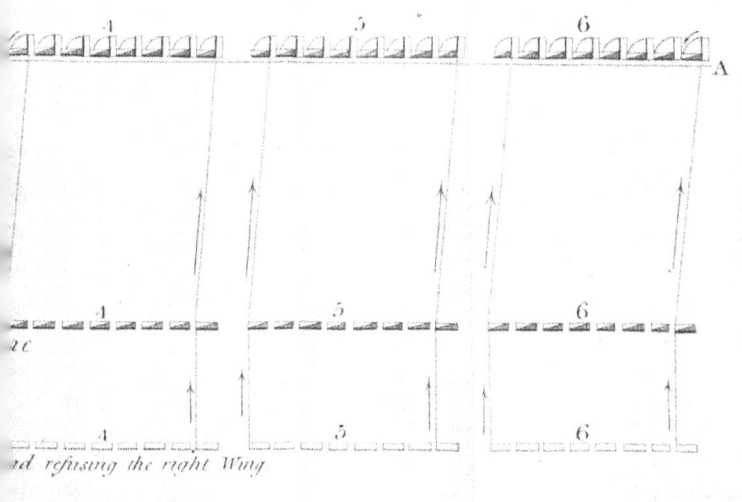

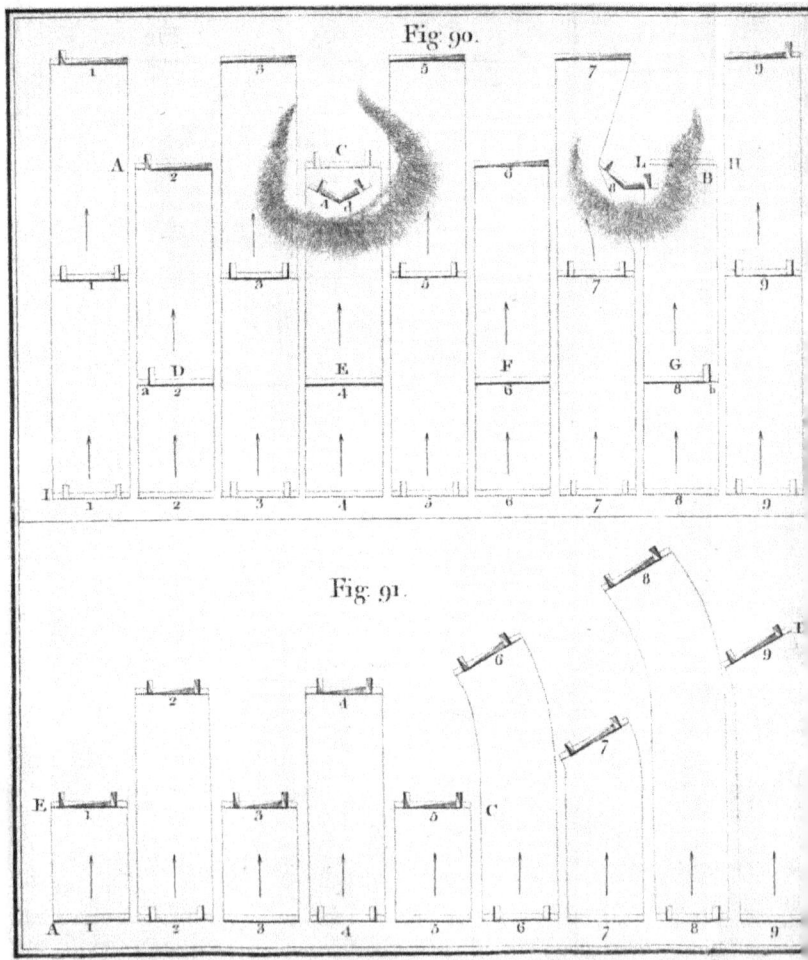

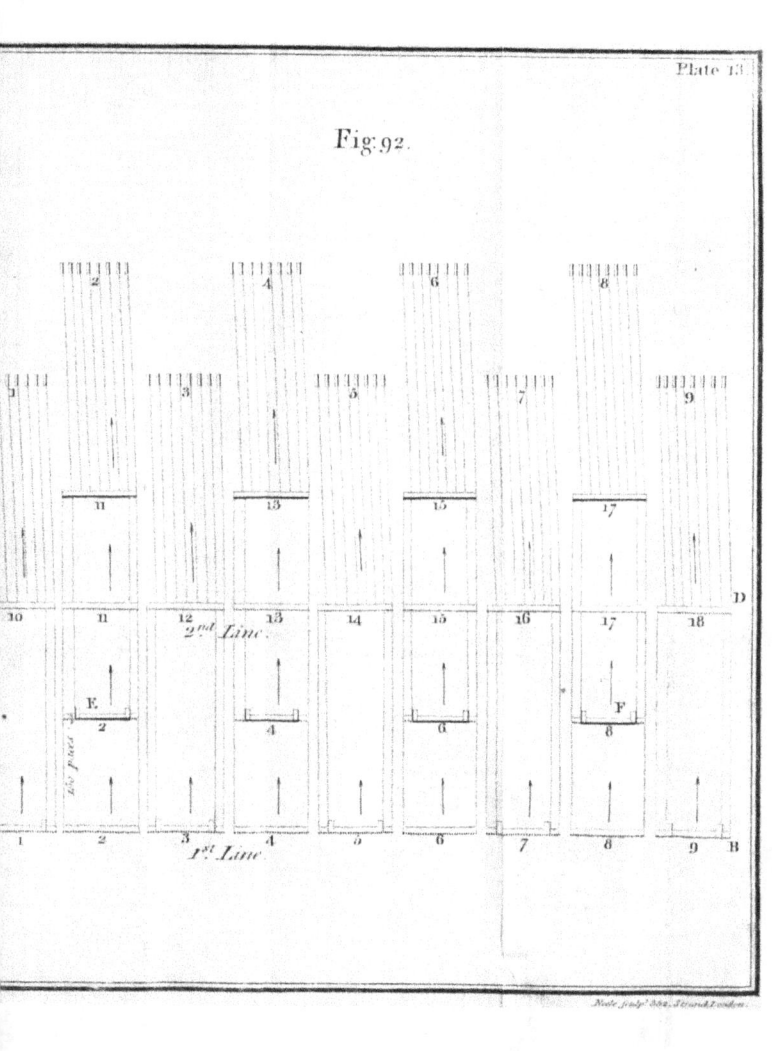

Fig. 92.

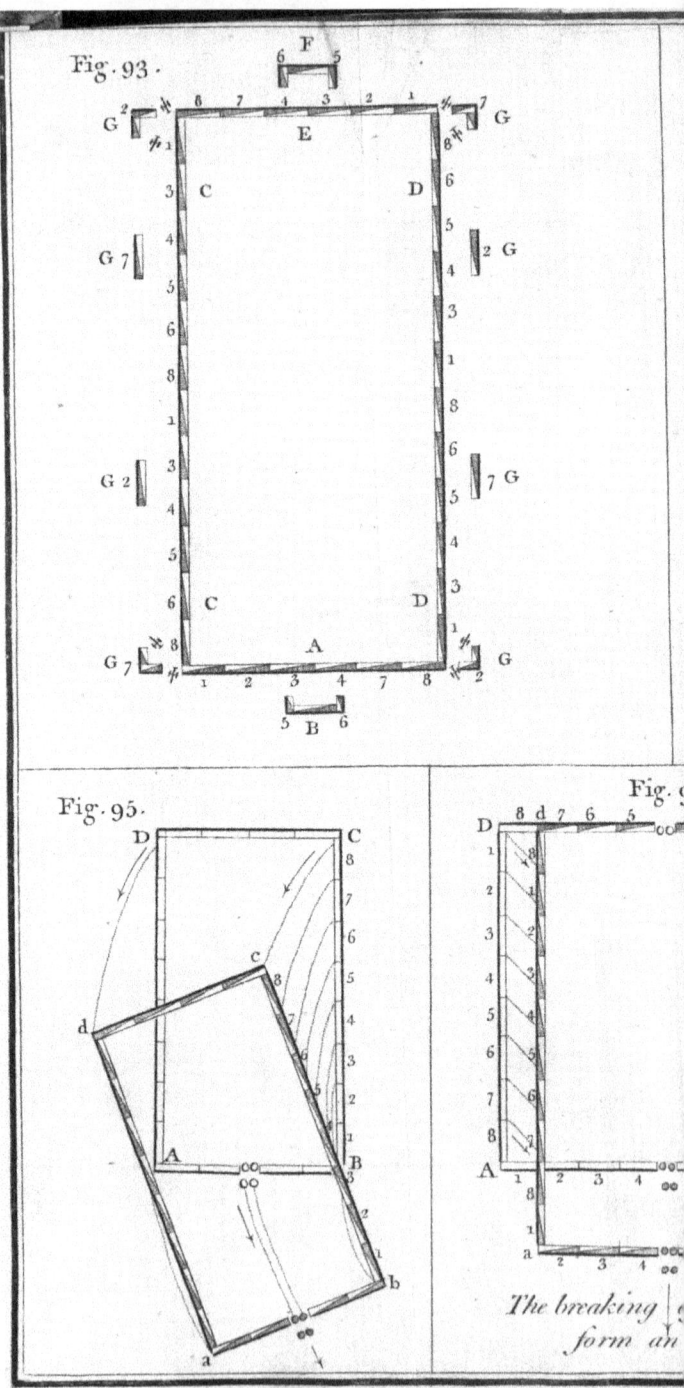

The breaking
form an

Pl: 14.

Fig. 94.

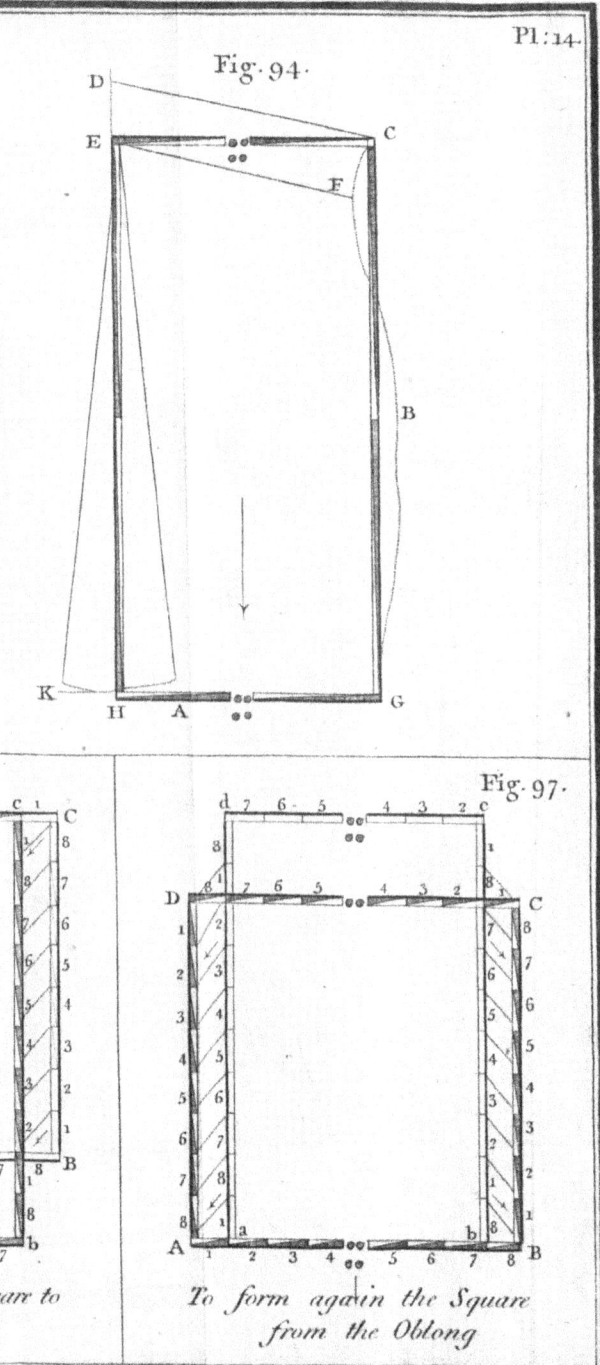

Fig. 97.

To form again the Square from the Oblong

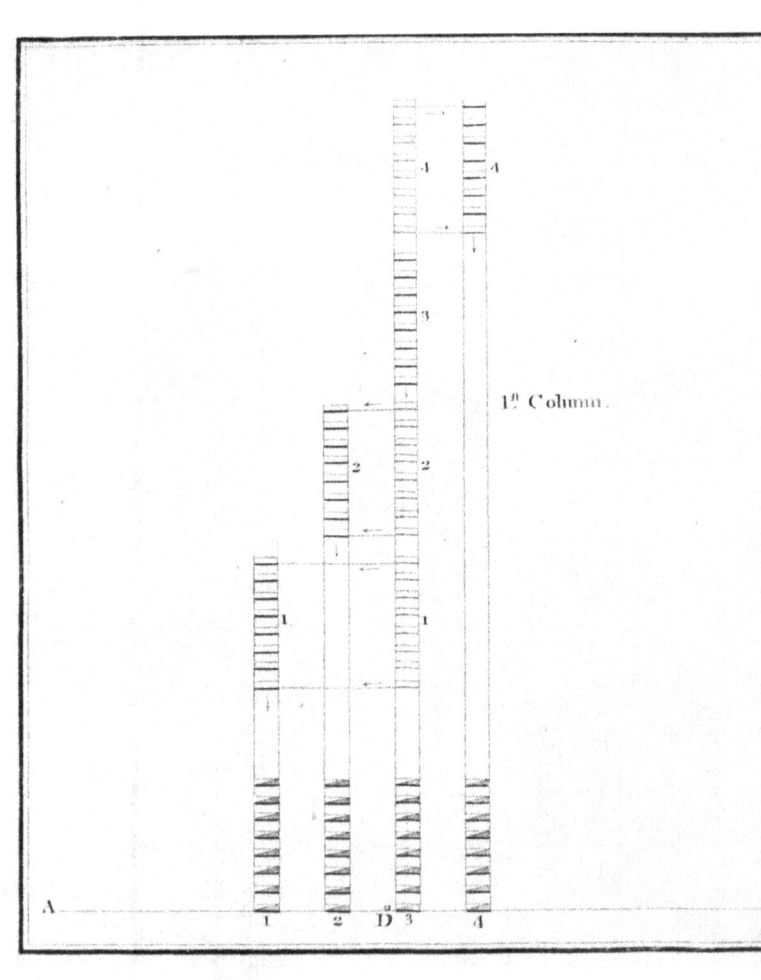

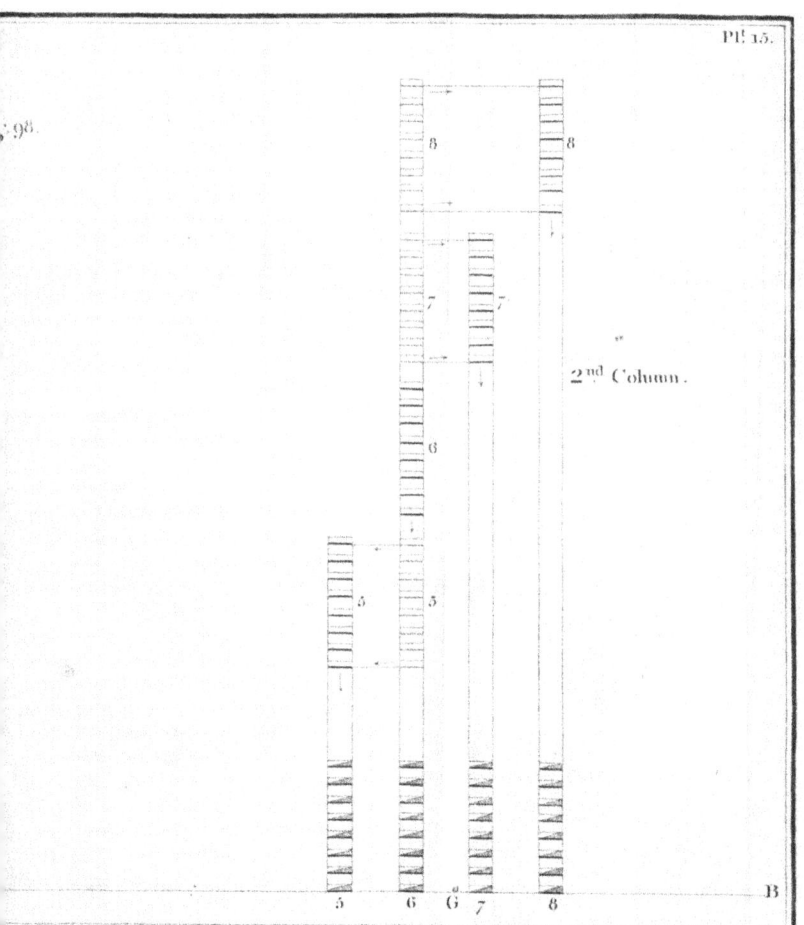

Pl. 15.

2nd Column.

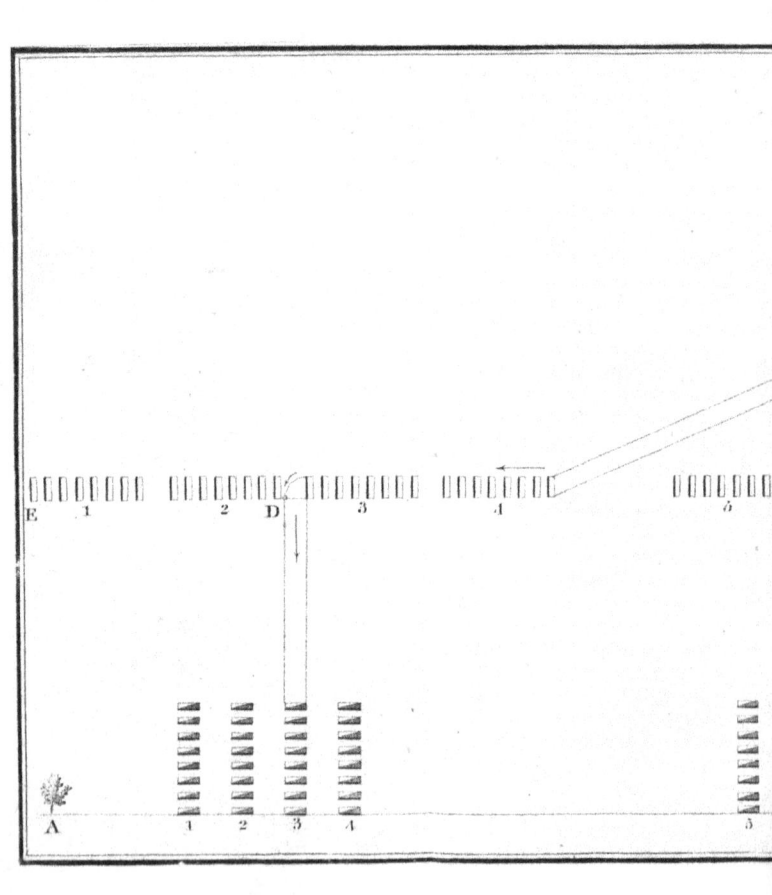

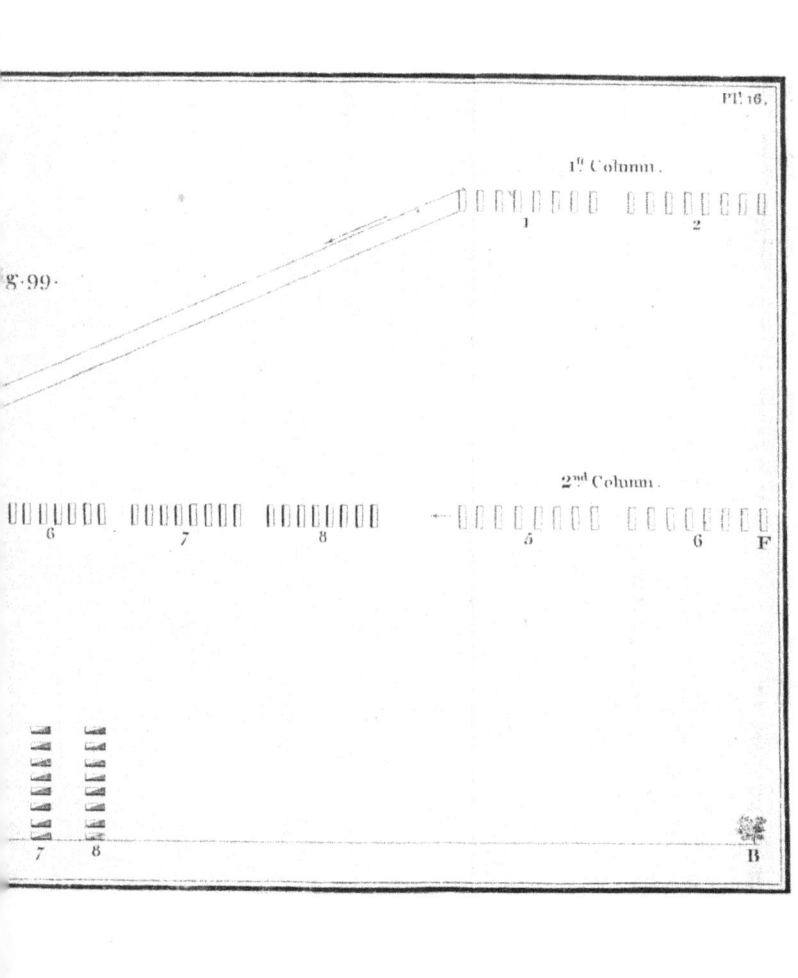

Pl. 16.

Fig. 99.

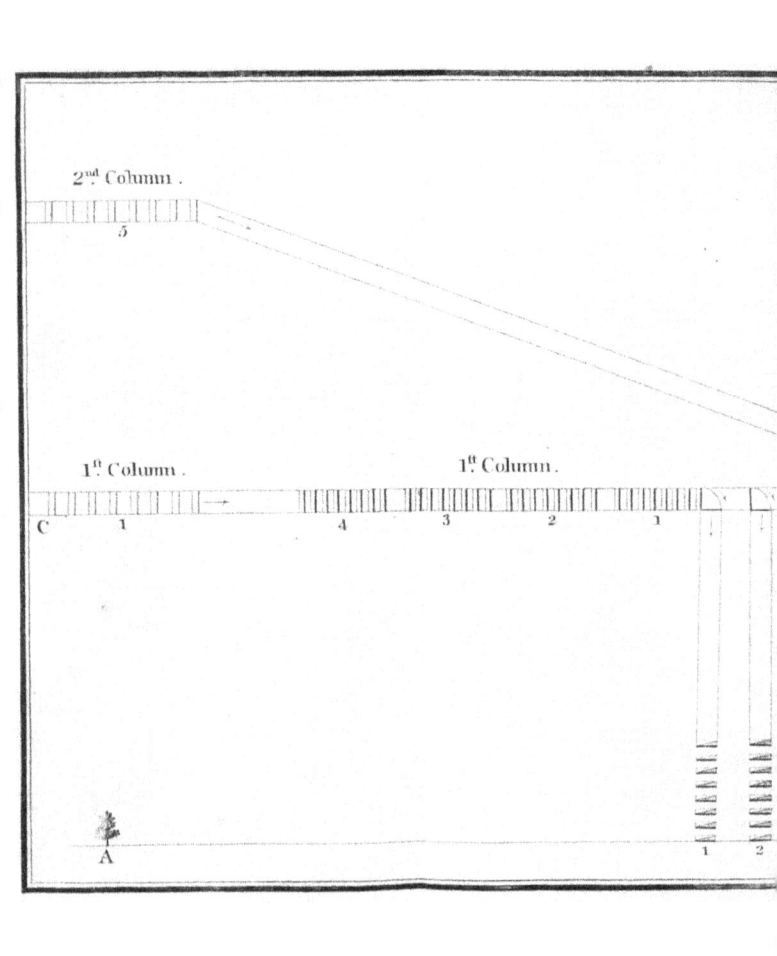

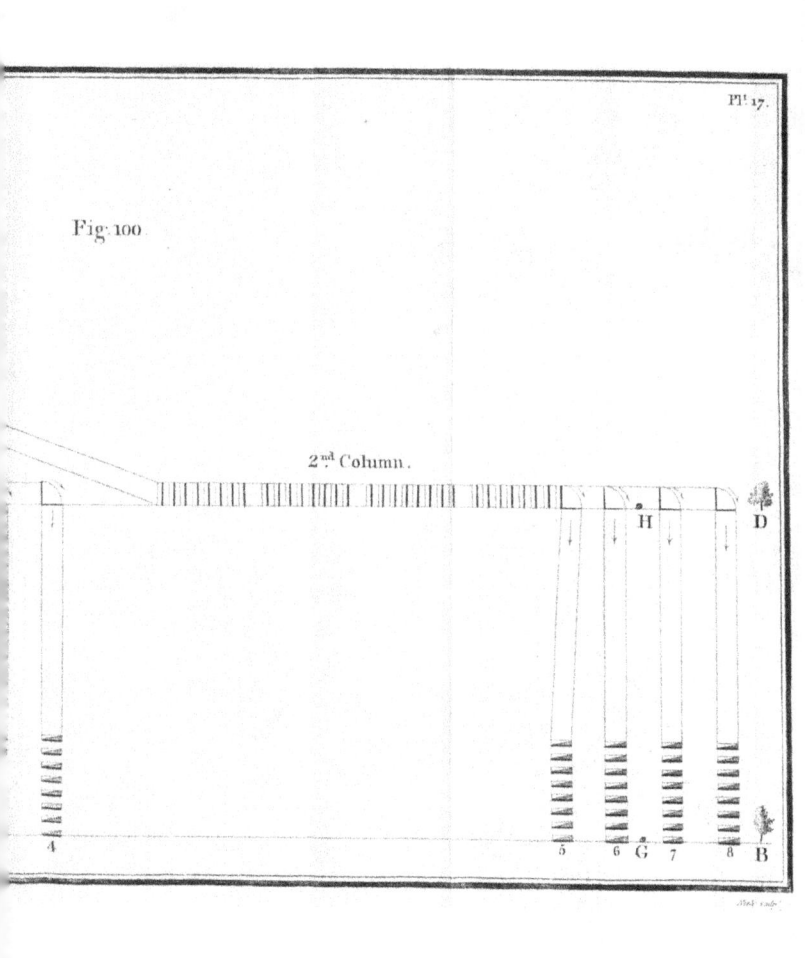

Fig. 100

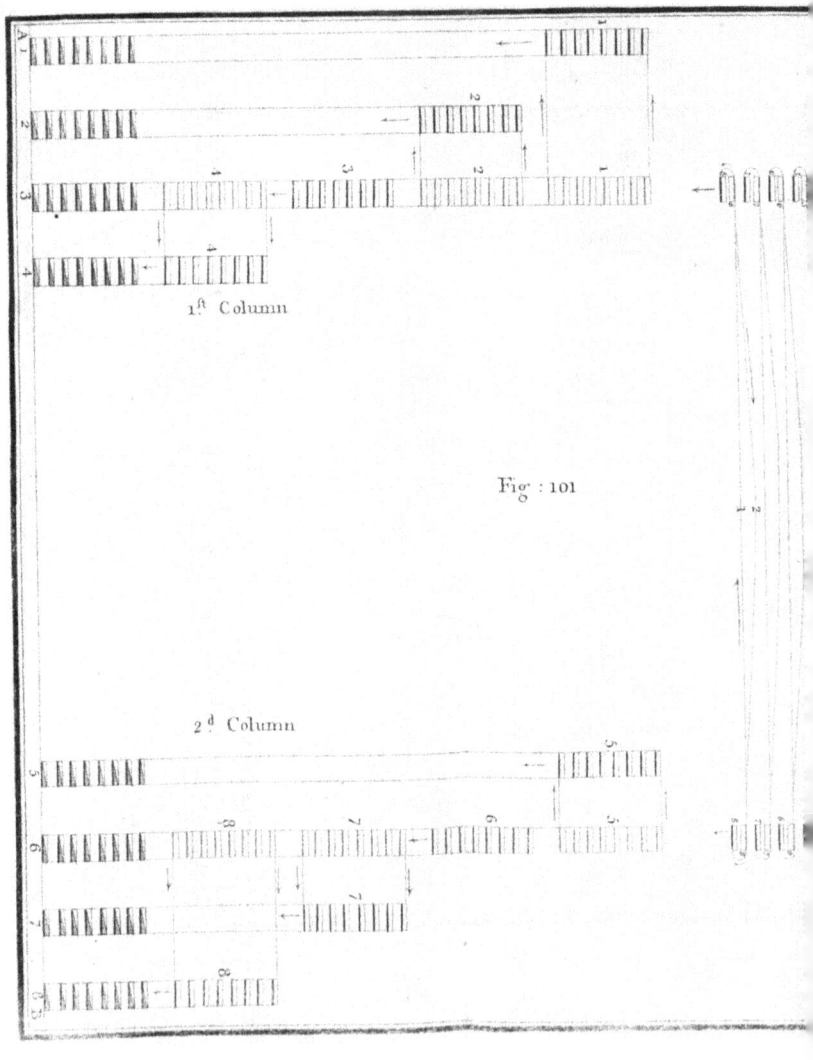

Fig: 101

1st Column

2d Column

Pl: 18.

1st Column in the position where the 2d stood before

Counter-march by Divisions

Lines shewing how the two Columns have been changed

Countermarch by Divisions

2d Column in the position where the 1st stood before

www.ingramcontent.com/pod-product-compliance
Lightning Source LLC
Chambersburg PA
CBHW070958160426
43193CB00012B/1826